the COIN COLLECTORS SURVIVAL MANUAL

the COIN COLLECTOR'S SURVIVAL MANUAL

SCOTT A. TRAVERS

ARCO PUBLISHING, INC.
NEW YORK

All photographs not credited are courtesy
of the author.

Published by Arco Publishing, Inc.
215 Park Avenue South, New York, N.Y. 10003

Library of Congress Cataloging in Publication Data

Travers, Scott A.
   The coin collector's survival manual.

   Includes index.
   1. Coins—Collectors and collecting—Handbooks, manuals,
etc.   2. Coins, American—Collectors and collecting—
Handbooks, manuals, etc.   I. Title.
CJ81.T73   1984   737.4'075   84-485
ISBN 0-668-05683-5 (Cloth Edition)
ISBN 0-668-05695-9 (Paper Edition)

Printed in the United States of America

10 9 8 7 6 5 4 3 2 1

To my parents, Barbara and Harvey Travers, who encouraged me and provided me with the loving supportiveness necessary to embark on and complete this project.

To Florence Schook, vice president, American Numismatic Association, who encouraged me, rewarded me, and motivated me when I was a young numismatist.

To Margo Russell, editor of *Coin World*, who recognized me at an early age and publicized my efforts.

And to Anthony Swiatek, my good friend and colleague, who introduced me to Arco and served as a driving force in making this book a working reality.

Contents

vii

Contents

Acknowledgments

Credit is due the following individuals who gave of their knowledge and expertise:

Stanley Apfelbaum; Richard Bagg; Q. David Bowers; Morris Bram; Walter Breen; Kenneth E. Bressett; Ruthann Brettell; Clarence Clarkson; Pedro Collazo-Oliver; Thomas K. DeLorey; Pierrette M. DiVenuti; Sanford J. Durst; Martin H. Firman; William Fivaz; Harry J. Forman; Les Fox; Michael Fuljenz; David L. Ganz; Philip Gottesman; David Hall; Kenneth Hallenbeck, Jr.; James L. Halperin; Thomas V. Haney; David C. Harper; Allen Harriman; George D. Hatie; Ed Hipps; Charles Hoskins; James J. Jelinski; Donald H. Kagin; George Klabin; Chester L. Krause; Julian Leidman; James Miller; Thomas Mulvaney; Bernard Nagengast; William J. Nagle; John Pasciuti; William P. Paul; Donn Pearlman; Henry Rasof; Robert S. Riemer; Steven Ritter; Edward C. Rochette; Bob Rose; Joseph H. Rose; Maurice Rosen; Margo Russell; Thomas W. Sharpless; Anthony J. Swiatek; Paul F. Taglione; Sol Taylor; Michael J. Toledo; Julius Turoff; Adolf Weiss; Bob Wilhite; and Keith M. Zaner.

Credit is also due the following institutions and companies:

American Numismatic Association, American Numismatic Association Certification Service (ANACS); Amos Press, Inc.; International Numismatic Society Authentication Bureau; Krause Publications, Inc.; Miller Magazines, Inc.; National Collectors Laboratories; and Western Publishing Company, Inc.

The following individuals are due credit and special thanks for their generous contributions of photographs and other materials, time and advice, and support:

Kenneth E. Bressett, director of the A.N.A. Certification Service, who carefully reviewed the grading chapter and made invaluable suggestions, and who provided the most explicit photographs of hairlines on a Proof I've ever seen.

Pedro Collazo-Oliver, owner of National Collectors Laboratories, who provided each and every photograph for the chapter concerning altered and counterfeit coins, and who closely read the manuscript for this chapter and made some sensible revisions.

Thomas K. DeLorey, senior authenticator of the A.N.A. Certification Service, who interrupted his duties at ANACS and spent endless weeks compiling photographs from the ANACS photofiles to illustrate clearly the subtle nuances of coin grading; who persuaded ANACS to author an in-depth analysis revealing how it grades; who spent many tiring hours examining the manuscript and making important revisions; and who served as my constant telephone consultant at A.N.A.

William Fivaz, A.N.A. seminar instructor, who provided me with outstanding photographs of striking characteristics of coins, first points of wear, and Proof and non-Proof rims, and who made valuable suggestions after reading the grading chapter.

David L. Ganz, attorney, who reviewed and analyzed Chapter 9.

George Klabin, author of preservation articles and president of Equi-Safe Corporation, who spent many telephone hours alerting me to the dangers of storing coins in polyvinylchloride (PVC) holders; who provided me with copies of a scientific study alleging a link between PVC and coin corrosion; who edited the two chapters relating to coin storage; and who gave me many photographs which illustrate the problems of coin preservation and storage.

Maurice Rosen, editor/publisher of the *Rosen Numismatic Advisory*, for permission to reprint the most valuable interview he has ever published: "Confession of A Rip-off Coin Salesman"; and who reviewed many of the survival strategies suggested in this book.

Henry Rasof, my editor at Arco, who refined the organizational texture of the manuscript, and who listened attentively when I told him that certain sections did not need their organizational texture refined.

Anthony J. Swiatek, editor/publisher of *The Swiatek Numismatic Report*, who spent countless hours reviewing the manuscript; who gave me photographs illustrating the effects of "dipping"; and who allowed me to reprint the results of his study concerning artificial toning.

Paul F. Taglione, president of New England Rare Coin Galleries, Inc., who spent many days writing a candid analysis of how ANACS grades, and who made valuable suggestions concerning liquidation.

Bob Wilhite, "Coin Market" value guide editor for Krause Publications, Inc., who candidly shared with me his method for determining price-guide values.

Preface

For those who don't possess a degree of healthy skepticism, the coin field is a tough one to make money in. The coin market is like an ocean of hungry sharks, waiting for a powerless victim into whom they can sink their teeth. This book should help you to survive in that ocean.

In *The Coin Collector's Survival Manual*, you'll learn everything the pros know, from how to look at a coin to how to negotiate with a coin dealer. You'll find out why magnification and lighting could play an important role in your coin purchases, what the motives of certain dealers are, and why you should always keep your guard up.

The greatest losses to buyers of coins center around the grading of coins. Tiny differences in a coin's appearance can mean a huge difference in a coin's value. I have compiled a vivid set of self-help coin grading enlargements to clarify the subtle nuances of grading. And a special grading survey is presented so you can see how some of the country's leading experts grade coins.

Simple methods of detecting counterfeit coins are presented, along with many photos carefully selected to show you how to spot fakes. You'll also learn why price guides don't really show what your coins are worth, what to watch out for when you deal with a coin dealer, how not to get ripped off if you buy through the mail (and how to take action if you are), and how to profit from coin conventions—financially and educationally.

There's an entire section about caring for your coins. An improperly stored coin can be as undesirable as an overpriced one. There's information about how to choose coin holders that won't damage your coins, safe-deposit box storage, and home security.

Whether you are a casual collector or a serious investor, or someone in between, I'm sure you will find the advice given in the following pages useful in your quest for coins.

Scott A. Travers

New York City

Introduction

The collecting of coins is an endlessly fascinating hobby. Coins are a mirror of our civilization; they reflect political and social turmoil, artistic and cultural triumph, and both obstructed and unobstructed societal evolution. Ionian merchants collected the first coins in the fifth century B.C. when coins were first made.

The coinage of America is the coinage of a special people. The beauty of rare coins is appreciated by connoisseurs, just as works of art are treasured by art lovers. Coin collecting, once termed "the hobby of kings," has been a source of pleasure and profit to king and nonking alike. For many years, though, the acquisition of high-quality rare coins was dominated by the elite: King Farouk of Egypt, Baron de Rothschild, and the DuPont and Lilly families. The proliferation of educational materials and, thus, of artistic appreciation has brought about a surge of interest in rare coins from people in all walks of life.

Frustration with the performance of paper assets such as stocks, bonds, and commodities has encouraged an increasingly greater number of people to buy rare coins, a *tangible* asset with a sparkling performance record.

But it's the collecting instinct that encourages all of us to collect something we can hold, touch, and feel. There are three basic types of individuals who buy coins: the collector, the collector/investor, and the investor. Even the unknowledgeable investor is touched, sooner or later, by the collecting instinct.

Collectors buy coins for their artistic, cultural, and historic significance. They are not overly concerned with price, just with having a particular coin to complete a particular set. They want each and every date for that set, and they would sell their houses or cars or clothing to get that coin. If a collector buys a coin for $50 which increases in value to $500 a year later, chances are he or she won't sell it.

The collector/investors also appreciate the artistic, cultural, and historic significance that coins have to offer. But they buy coins to make a profit. It's like the doctor who invests in rare paintings but hangs them on his or her wall for their beauty. While collector/investors own the coins, they look at them and admire their breathtaking magnificence. But if the value increases substantially in a short period of time, chances are those coins will get sold.

Unknowledgeable investors buy coins to make a profit. They are only interested in one thing: the bottom line. But ironically, many unknowledgeable investors become dedicated collectors. Just holding a rare coin is a thrill; and many unknowledgeable investors are educated and culture-oriented individuals to begin with, seeking to diversify their holdings.

In short, almost everyone who buys coins learns to appreciate them sooner or later. *The Coin Collector's Survival Manual* will intensify this appreciation by showing you how to protect yourself when you enter the market. Whether you're a collector, collector/investor, or unknowledgeable investor, be careful when you buy or sell coins; be *very* careful. One wrong step could spoil your appreciation for the world's greatest avocation.

Glossary

Knowledge of the language is an essential element of survival. Take some time to familiarize yourself with the words used by coin collectors and dealers. It could mean the difference between surviving and not surviving.

abrasion—an acquired mark or nick that mars a coin's surface and lowers its eye appeal.

abrasive—the category of chemicals or substances which, if used on coins, will abrade or scrape away the top layer of metal.

accumulation—a hoard or group of coins being held at a common location.

album—used by collectors to store coins of a series. A useful way of assessing progress in completing a collection.

almost—often used to describe a coin which is near a higher grade, but isn't that grade.

altered—usually a genuine but common coin that has been tampered with by an unscrupulous person in order to make it resemble a rare coin.

A.N.A.—American Numismatic Association, world's largest coin collector organization.

ANACS-certified—authenticated, or authenticated and graded by the American Numismatic Association Certification Service (ANACS). The coin should be accompanied by a photocertificate issued by the Service.

appraisal—a professional opinion offered by a dealer. These are rarely objective because dealers like to buy coins for less than they are worth.

ask—the "Ask" column of the *Coin Dealer Newsletter*. Refers to "wholesale" prices dealers are asking for particular coins.

attribution—the description and background information given a coin in a dealer's retail catalog, auction catalog, etc. Does not refer to grade.

bag-mark—a mark on a coin's surface which has been acquired through contact with another coin or coins banging around inside a Mint-sewn bag.

bid—the "Bid" column of the *Coin Dealer Newsletter*. Refers to "wholesale" prices dealers are offering to pay for certain coins.

bidder—a person bidding at an auction or making serious offers to buy a coin or coins in competition with others wanting that same material.

book—the list of mail bidders and submitted competitive bids to buy coins at public auction.

bourse—the room where dealers gather to buy and sell rare coins.

Breen—*Walter Breen's Encyclopedia of United States and Colonial Proof Coins.*

Brown & Dunn (B&D)—*A Guide to the Grading of United States Coins,* by Martin R. Brown and John W. Dunn, a once widely used grading guide with line drawings to illustrate wear.

bullion—uncoined gold or silver in ingots or bars.

business strike—the coin manufactured by the Mint for everyday use.

cabinet friction—a specific type of wear on a coin which has circulated slightly. The term originated in dealers' catalogs years ago when coins were stored in elaborate cabinets with velvet trays. The coins slid about on these trays and developed "cabinet friction" on their highest points.

cameo—usually denotes a contrast between frosted fields and reflective devices.

capital gains—the tax category under which profits from rare coin investments are declared.

carbon flecks/spots—usually those spots which are not really carbon, but dense areas of toning on a coin's surface. These spots, attributed to "mishandling," are darkened areas resulting from contact with saliva.

cataloger—the individual who assigns a grade to a coin or coins in a dealer's catalog (e.g., retail or auction).

Choice—adjectival qualifier adopted by the A.N.A. to help better describe most grade categories. It is most popularly used to describe a Mint State-65 coin.

Coin Market Prices—the coin market price guide by that name published weekly as a supplement to *Numismatic News.*

collection—a meticulously assembled holding of coins.

condition census—the finest existing condition of a given coin. Does not refer to the finest condition ever known or finest condition possible.

consignor—a person whose coins are sold by an auction company.

counterfeit—a fake coin.

cycle—the historical boom-and-bust price performance tendency of the coin market.

detraction—an imperfection, either Mint-made or acquired, which subtracts from a coin's grade or value or both.

devices—the parts on a coin that stand out, such as the lettering, portrait, and stars.

die—a metal object engraved with a coin's design, used to strike or stamp out coins.

doubled die—coins with doubling of the letters and date resulting from the die itself having been struck twice.

edge—a coin's side: the part you touch when you hold a coin properly. This is not to be confused with obverse or reverse.

estimate—a dealer's written approximation in his or her auction catalog of what a coin is worth and might sell for at that auction.

exhibit—a display of coins with educational information shown at a coin show and competing for a prize.

eye appeal—a controversial ingredient of coin grading that encompasses a coin's color or quality of toning and strike.

face value—the amount of money the coin represents as a medium of exchange. For example, the face value of a nickel is 5 cents.

fields—the part of the coin that serves as background and doesn't stand out.

flip—a pliable, two-pocket coin holder which folds over. The coin is inserted in one pocket; a written description of the coin is inserted in the other pocket.

Gem—official A.N.A. grading terminology for Mint State-67, a nearly perfect coin.

grade—the universal language which coin enthusiasts use to describe what a coin looks like or how much wear and tear it has endured; depends upon level of preservation and overall beauty.

Gray book—*Official A.N.A. Grading Standards for United States Coins,* by the American Numismatic Association.

Gray sheet—*Coin Dealer Newsletter* (*CDN*), a weekly publication essential for successful coin transactions, and *The Monthly Summary,* the *CDN*'s monthly publication. These are the most relied upon guides for accurate prices.

hairlines—a patch or patches of light, almost unnoticeable scratches on Proof coins. Usually caused by cleaning.

insert—a sturdy piece of paper with a description of a coin which is inserted into one pocket of a flip-type coin holder.

Judd—the popular reference work written about pattern coins: *United States Pattern, Experimental and Trial Pieces,* by J. Hewitt Judd, M.D. Each pattern is given a "Judd number." These numbers are referred to almost any time a pattern is offered for sale.

junk dealer—a dealer who sells inexpensive and relatively common circulated coins, as well as rolls of Uncirculated recent-issue coins.

Kointain—a trademark and popular name for a transparent, curvilinear triacetate coin capsule that fits snugly around the coin and is used to protect it.

Lucite-type holder—the Lucite sandwich-type holder manufactured by Capital Plastics, Inc. These holders are composed of three small sheets of thin acrylic (really Plexiglas). The middle sheet has a space for the coin.

luster—the circular pattern in which a true Uncirculated coin reflects light.

Mint error—a coin error that occurred during the actual manufacture of a coin. Some collectors collect only Mint errors.

Mint-mark—the letter on a coin that indicates where it was minted: No Mint-mark—Philadelphia or West Point; P—Philadelphia; O—New Orleans; CC—Carson City; S—San Francisco; D—Denver.

Mint State—a coin which has not circulated. Mint State coins should not exhibit wear. The terms *Mint State* and *Uncirculated* are the same.

national show—a coin convention attended by dealers from throughout the country.

nonabrasive—the category of chemicals or substances which, if applied to coins, will not remove the top layer of metal. Nonabrasives are usually not harmful to coins.

numismatics—the study of coins, medallic art, and paper money.

obverse—the front of a coin.

overgrading—describing a coin as being in a higher grade than it actually is in.

overpaying—paying more money for a coin than the coin is worth.

overtones—traces of toning colors on a coin that is toned one primary color.

patina—the brownish color that forms on the top layer of metal on copper coins.

pattern—a coin struck by the Mint to see how an experimental design would look if made into a coin.

Perfect—an official A.N.A. grading term referring to a coin with no imperfections or detractions of any kind. Graded Mint State-70.

periphery—the outermost area of a coin's obverse or reverse. Can be identified by a thin imaginary ring around the obverse or reverse.

Photograde—the grading guide by James F. Ruddy with photographs of coins. Helpful guide to grading circulated coins.

polyvinylchloride (PVC)—a plasticizer found in many popular coin holders. Destructive to valuable Uncirculated coins.

premium—the amount of money a coin is worth above its face value. This value is set in the rare-coin marketplace.

preservation—refers to how well a coin has been kept since it was made by the Mint. Careful steps have to be taken by the collector to make sure that coins that have been meticulously stored remain well preserved.

prices realized—the list of prices of coins sold by auction and usually available from the auction house within a few weeks after the auction.

Proof—the coin struck by the Mint especially for collectors to save. Proof coins were (and are) struck twice on specially polished dies and specially selected planchets to assure a chromiumlike brilliance.

Prooflike—a coin made by the Mint for circulation which looks like a Proof. A Prooflike coin has similar reflective properties to a Proof.

Red Book—*A Guide Book of United States Coins,* by Richard S. Yeoman.

regional show—a coin convention attended by dealers from a number of nearby states.

restrike—a genuine coin struck by the Mint at a later date with dies which designate that the coin was struck at an earlier date.

reverse—the back of a coin.

rims—the raised rings which encircle obverse and reverse and protect the coin from wear.

rip—a coin bought for considerably below its real value.

roll—in general, a stack of coins of the same denomination, year, and Mint-mark. The number of coins composing a roll is often, but not always, fifty.

Select—an official A.N.A. grading term. It refers to a Mint State-63 coin, "an example with attractive Mint luster, but noticeable detracting marks or minor blemishes."

series—a collection of an example of each coin date and Mint-mark issued for a specific type coin design.

Sheldon—the late Dr. William Sheldon, author of *Penny Whimsy*, the book about large cents in which the coin-grading scale of 1–70 was introduced.

slider—a lightly circulated coin that appears to be Uncirculated.

stick—a term used by mail-order coin dealers. Usually refers to an over-priced and less than desirable coin sold through the mail and not returned for a refund by the buyer.

striations—light patches of a raised scratchlike texture that result from polishing of the die.

strike—the quality of design detail present on a coin after it is Minted.

Swiatek & Breen—*The Encyclopedia of United States Silver and Gold Commemorative Coins*, by Anthony Swiatek and Walter Breen.

switch—occurs when a valuable coin is switched by an unscrupulous person for a less expensive coin.

table—a booth at a coin convention rented by a dealer from which to conduct business.

teletype—any of a number of networks used by dealers to communicate and do business with each other. Although many dealers use the teletype for contacts, these same dealers often confirm terms and negotiate prices over the telephone.

toning—a slow, natural, regular process by which a coin oxidizes over a period of months and years.

Trends—the coin price guide supplement of *Coin World* (the popular weekly coin publication).

Type—an example of a major design of coin (e.g., Barber quarters and Liberty Seated halves). Does not refer to different metals of the same coin Type. Sometimes used to refer to variety (e.g., Type I).

Uncirculated—a coin that has never circulated or been spent and, most importantly, has no wear on its highest parts.

underbidder—the person bidding on an auction lot in an unreserved public auction who does not bid high enough to acquire the coin he or she is bidding on, but whose bids are second highest.

undercounting—an unscrupulous practice by which, for example, a "fifty-coin-roll" containing only forty-nine coins is sold at the fifty-coin price.

undergrading—describing a coin as being in a lower grade than it actually is in.

vest-pocket dealer—a dealer who works the coin shows with an inventory of coins in his or her vest pocket. Vest-pocket dealers rarely take tables at coin shows and often deal in coins on a part-time basis.

view—looking at coins to be sold at auction at a set later date. During this presale viewing, prospective buyers have the opportunity of assessing a coin's suitability, grade, authenticity, etc.

virtually—a popular term used to gloss over a coin's shortcomings. "Virtually free of scratches" means the coin has scratches.

wear—the smoothing or abrading of a coin's top layer of metal caused by circulation.

whizz—artificially simulating Mint luster by removing the top layer of a coin's metal with a circular wire brush and/or abrasive chemical.

the COIN
COLLECTOR'S
SURVIVAL MANUAL

1

Refining Your Method of Looking at Coins

The wooden floor creaked as the middle-aged gentleman walked across to the counter of the small coin shop. As he reached the display case, he noticed the subtle contrast between the blue velvet trays and the white cardboard coin holders which filled them. As the man glanced down at the counter, he expected to see the types of coins that he was accustomed to viewing: the half cents, the large cents, the silver dollars, the twenty-dollar gold pieces, and a variety of other coins in between—circulated coins and uncirculated ones, too. He was a collector of rare United States coins, specializing in Liberty Seated half-dollars of the highest Mint State designations (coins which are Mint State—i.e., look new and have never been circulated—are not all equal; some Mint State or Uncirculated coins are better than others), and to him each specimen had always seemed highly intriguing. His procedure of scanning the coins under the fingerprinted glass of the counter was always the same. He would check out the coins in his specialty, then admire the displayed specimens of other coin types, soon returning to his specialty, perhaps to select a coin suitable for his collection.

But this visit was different. Before the gentleman had time to examine any of the coin types outside of his specialty, an 1878 Liberty Seated half-dollar activated his collecting instincts. Its rich, natural *toning* * immediately caught his attention, for that coin possessed the most desirable toning imaginable. The center was a golden color, and it faded into rings of red, purple, and blue. The collector couldn't have seen any imperfec-

---

* *Toning* is the slow, natural, and regular process by which a coin oxidizes over a period of months and years. Collectors pay more for coins with beautiful toning because the colors are so attractive and make the coin stand out from others which are not toned. However, toning often covers up imperfections.

1

tions on that coin if he wanted to. His attention was focused on the coin's overwhelming positive characteristic—its natural toning. He studied Ms. Liberty through the display case and coin holder, and how graceful she looked with halos of beautiful color about her. The collector didn't look at the price, for that seemed secondary. He would have paid almost any price.

The shop's proprietor stood inconspicuously in the corner, so as not to interfere with the collector's coin viewing. But the proprietor soon made himself known. He asked if the collector desired to look at anything from the case. The collector, who didn't bother looking up, pointed to the 1878 half. The proprietor took the toned half in his left hand and a piece of red velvet in his right. "Pull up a stool and sit down," he told the collector.

The shop had four tall, old wood stools at its counter. And it looked like a scene out of an old John Wayne movie as the collector pulled a stool up to the counter and sat down in front of the proprietor, a man who hadn't shaved for days and who wore a T-shirt and cowboy hat. "This here half is a real Gem,"* insisted the proprietor as he spread the velvet across the counter. The collector needed no assurances, for he possessed the ability to recognize original toning. "May I take it out of the holder?" the collector asked. "Go ahead. That's what the velvet is for; just be careful," the proprietor responded. The collector was careful to remove the four staples before taking the coin out of the holder, so as not to subject the coin to any unnecessary sliding or scratches.

The collector was even more overwhelmed by the attractive toning when he looked at the coin up close, for the same effect appeared on the reverse. He found the bright red from the velvet to be slightly distracting, but he thought he was able to overlook that. "Gem B.U.,"† read the holder. "$4,000," read the price. He bought it.

For two days in a row he carefully studied and admired his new acquisition, each time reassuring himself of his great buy. But on the third day, he became used to the toning and was able to develop a more objective perspective on the half's negative characteristics. And there were many which had gone unnoticed. There were several large scratches on the reverse which the collector spotted all at once. Since he hadn't seen them before, he wondered if they were there when he bought the coin. Then he spotted two rim nicks. As he was studying the obverse, he saw a scrape across Ms. Liberty which he hadn't noticed before. He still

---

* Gem—a nearly perfect coin which looks brand new, has never been circulated, and is free from wear and tear.

† B.U.—"Brilliant Uncirculated."

was pleased with his acquisition because it was genuinely Mint State, and the toning was original. But had this gentleman refined his method of looking at coins, he might have been able to identify the negative characteristics before he made the purchase. If this specimen had had slight wear on its high points, it could have been overlooked. This collector was fortunate. If he doesn't refine his method of looking at coins, though, his fortune may change.

Many numismatists need to refine their coin-viewing methods so that a coin's negative, as well as positive, characteristics can be identified and all factors may be considered during grading and, thus, buying decisions. Collectors should also know how to maintain the coin's level of preservation during the viewing process.

This section deals with *how* to look at coins so as to become familiar with each specimen's intricacies. I suggest that you systematize the process by which you look at coins so as not to be overwhelmed by any characteristic. This chapter also deals with the fundamentals of preserving the coin while you are looking at it.

COIN-VIEWING ATTITUDES AND TECHNIQUES

There are four basic coin-viewing attitudes:

1. Looking for beauty and admiring as a work of art
2. Looking for strengths
3. Looking for imperfections or detractions
4. Looking for both the strengths and the imperfections, while saving your appreciation for the coins you own.

The rare-coin enthusiast may have the ability to combine successfully the above attitudes with an adequate coin-viewing method. However, for practical purposes, attitude 4 is probably the best to adopt.

Numismatists are actively encouraged to appreciate the cultural, historic, and artistic significance that each coin represents. However, when a buying decision is being made and money is involved—sometimes great sums—it is important to look at the coin's physical well-being only. It has been stated that when a coin is offered for sale, the seller only "sees" the positive characteristics, while the buyer only "sees" the negative characteristics. There probably is some truth to this conventional wisdom. So the collector must make a concerted effort to be objective and look at the entire coin—each and every part of it.

Looking at a coin is like proofreading a letter. You probably won't find any mistakes if you just skim its contents. But if you scrutinize it word by word, letter by letter, you stand a much greater chance of discovering an error. The same principle applies to coins. A quick glance at a coin won't necessarily reveal its detracting characteristics to most collectors. And if the coin has any overwhelmingly positive characteristic(s), some numismatists accidentally overlook rather obvious detractions. Study the coin closely. However, unlike a letter, a coin can't be read line by line, from left to right. You have to develop a method of reading coins for strengths and detractions. You can choose the one you feel most comfortable with—or combine techniques in order to form an effective approach.

Coins and the Clock

In order to provide for mutual understanding and uniform description, numismatists have agreed that each coin's characteristics can be described by referring to the coin's corresponding position on the clock. For example, if a coin has a scratch on the obverse near the top, this imperfection may be described as, "obverse scratch at 12:00." (Some individuals, particularly left-handed ones, may feel more comfortable scanning in a counterclockwise direction.)

NOTE: The coin-viewing methods presented are for study purposes. Before taking a coin out of its holder, read the explanation on pages 7–8 of how to protect coins during the viewing process.

The Basic Clockwise Scan

- Scan the obverse in a clockwise direction.
- Repeat the process on the reverse.
- Carefully tilt and rotate the coin while viewing the obverse so that it can be viewed from more than one angle, and repeat this for the reverse.
- Scrutinize the rims from the obverse, reverse, and side.
- View the coin in its entirety.

The Clockwise Fields and Devices Scan

- Scan the obverse *fields* in a clockwise direction.
- Scan the obverse *devices* in a clockwise direction.
- Repeat scanning of both fields and devices on the reverse.

- Carefully tilt and rotate the coin while viewing the obverse so that it can be viewed from more than one angle, and repeat this for the reverse.
- Scrutinize the rims from the obverse, reverse, and side.
- View the coin in its entirety.

The Division Scan

- Divide the coin into equal, imaginary sections as you would slice a pie into pieces of the same size. You can choose as many or as few sections as you desire—two, three, or, preferably, four.
- Choose a section, and scan it in a clockwise direction. Move to the next section in a clockwise direction, repeating the viewing action.
- Repeat the obverse viewing action on the reverse.
- Carefully tilt and rotate the coin while viewing the obverse so that it can be viewed from more than one angle; repeat this for the reverse.
- Scrutinize the rims from the obverse, reverse, and side.
- View the coin in its entirety.

The Divisional Fields and Devices Scan

- Divide the coin into equal, imaginary "pie" sections of the same size. You can choose as many or as few sections as you desire—two, three, or, preferably, four.
- Choose an obverse section, and scan its *fields* in a clockwise direction. Then scan the *devices* of that obverse section. Move to the next section in a clockwise direction, repeating the viewing action.
- Repeat the process for the reverse.
- Carefully tilt and rotate the coin while viewing the obverse so that it can be viewed from more than one angle; repeat this for the reverse.
- Scrutinize the rims from the obverse, reverse, and side.
- View the coin in its entirety.

These viewing methods present the basic elements of examining coins. Practice these methods so that you can decide which technique is most effective. The methods described can be used with or without magnification.

The obvious points that detracted from the value of the Mint State half-dollar described earlier, and which the collector missed, are not an unusual example of overlooked detractions. On the contrary, it is common for detractions to go unnoticed for an extended period of time.

TESTING YOUR DEALER

Dealers are human, too, and they buy coins in much the same way collectors do, for there isn't a wholesale coin source. At one coin convention, a dealer friend rushed over to show me a coin he called a "terrific buy." It was a Mint State Peace dollar—brilliant and fully struck. I scanned the reverse and noticed a large planchet crack (the *planchet* is the blank circular piece of metal on which a coin is struck. Sometimes, planchets are imperfect before the coin is struck, causing the coin itself to be imperfect.) The dealer said that he had looked at the coin for hours and never noticed the imperfection! Many dealers, too, need to refine their coin-viewing methods.

You can easily test your local dealer's astuteness by looking at his or her coins in inventory. Ask to look at the 1921 Lincoln cents. The 1921-P is worth under a dollar in the average circulated grades. But the 1921-S is worth about double the value of its plain counterpart. The "S" is weakly struck on quite a few 1921-S cents, and many '21-Ss are masquerading as '21-Ps. Study the coin and look closely for the Mint-mark. Use a magnifying glass if you wish. If you've spotted the Mint-mark and the coin is described and priced as a 1921-P, you know that your dealer has made an honest mistake. Stories have been told about rolls of Mint State 1921-P Lincolns being bought with several Mint State 1921-S cents in the roll.

Some professional numismatists can look at a coin in a matter of seconds and see both its negative and positive attributes. Extensive experience has made these individuals practiced coin viewers, and no methods other than the ones described (or variations of them) are used. However, the viewing action is performed with split-second timing. These professionals must develop this skill, for when viewing hundreds of lots during an auction presale viewing session, one can't spend a great deal of time with each coin.

Although the Liberty Seated half-dollar collector overlooked imper-

Fig. 1–1. Barely visible Mint-mark. This 1911-D has its "D" Mint-mark barely visible. The coin was manufactured like this. Sometimes a dealer will not notice a Mint-mark and sell a coin at too low a price.

fections, he performed some actions correctly. He removed the staples from the holder before removing the coin. He took the coin out of the holder in order to examine it thoroughly. He looked at the coin over a piece of soft fabric so the coin would be cushioned if it was unexpectedly dropped. He held onto the half-dollar firmly enough so it wouldn't drop, and he was careful not to talk over the coin while it was exposed to airborne pollutants. In other words, he preserved the coin while taking it out of the holder and looking at it.

HOW TO HANDLE COINS

The average collector would be amazed at the number of *once* exceptional rare coins—those ruined by improper removal from holders. The viewing of such a piece is disturbing. Picture a silver Proof coin (a "Proof" is a coin made especially for collectors; it is struck by a special process and possesses a chromiumlike brilliance) over one hundred years old with dazzling mirror fields and frosted devices—a coin which immediately captures the viewer's attention. But when you look upon its nearly perfect obverse surfaces, scratch marks from a staple are visible. The origin of the scratch marks may be traced back to a numismatist who wanted to look at the coin out of the holder and didn't remove all of the staples. Both the premium and aesthetic value of the coin are lowered considerably by such an action. And future generations of collectors are deprived of appreciating a coin whose high level of preservation could have been maintained. So don't try to save time. Remove every staple before taking a coin out of its holder.

Whenever possible, remove each coin from the holder in order to examine the rims. However, during an auction presale viewing session, this may not be allowed. This shouldn't deter you from buying. Usually the coin is displayed in a clear plastic envelope, such as a polished vinyl flip. This allows you to see the rims. If the coin is in such a holder, study the holder to determine what imperfections are in the plastic. This enables you to evaluate the coin without confusing holder imperfections with coin ones.

Here are some other things you can do to examine coins without causing possible damage.

- If the coin is in a Lucite sandwich-type holder, the coin needs to be removed so that the rims can be examined. To do this, first tap the holder lightly, obverse downward, to loosen the coin. Next, remove all screws, but keep the holder together. Place the screwless holder, obverse downward, on a flat surface, cushioned by some type of fabric. Remove the top piece of plastic, and ease the coin out of the holder by applying light pressure to the coin's reverse with a piece of soft plastic, such as a polished vinyl flip coin holder.* Remove the second layer of plastic, and the coin will be resting, reverse upward, on the bottom Lucite piece. Further instructions concerning the removal of coins from holders are provided in chapter 13.

- Make sure a piece of soft fabric, such as velvet, is under the coin during viewing. However, the color should not be distracting to the collector, as was the red velvet described earlier. Black or blue are satisfactory, neutral colors.
- Hold coins firmly by the rims with thumb and forefinger. It's an interesting phenomenon that both collectors and dealers drop the valuable coins and not their less valuable counterparts. This can be simply explained. People get nervous holding expensive pieces. Either their hands shake or they handle the coins so gingerly that the coins fall.
- A number of collectors have posed the question of whether holding a coin on the edge may cause fingerprints. It may. And if that concerns you, wear cloth or sulfur-free gloves while you are holding the coin. However, most collectors like the thrill of actually holding each coin. And if you are like most collectors, you will want to experience this same excitement. Also, realize that the dealer from whom you purchased the coin probably held it without gloves, and in years to come you might see his or her fingerprints on the edge. (The *edge* is *not* the coin itself. See the Glossary for a definition.)
- Don't talk while your coins are out of their holders and anywhere near your mouth or within "spitting" distance. Small drops of saliva can land on the coin and cause "carbon" spots. Such spots really aren't carbon, just toning areas which resulted from mishandling.

When you look at a coin, look closely. Handle it carefully, but firmly. Don't talk over the coin. These viewing methods help to set the foundation for you to appreciate and prosper from numismatics—both financially and aesthetically.

---

* Perform this process with utmost caution. Each coin has a light oxide coating on its surfaces, and this coating can be easily disturbed. Too much pressure from the pliable plastic touching the reverse can disrupt this coating. The injury has the potential of healing unevenly, thus very slightly lowering the aesthetic appeal.

2

Magnification
and
Lighting

"No matter how you look at it, it's still Mint State." Right? Not necessarily! The magnification used to view coins and the lighting in which they are viewed have a potentially significant impact on the grade a coin is given. If you grade coins under unusually high power magnification, you're likely to lower the grade unnecessarily, because small imperfections will appear large and be blown out of proportion. And if you grade coins under lighting conditions favorable to the seller, you're likely to raise the grade considerably. These rules are particularly applicable to Mint State or Uncirculated (refers to a coin that has never been circulated) coins, whose grades are affected by minute imperfections and are often graded according to the quality of the way in which they reflect light. Further, a coin which has light but almost unnoticeable wear on its highest points—an "About or Almost Uncirculated" coin—can appear Mint State if viewed under too little magnification or if viewed under certain types of light.*

Magnification has two primary numismatic uses: as an aid in grading and as an aid in authenticating.

---

* The American Numismatic Association's official grading terminology specifies that the words *About Uncirculated* be used to describe a coin that is very close to Uncirculated but has slight wear. Most coin dealers use the words *Almost Uncirculated* to describe these coins because *almost* is a better descriptive word than *about* in referring to a coin which is nearly or "almost" Uncirculated.

MAGNIFICATION FOR GRADING

In grading, the purpose of magnification is to be able to view an entire side of a coin, not look at small sections of it under high-power magnification. I recommend a 5-power (5×) or 10-power (10×) glass for grading.* If you use, say, a 20× glass, you will be tempted to downgrade a coin for having some trivial imperfection that you can't see with the naked eye. As you can see from the Bausch & Lomb chart (Fig. 2–1), the greater the magnification, the smaller your field of vision. If you're buying a magnifying glass for grading, buy one large enough for you to be able to look at one side of whatever kind of coin you collect.

Although I recommend against using a stereoscope or high-power magnifier to grade, the most advanced numismatists do use these tools as grading aids. I look for things that would normally go unnoticed when under low-power magnification, such as *large* hidden scratches and artificial reengraving of certain details done to make the coin appear better than it is. When this approach is used, it's important to discount the appearance of minute imperfections. No coin is perfect. And even the best of the best have tiny nicks that do not count in grade determination. *The most important aspect of using magnification is consistency in the power you use.* Don't use a 5× to grade one coin and a 10× to grade another.

MAGNIFICATION FOR
AUTHENTICATION

The magnification used to determine whether a coin is real or counterfeit, unaltered or altered, is significantly different from the magnification used for grading. If you're looking at Mint-marks, a 20× glass is recommended. This power glass just about allows you to see the Mint-mark (the letter on a coin which indicates where it was minted) and a little surrounding area. If you want to check out a coin overall for being authentic by gaining a sense of its surface, a stereomicroscope is necessary. A stereomicroscope has lenses for *both* eyes rather than just one. The depth and quality of what you are looking at is remarkably improved by the use of two sets of lenses. Quality varies considerably. When shopping

---

* Magnification "power" refers to the number of times a coin is magnified. For example, 1 power (1×) refers to the coin without magnification; 2 power (2×) refers to the coin appearing twice as large as its actual size, and so on.

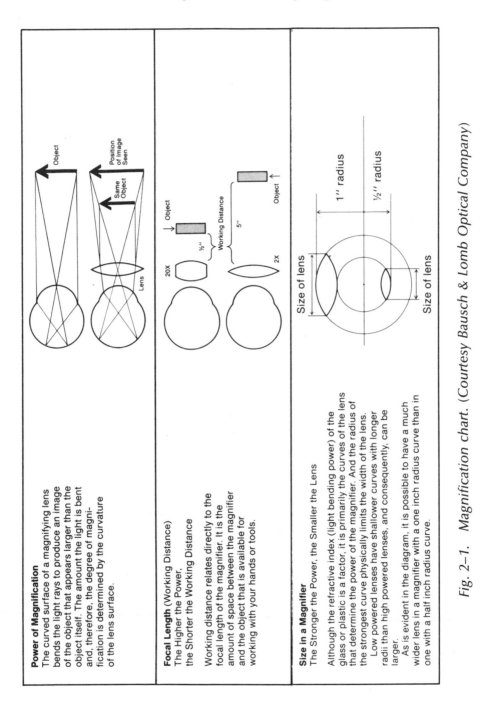

Power of Magnification
The curved surface of a magnifying lens bends the light rays to produce an image of the object that appears larger than the object itself. The amount the light is bent and, therefore, the degree of magnification is determined by the curvature of the lens surface.

Focal Length (Working Distance)
The Higher the Power,
the Shorter the Working Distance

Working distance relates directly to the focal length of the magnifier. It is the amount of space between the magnifier and the object that is available for working with your hands or tools.

Size in a Magnifier
The Stronger the Power, the Smaller the Lens

Although the refractive index (light bending power) of the glass or plastic is a factor, it is primarily the curves of the lens that determine the power of the magnifier. And the radius of the strongest curve physically limits the width of the lens.

Low powered lenses have shallower curves with longer radii than high powered lenses, and consequently, can be larger.

As is evident in the diagram, it is possible to have a much wider lens in a magnifier with a one inch radius curve than in one with a half inch radius curve.

Fig. 2–1. Magnification chart. (Courtesy Bausch & Lomb Optical Company)

for a stereoscope, select one which gives you a feeling of unlimited view, as opposed to one which makes you feel as if you're looking through two tubes. The most popular stereoscopes for coins are made by Nikon and Swift.

LIGHTING

Lighting is the most important environmental variable that affects how coins are graded. It's no longer a secret that lighting can be arranged so that an About Uncirculated coin will appear Mint State. This is startling when you consider that the difference in price between an About Uncirculated coin and its Mint State counterpart can be hundreds or even thousands of dollars.

A Mint State coin reflects light in a fully circular pattern as you rotate it under a pinpoint light source. This circular pattern must be complete for the coin to be Mint State. Imagine a circle. A coin which is About Uncirculated reflects light in an incomplete or disturbed pattern. Imagine a pencil-drawn circle with a few small sections erased. A cleaned coin reflects light in a uniform pattern, all at once, with no trace of a circular pattern.

From this, it sounds as if it might be easy to differentiate About Uncirculated from Mint State. It isn't. If viewed under certain types of lighting conditions, a coin with a grade of About Uncirculated might appear to be Mint State to every expert who looks at it. For example, floodlights increase the brilliance yet *decrease* your ability to identify detracting marks and wear. If viewed under floodlights (popular at coin conventions), a coin of the About Uncirculated grade would reflect light in that *almost* complete circle but would appear to reflect light in a *complete* circle and, thus, appear to be Mint State. To further complicate matters, chandeliers create a delightful glowing effect by means of the glass and bare filament. If certain About Uncirculated coins were looked at under both floodlights and chandeliers, not only would they look Mint State, but they also would look Choice or Gem Mint State.

The solution is to view coins under a tensor-type lamp, with fluorescent lighting as a background light. Tensor provides a high-intensity pinpoint light satisfactory for grading. Fluorescent light spreads light evenly. Make certain that you are consistent in using the same type of light whenever you grade. If you go to a dealer's store or a coin show, don't be afraid to ask the dealer to allow you to examine the coin under a pinpoint light source. If one isn't available, ask to borrow the coin so that you can bring it to your own light source. If you're not granted permission, don't buy the coin.

The following is a chart of the effects of certain types of light on certain types of coins:

Light Source	Actual Grade	Apparent Grade Under Light
sun	Gem Mint State	About Uncirculated, scratches
fluorescent	Gem Mint State	Mint State with scratches
incandescent (light bulb)	Gem Mint State	Gem Mint State with "identity loss"—some details overlooked
diffused (floodlight)	About Uncirculated	Mint State
bare filament	Mint State (and ugly)	Gem Mint State and attractive
floodlight & bare filament	About Uncirculated	Gem Mint State

Circulated Coins and Lighting

Although the previous chart refers primarily to coins with high grades, circulated coins are also affected by light. Dull circulated coins often display an attractive glisten when displayed under floodlights and chandeliers. And they are subject to having their defects hidden by the same types of light which hide defects of the Mint State coins.

Remember, magnification and lighting problems can be minimized if each is used consistently. Use the same type of magnification under the same type of lighting to view all of your coins.

3

The Grading of
United States Coins

As the system for grading has been refined to include more levels of grading, there is more latitude for misrepresentation of specimens. This practice is not only harmful to the collector, but serves to degradate the efforts of reliable coin dealers who are attempting to compete in the coin market on an equitable basis. Secondarily, as coins have become more valuable in all categories, small discriminations, which at one time might not have seriously affected the value of the coin, are today important in assessing its value. The highest quality coins have appreciated the most and at this point in time, minute differences among these high quality coins are crucial in terms of competitive value. The science of grading coins has not kept pace with the growing need for finite and highly specific valuation.

—Dr. Richard Bagg and James J. Jelinski
The Numismatist

Grading. It sounds like a simple word and a description of a simple process. The word itself may be simple, but the process it describes in the field of coins couldn't be more complex. The variables related to grading are endless. The debate among knowledgeable numismatists about what affects grade or why coins are graded remains unsettled. The country's foremost numismatists are undecided as to what grading really is. In my attempts here to simplify a complex art and state why coins are graded, I must apologize to some of my professional colleagues in the coin field. About a third will agree with what I have to say, singing my praises and hailing me as a numismatic prophet and savior of the industry. Another third will give my presentation a lukewarm reception, pointing to areas with which they agree and other areas with which they do not. The last third will harshly criticize my explanations, pointing out that I have oversimplified a complex process which must remain complex.

WHAT GRADING IS AND WHY COINS ARE GRADED

Grading is the universal language which numismatists use to describe coins. Coins are graded on a 3–70 scale, on which 3 is the lowest and 70 is the best. The amount of wear and tear a coin has endured will to a large degree determine its grade. A grade, then, is a description, a numismatic shorthand for what a coin looks like. Numismatists have agreed that the best way someone can draw a mental picture of what a coin looks like is for a coin to be graded without regard to imperfections, then for the imperfections to be described separately. In other words, if a well-worn coin has a scratch, grade the coin as if it didn't have a scratch—then describe the scratch. This concept itself is controversial, for many professionals tend to price coins first, then grade them. Students of grading grade coins first, then price them; it's far easier to learn grading without paying attention to price. When you learn grading this way, though, it's important to realize that the grade you assign a coin will not immediately let you price the coin if the coin has *any* imperfections.

Coins are graded so that they can be sold to people through the mails who don't see the coins before ordering; so people who do see the coins they are buying will have an idea of the value of the coins by looking up their values in price guides; so you can compare dealers' offerings; and so you can describe your collection and be able to draw a mental image of what it looks like when it's sitting safely in a bank safety deposit box. It all comes down to one thing: money. In general, the higher the grade, the higher the price.

THE AMERICAN NUMISMATIC ASSOCIATION CERTIFICATION SERVICE AND ACADEMIC GRADING

The American Numismatic Association (A.N.A.)—P.O. Box 2366, Colorado Springs, Colorado 80901—has set up a certification service that grades coins for a small fee. Academic grading (grading the coin without regard to imperfections; then describing the imperfections) is used. The Association's certification service is of supreme concern to dealers and collectors alike. Because of widespread respect for the Association itself, collectors believe that the opinions offered by the service are gospel— which they aren't. However, although the A.N.A.'s certification service isn't always correct in the grades it assigns to submitted coins, it is correct in its academic approach to grading.

Strike, which refers to the degree of detail appearing on a coin at its manufacture by the Mint (e.g., a "weakly struck" Uncirculated coin is one which has never been circulated but which was manufactured missing much detail of its design), is not taken into consideration by the A.N.A.'s service when the numerical grade is assigned. But you can be absolutely certain that two identically graded Uncirculated coins, one sharply struck and the other weakly struck, do not carry the same value. The A.N.A.'s service has been harshly criticized because even when it properly follows its own parameters, its assigned grades don't always relate to price.

WHAT CONSTITUTES GRADE

A coin's *grade* depends upon its *level of preservation* and its *beauty*. However, the amount of emphasis that each factor is given during the grading process is the subject of debate.

Level of preservation refers to how well a coin has been preserved since it was minted. A coin that has had a hole drilled in it, that has many scratches, and that is well worn with no detail left is in a low level of preservation. A coin that has been carefully stored and looks as new as when it was minted is said to be in a high level of preservation. There is wide agreement that level of preservation constitutes the major percentage of a coin's grade.

Many dealers consider "beauty" of immense importance and weight when considering what grade to give a coin; the A.N.A. and its certification service take an academic approach and give little weight to beauty, with some exceptions. In my use of the word "beauty," I'm *not* referring to a coin's design. Rather, I'm referring to factors such as *toning*, the slow, regular, natural process through which a coin acquires a patina or color. The commercial segment of the coin-collecting hobby and business weights the quality of this color heavily; the academic segment discounts the importance of this color.

COINS MADE FOR CIRCULATION

A coin is most valuable if it has been *well preserved* and, thus, looks the same as it did the day it left the Mint, with the exception of toning. Collectors call these coins *Mint State* (MS) or *Uncirculated* (Unc.). Coins which are Brilliant Uncirculated are often referred to as *B.U.* After a business strike coin—one made for general circulation—is minted, it is distributed to the Federal Reserve System, which distributes it to the banks; the banks then distribute the coin to the public. This distribution system has been in effect since 1913. As a coin passes from person to person or circulates, it becomes worn from being handled. Such coins are called "circulated" coins by collectors and are far less desirable than the coins which are Mint State, for the wear causes a great deal of luster and detail from the coins to be lost which can never again be recovered. There are numerous distinctions within both the MS and circulated grade categories.

A coin's grade is an indirect statement of value. It is therefore imperative that you be familiar with coin grading or be able to trust someone who is. But the fact that you are a scholar, able to grade every coin meticulously and accurately, doesn't mean you can necessarily know a coin's value, as explained in chapter 7. Grading habits of dealers change according to the mood of the coin market.

HOW THE A.N.A. VIEWS EYE APPEAL

Although coin grading is a subjective process of evaluation, the most subjective element of a coin's appearance, its overall beauty, is not always incorporated into the grade. The very thought that beauty is not taken into consideration infuriates both dealers and collectors. When a dealer is confronted with the allegation that many of his or her colleagues don't take overall beauty into consideration, the dealer's immediate reaction is to claim that the American Numismatic Association Certification Service (ANACS) doesn't take eye appeal into consideration when assigning a grade, which is only partially true.*

If all of the dealers all of the time strongly believe that a particular type of toning on a particular coin is awesome, phenomenal, and overwhelmingly attractive, ANACS would feel justified in raising its grade by half of a grade (e.g., MS-63/65 raised to MS-65/65). The trouble is, this

---

* ANACS is an arm of the world's largest and most influential nonprofit rare-coin organization, the American Numismatic Association. The service states its opinion of authenticity and grade and issues photocertificates for a nominal fee. The grades are arrived at through examination by a panel of graders employed by the service. If ANACS is uncertain of grade or authenticity, the coin is sent to an independent consultant(s) for a supporting opinion(s).

concept is one which can only be written about because all of the dealers all of the time are never in complete agreement as to any type of toning always being attractive. Consequently, it has given some coins the benefit of a slightly higher grade for being beautiful, when many dealers thought the coin was ugly with terribly unattractive toning.

SUBJECTIVITY

Grading is subjective, but not as subjective as some dealers would like you to think. These dealers might sell you a coin, give it a high Mint State grade, then refuse to take it back when you find out it isn't Mint State, but has slight wear, claiming that grading is subjective and that there are legitimate differences of opinion. Most dealers know what makes a coin universally beautiful or universally ugly. The "grading is subjective" argument carried to extremes is a defense of unethical grading practices.

Many would agree that the purpose of grading is more to communicate how well a coin has been preserved than how nice it looks. The fact remains, though, that in most cases the higher the grade, the better the appearance. A universally ugly coin doesn't deserve a high grade no matter how high its "technical level of preservation."

PROOF—A METHOD OF MANUFACTURE, NOT A GRADE

When coins were first assigned grades, only a few grades existed: Unc., Fine, Good, Fair, Poor, and mutilated or basal state. Of course, these grades refer to business strikes. The term *Proof* was also used. But Proof doesn't refer to a grade; rather, it refers to a method of manufacture. A Proof is a coin struck *at least twice* on specially polished dies and specially selected planchets to assure a chromiumlike brilliance (1982-S, and possibly later date, commemorative Proof coins were struck three times because of the higher relief design; virtually every other Proof coin was struck twice). Proofs are sold to collectors during the year of issue at a premium—a price above the face value of the coin. Brilliant Proof coins are among the most beautiful, for there is often a cameo contrast between the reflective fields and the frosted devices. The *Matte Proof* has a different appearance and is produced by a different process. For example, some Proof coins struck during 1908–1916 by the Philadelphia Mint appear grainy because either the dies or the coins were sandblasted. This area is explored fully in chapter 5.

GRADING GUIDES

As the coin business has become more sophisticated, so have grading philosophies. More and more grades have been added. A good review of these philosophies, some of which are still adhered to today, is provided in *Grading Coins: A Collection of Readings*, edited by Richard Bagg and James J. Jelinski (Essex Publications 1977). The first major grading guide to gain universal acceptance was *The Guide to the Grading of United States Coins*, by Martin R. Brown and John W. Dunn, which became known as the "Brown & Dunn" method of grading. The authors allowed the reader to grade coins by looking at line drawings and comparing the representations to the coins. The authors stressed that graders familiarize themselves with coin design by closely examining well-struck Mint State coins. This would allow for better understanding of what parts of a coin's design were missing from circulated specimens, thus allowing ease of grading for circulated coins.

The Brown and Dunn method was a good start in promoting standardized grading practices, but it is far from adequate today, although some dealers still use it. The Retail Coin Dealers Association (R.C.D.A.) recommends it over other grading guides. This guide is popular with dealers who desire a less specific set of grading parameters than those of the A.N.A. The importance and popularity of this guide is exaggerated by the dealers who like its general definitions.

In 1970, *Photograde* (see Fig. 3–1), by James F. Ruddy, made its mark on the numismatic community. This was a truly revolutionary book which can still be used to supplement grading knowledge. In it, every major United States coin design is illustrated with black-and-white photographs. This book is a must for the inexperienced collector, for coins can be compared to their photographic likenesses and accurate grades arrived at. *Photograde* is a general reference and should be used in conjunction with *Official A.N.A. Grading Standards for United States Coins*, by the American Numismatic Association (Fig. 3–2). The shortcoming of *Photograde* is its lack of depth. It only shows how to grade circulated coins. There are no photos of Mint State coins. And there is only one level of quality given for each major grade, thereby not acknowledging that although a particular circulated coin may be assigned a grade, that coin may be a strong example or a weak example of that grade.

FINE

Obverse: The date will be sharp. The shield will be complete around its outer edge. Liberty's right leg will be worn flat.
Reverse: Approximately half of the feathers will show.

VERY FINE

Obverse: Liberty's right leg will be rounded but worn from above the gown to the foot. About half of the mail covering the breast will show.
Reverse: The eagle's body will be worn smooth.

EXTREMELY FINE

Obverse: Liberty's right knee and the tip of her breast will show slight wear.
Reverse: All of the feathers will show but will be worn on the high spots.

ABOUT UNCIRCULATED

Obverse: Only a trace of wear will shown on the knee cap, breast, and center of shield.
Note: Usually struck with a flat head. An Uncirculated coin with a fully detailed head is worth a premium price.
Reverse: Only a trace of wear will show on the front edge of the eagle's wing and the high points of the breast.

LIBERTY STANDING QUARTERS
1925-1930

ABOUT GOOD

Obverse: The rim will be worn down into the date and letters.
Reverse: The rim will be worn down into the lettering and stars.

—Page 77—

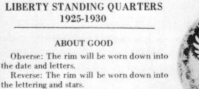

Fig. 3–1.   A page from Photograde, *by James F. Ruddy.* Photograde *is published by Bowers and Merena Galleries, Inc., Box 1224, Wolfeboro, NH 03894. (Courtesy Bowers and Merena Galleries, Inc.)*

SMALL CENTS—LINCOLN 1909 TO DATE

MINT STATE *Absolutely no trace of wear.*

MS-70   UNCIRCULATED *Perfect*
A flawless coin exactly as it was minted, with no trace of wear or injury. Must have full mint luster and brilliance or light toning. Any unusual die or planchet traits must be described.

MS-67   UNCIRCULATED *Gem*
Virtually flawless but with very minor imperfections.

MS-65   UNCIRCULATED *Choice*
No trace of wear; nearly as perfect as MS-67 except for some small blemish. Has full mint luster but may be unevenly toned or lightly fingermarked. A few barely noticeable nicks or marks may be present.

MS-63   UNCIRCULATED *Select*
A mint state coin with attractive mint luster, but noticeable detracting contact marks or minor blemishes.

MS-60   UNCIRCULATED *Typical*
A strictly Uncirculated coin with no trace of wear, but with blemishes more obvious than for MS-63. May lack full mint luster, and surface may be dull or spotted.
    Check points for signs of abrasion: high points of cheek and jaw; tips of wheat stalks.

ABOUT UNCIRCULATED *Small trace of wear visible on highest points.*

AU-55   *Choice*
OBVERSE: Only a trace of wear shows on the highest point of the jaw.
REVERSE: A trace of wear shows on the top of wheat stalks.
    Almost all of the mint luster is still present.

AU-50   *Typical*
OBVERSE: Traces of wear show on the cheek and jaw.

[81]

Fig. 3–2.   A page from the official A.N.A. grading guide. (Permission for reproduction of page number 81 from Official A.N.A. Grading Standards for United States Coins *has been granted by the copyright holders, American Numismatic Association, Colorado Springs, Colorado, and Western Publishing Company, Inc., Racine, Wisconsin)*

A.N.A. GRADING STANDARDS

In 1977, the American Numismatic Association introduced its *Official A.N.A. Grading Standards for United States Coins.* Every United States coin was illustrated by line drawings. Finally, it was thought, the numismatic industry would have a set of uniform, agreed-upon standards. The guide grades coins based on a scale of 1–70, in which 1 is poor or basal state and 70 is perfect. The official A.N.A. grading system scale, as revised in 1981, is as follows:

Adjectival Designation	Numerical Grade	Adjectival Qualifier
Mint State	70	Perfect
Mint State	67	Gem
Mint State	65	Choice
Mint State	63	Select
Mint State	60	Typical
About Uncirculated	55	Choice
About Uncirculated	50	Typical
Extremely Fine	45	Choice
Extremely Fine	40	Typical
Very Fine	30	Choice
Very Fine	20	Typical
Fine	12	—
Very Good	8	—
Good	4	—
About Good	3	—

This numerical system is based on a grading formula devised by the late Dr. William Sheldon for his book *Penny Whimsy*—an authoritative text on large cents. Dr. Sheldon introduced this scale in the late 1940s and early 1950s as an algebraic pricing formula for large cents:

$$\text{Book Value} = \text{Basal Value} \times \text{Numerical Designation}$$

In other words, by multiplying the value of a particular specimen in basal state ("basal" means barely identifiable as to type of coin) by the numerical grade, the value could be computed. For example, if coin X, an Extremely Fine-40, was valued at $2 in Basal State-1, its book value would have been $80:

$$\underset{\text{Book Value}}{\$80} = \underset{\text{Basal Value}}{\$2} \times \underset{\text{Numerical Designation}}{40}$$

Theoretically, the correct grade of a large cent could have been found with just the book value stated. As in any algebraic formula, you can always solve for the unknown with two knowns. This formula is outdated today, for minute differences in a particular coin's grade can mean a considerable difference in price.

The second edition of *Official A.N.A. Grading Standards for United States Coins* (Whitman Coin Products division of Western Publishing Company, Inc., 1981) (see Fig. 3–2) is essential for grading all U.S. coins. When buying coins, insist that the seller use these standards. If the seller uses what he or she calls "my own standards," then he or she is not legally bound to use any system and is free to overgrade.

OVERGRADING AND UNDERGRADING

Overgrading is the describing of a coin as being in a higher level of preservation than it actually is. Undergrading is the describing of a coin as being in a lower level of preservation than it actually is. Although both can be used to take advantage of you, market fluctuations can lead to both. Just because a dealer doesn't overgrade doesn't mean that he or she is honest. The dealer may undergrade to try and catch you off guard—then grossly overprice!

Impact of Market Fluctuations on Grading Standards

In a boom market, grading standards become very liberal. In a depressed market, grading standards become tight and potential buyers become highly selective: people tend to believe a coin is in a lower grade than is in fact the case. During a business-as-usual market, coins tend to be graded more accurately than during a boom or a bust phase.

During a boom market, desirable coins are in short supply because so many people want them and are paying top dollar to get them. Let's use an accurately graded 1880 Liberty Seated quarter (Proof-63) as an example. During a boom market, dealers would call this coin a Proof-65 or better because there are so few actual Proof-65s around to satisfy demand.

During a depressed market, grading standards become very tight because it is difficult to sell coins. So everyone scrutinizes each coin closely. The Proof-63 quarter becomes a Proof-60 quarter. Suddenly that light, almost unnoticeable nick on the knee becomes a gigantic gouge, blamed for almost eliminating Ms. Liberty. Everyone is looking for a reason not to buy, so trivialities become major imperfections. This partially accounts for ANACS being accused of overgrading during the slump of 1981–1982. Dealers deluged the service with coins during this period because they wanted MS-63 certificates for coins which they and other dealers believed were MS-60s. Dealers who weren't satisfied with a grade would discard the certificate and send the coin in again. Guess what happened? Sometimes they got a different grade because the staff was overworked, overwhelmed, and not able to handle the load. Some big mistakes were made by ANACS during this period, and these mistakes seriously impaired the Service's reputation. *Remember: If properly preserved, the coin's grade doesn't change. Only dealer coin-grading attitudes change.*

As you can well imagine, these moods have a hectic impact on value guide accuracy. This is explored in chapter 7.

How Some Dealers Rip Off Their Customers by Overgrading

There are three basic categories of overgrading: *vindictive, blue collar,* and *white collar.*

Vindictive Overgrading.   This refers to a coin being sold which has little or no premium value (the amount of money a coin is worth above its face value) and has, for all practical purposes, no chance of ever gaining a premium value. Most vindictively overgraded coins are either grossly overgraded or whizzed.

Whizzing is a process used to simulate mint luster on a circulated coin through use of a wire brush (perhaps a rotary electric one) and/or an abrasive chemical. The top layer of metal is modified so that high point wear is not visible. Whizzed coins can often be spotted because the cleaning is often crude, the surface is highly porous, and the coin often appears with loss of detail. A whizzed 1832 half-cent displays a peculiar graininess and surface porosity. A closeup of the "LIBERTY" on that same coin as shown in Fig. 3–3 points up the unnatural rippled effect. A genuine Mint State coin would be smooth, with the natural luster beaming from the surfaces if viewed with the naked eye. If viewed under a microscope, the Mint State coin would exhibit "flow lines" (lines that result from the minting process and spread out from the center to the rim, where they are most prominent). The word "whizz" is used to describe the process because of the noise it was originally associated with.

The whizzed coin is relatively easy to spot and has received so much publicity that it has been virtually eliminated from the marketplace. But watch out for whizzed coins in places such as flea markets where reputa-

Fig. 3–3. Blowup of a whizzed half-cent. The appearance is granular and unnatural, indicating the coin was brushed. (ANACS photograph)

ble dealers are not the primary sellers. In general, whizzed coins are unsalable. ANACS will grade whizzed coins and add "whizzed" to the description.

Blue-Collar Overgrading. Blue-collar overgrading, the gross overgrading of coins with value, comes in two types. The most common involves circulated coins, the other, less common type, concerns subtle, but still gross, overgrading of Extremely Fine and low-grade About Uncirculated (50) coins.

The first type of blue-collar overgrading is the overgrading of circulated coins and of coins in which very little money is made by overgrading. An example of this kind of blue-collar overgrading would be a dealer's grading a particular Buffalo nickel "Choice Extremely Fine-45," even though it is actually a Very Good-8. And the dealer might charge $15 instead of $2, even though a real EF-45 should be, let's say, $35. It's the bargain-hunter instinct in the beginning collector that leads him or her to buy an overgraded, overpriced coin.

The other kind of blue-collar overgrading involves the sale of coins as "Mint State" which clearly are *not*. Dealers who engage in this type of overgrading can be identified by their mail-order advertisements, which offer "GEM BRILLIANT UNCIRCULATED COINS AT A FRACTION

OF THE GOING PRICE." Despite such claims, the rule still is, you get what you pay for. Or as Lee Hewitt, former editor of the *Numismatic Scrapbook* (which merged with *Coin World*), once said, "There is no Santa Claus in numismatics." Nobody is going to offer you any coins (especially not Gems!) at a fraction of the going price. Those "Gems" usually turn out to be either Extremely Fine or About Uncirculated (no higher than 50) or somewhere in between. Occasionally, United States gold pieces will be graded "Choice B.U." or "Gem B.U." and be no better than Very Fine. Gold coins retain their original mint luster almost indefinitely, and sometimes even heavily circulated gold coins will have mint luster. Although these coins are collectible and have value, their value is a mere fraction of the original price paid. To avoid being a victim of blue-collar overgrading, *deal with reputable dealers.*

White-Collar Overgrading. White-collar overgrading is subtle, sometimes almost unnoticeable, overgrading,* and it is what gives the coin industry a black eye. It is of potential harm not only to collectors and investors, but to dealers, too, who also must buy coins.

These white-collar overgraders make money by selling strong, no-question Mint State-60s and 63s as "MS-65s," "MS-67s," and sometimes even as higher-grade coins. They also make a habit of selling borderline Uncirculated coins (AU-55 or AU-58) as Mint State, sometimes calling these ever-so-lightly circulated coins "MS-65s." The important factor concerning white collar overgrading is that it's subtle. Probably a few unscrupulous individuals engage in this practice all the time.

Differences of Opinion and Overgrading

It is important to remember that differences of opinion *do* exist. Let's say that a Barber quarter graded MS-65 is brought to ten top dealers for confirmation of grade. If three dealers believe the coin is MS-65, three believe it is MS-63/65, and four believe it to be MS-64, there obviously is some difference of opinion. (For the purpose of discussion, we have to assume that these dealers are competent graders, but more about that later.) That quarter probably isn't white-collar overgraded. The subjective element of grading cannot be removed.

But imagine another coin: a Barber half-dollar graded MS-69, complete with photograph in some dealer's catalog. The coin is priced at

* Overgrading, in the strictest academic sense, as defined by the A.N.A., refers to a coin being graded at least a full grade higher than it actually is. In other words, by A.N.A. standards, a circulated coin described as Uncirculated is overgraded, but an MS-60 described as MS-65 is not.

$7,250 (even though the MS-65 price is, say, $3,500) because it is supposed to be so much rarer and more desirable than its MS-65 counterpart. The same ten competent dealers are surveyed. Three of the dealers are emphatic about the coin being nothing more than MS-60; another three insist that the reverse is a little nicer than the obverse, thereby warranting that the coin be graded MS-60/63; two other dealers claim that they saw that Barber half or one exactly like it with ANACS papers certifying it to be MS-63/63 in an auction on the West coast (and swear it only brought $1,100 plus a 10-percent buyer's fee); and the other two dealers make a strong argument for the coin being a "technical" MS-63 which was lightly cleaned and artificially retoned. Sounds like a case of white-collar overgrading!

The Barber half was probably no better than MS-63. A grade of MS-65 would still classify the grader as a white-collar overgrader. But MS-69 shows him or her to be a no-question white-collar overgrader. The difference of opinion argument would only be valid if the dealer called the coin MS-63 (or even MS-63/65, with an appropriate price well below MS-65). If you questioned his or her grading in person (which I strongly urge you not to do), the grader might utter some rhetoric about grading being a matter of opinion.

What an Overgraded Coin Might Look Like

Sometimes white-collar overgrading is easy to spot. For example, look at the no-question Mint State 1903-O Morgan dollar in Fig. 3–4. There are no signs of wear, but the scratches on Ms. Liberty's cheek are large enough to be measured with a ruler. The cheek is one of the most grade-sensitive areas of the Morgan dollar (as well as of other "portrait" coins), and on this example, the face is so marked that it appears that Ms. Liberty got involved in a violent argument.

Now that these detractions have been brought to your attention, you might argue that nobody would ever buy a coin like this as a Mint State-65 or 67. Wrong! Pick up any dealer's catalog which has photographs of a good percentage of the coins offered. Chances are, you will be able to find at least one coin graded as MS-65 or better which has very obvious detractions—so obvious that they are apparent in the photograph. Compare that MS-60 with the 1884-O Morgan dollar graded MS-65/65 by ANACS that is depicted in Fig. 3–5. Pay particular attention to the exquisite satinlike luster which graces the cheek. This example also demonstrates that a coin does not have to be completely free from imperfections to earn the MS-65 grade.

People often think a coin shown in a photograph must be accurately graded. But many auction catalogs exhibit photograph after photograph of

Fig. 3–4.   MS-60 Morgan dollar obverse. This coin does not qualify for any higher grade because of the huge scratches on Ms. Liberty's cheek. This coin has no wear. (ANACS photograph)

Fig. 3–5.   MS-65 Morgan dollar obverse. The mark-free surfaces and satinlike luster make this example particularly desirable. It isn't perfect, but an MS-65 doesn't have to be. (ANACS photograph)

coins that display obvious and very detracting marks but are cataloged at grades approaching MS-70! Grading has a lot to do with common sense. If the coin has a number of scratches visible to the naked eye, chances are it isn't MS-70—or any grade approaching it.

SMALL IMPERFECTIONS, BIG GRADE DIFFERENCE

Examine the beautiful, original obverse of the 1909-S V.D.B. Lincoln cent shown in Fig. 3–6. (The letters "V.D.B." are the designer Victor David Brenner's initials, and were removed during the year of issue, thus creating four varieties: 1909-V.D.B.; 1909-S V.D.B.; 1909; and 1909-S. The "V.D.B." is on the reverse.) This example is wholly original, with the characteristic needle-sharp strike of the first year of issue. The piece displays a delightful cherry-golden tone and is almost a candidate for Mint State-65. But there's one problem: carbon spots, little black spots which are visible on both sides. Although copper coins are more susceptible to these unsightly spots than coins of other metallic content, a Lincoln cent cannot be graded MS-65 with such a detracting characteristic. Thus, the grade is MS-63. However, the coin is deceiving because its other characteristics are so exceptional.

This is the type of coin a dealer would buy as an MS-65—only to get it back to his or her shop, study it, and discover, much to his or her dismay, that the chicken-pox-like spots bring down the grade to MS-63. Lincoln cents and other copper coins with equally value-subtracting imperfections are sometimes advertised as being MS-67 and higher. Watch out for spots on copper coins. Even if the coin is desirable in every other respect, if it has a spot or spots, you will be penalized when the time

Fig. 3–6. MS-63 1909-S V.D.B. Lincoln cent obverse. This coin would grade MS-65 were it not for the scattered little black specks. A small difference in grade can mean a big difference in price. (ANACS photograph)

comes to sell. If you see the problem when you buy and get a good enough deal, that's fine. But do look for spots on copper coins. A little spot when you buy is a big problem when you sell.

Weak, Solid, and Strong Grades

The subject of weak, solid, and strong grades is controversial. Not every Mint State-65 Franklin half-dollar, for example, is exactly in the middle of the standards set for MS-65. Some barely make it, some are right in the middle, and others are borderline or candidates for MS-67. This rule applies to every grade. The 1956 Franklin half shown in Figs. 3–7 and 3–8 has been assigned the ANACS grade of MS-65/65. But most dealers would agree that the technical grade is MS-65/63. ANACS has given the coin the full 65 rating because of the incredible toning which everyone agrees is stunning: hues of golden-russet, sky-blue, and olive-green emanate from spotless surfaces. The reverse, however, has a rather prominent scratch on the left side of the bell. This coin would not be upgraded to 67 even if it didn't have the scratch. Therefore, the reverse is a borderline 65. This specimen does not deserve a premium above the MS-65 value. However, some coin dealers might lure you into paying a premium (possibly not even consciously). The scratch wouldn't be mentioned, and a photograph of the coin's obverse might appear in the dealer's catalog. (If you don't see the coin itself before buying or bidding, you don't know what the reverse looks like.) Extensive mention of the breathtaking toning might be made, with a sentence informing you that this coin is an ANACS-certified MS-65/65. Look before you buy. Just because a coin is graded MS-65/65 by ANACS and has a premium obverse does not mean that it should command that superpremium price.

MINT-MADE IMPERFECTIONS

A Mint-made imperfection is a defect that occurred at the mint during a coin's manufacture. One cause of dealer disillusionment with ANACS is the service's adherence to the principle of Mint-made imperfections not subtracting from a coin's numerical grade. However, many dealers believe that *although Mint-made imperfections do not subtract from the technical level of preservation, they do subtract from the price.* The 1921 Peace dollar shown in Fig. 3–9 has been well preserved, with exquisite hues of gold and cherry upon lustrous surfaces. But look in the left obverse field, in front of Ms. Liberty's nose. A flaw in the planchet has caused a most detracting depression. This coin is a technical MS-65, based on the rule that Mint-made imperfections do not subtract from a coin's numerical grade. But this problem piece would command nothing more than an MS-60 or MS-63 price, if you're lucky enough to find a

Fig. 3–7 (above left).   MS-65 Franklin half-dollar obverse. Beautiful toning graces the obverse, which is a solid MS-65. (ANACS photograph)

Fig. 3–8 (above right).   MS-65 Franklin half-dollar reverse. The reverse is just as beautifully toned as the obverse, but a scratch on the bell, indicated by the arrow, causes this coin to barely qualify for the MS-65 designation. Don't buy a "just-made-it" MS-65 for a high price. (ANACS photograph)

Fig. 3–9.   MS-65, with Mint-made defect, Peace dollar obverse. Notice the planchet depression, indicated by the arrow, which does not lower the grade, just the value, according to the A.N.A. (ANACS photograph)

buyer for it. Buying coins for their ANACS grades is not the wisest method of acquisition, for you cannot match the ANACS grade with the price guide grade to determine the value. Buy the coin, *not* the certificate.

WHITE-COLLAR OVERPRICING

Coins in legitimate high levels of preservation also can be used to separate you from your money. For example, coins which are not rare, but are almost perfect, are sometimes sent in to ANACS to be certified as MS-67 or PF-67. (PF is ANACS's abbreviation for Proof.) Late-date Proof half-dollars can occasionally be found graded PF-67/70 or PF-67/67 (see Fig. 3–10). These coins are offered at a premium, but are not worth the premium. Another good example is the 1943-S steel cent shown in Fig. 3–11. This coin is representative of a breed of coins that are scarce in high levels of preservation and rarely sent to ANACS to be graded. The example here is certainly a notable one: a dazzling contrast between the highly reflective fields and snow-white devices. The piece was graded MS-67/67 by ANACS. This coin is less rare, though, than some people, even dealers, think it is. But because it is such a "common" coin, few dealers bother sending it in to be certified. When one is sent in to be certified, a big fuss is made about it. In other words, this coin attracts hype. The owner of the specimen shown says he declined a dealer's offer of $125 for it. Its MS-65 price is under $10! Some coins are truly rare in MS-67, even when their MS-65 counterparts are relatively common. But this 1943-S steel cent is not an example of one of those rare coins. If this steel cent were offered for $500 or $600 as an MS-67, it would not be a case of white-collar overgrading; it would be a case of white-collar overpricing.

Fig. 3–10.   Proof-67 Kennedy half-dollar obverse. This gorgeous ANACS-certified Proof-67/67 is common and not very valuable. Don't pay a high price for a high-grade, highly common coin. (ANACS photograph)

Fig. 3–11.   MS-67/67 Steel Lincoln cent, obverse and reverse. This coin is almost as reflective as a Proof, but still isn't rare. Just because ANACS graded it MS-67/67 doesn't mean it's worth several hundred percent of the MS-65 price. (ANACS photograph)

HOW TO DISTINGUISH MINT STATE FROM ABOUT UNCIRCULATED

As I stated earlier, grading practices are based on common sense. If a coin has wear, that coin is no longer Mint State. But the important question to know the answer to is, "On what part of the coin should I look for wear?" The answer is based on common sense: *the high points.* The highest points on a coin are what show tell-tale signs of circulation (coins wear the way crowns on teeth do). Each coin is different (even coins of the same denomination and year). Therefore, there can be no completely accurate textbook explanation of how each coin wears. You just have to look for the high points.

It is important to know that the first step in evaluating high-point wear and its severity is to know to look for a change in color of the high points. The following chart lists the basic coinage metals and the color of the high points that each coin possesses after it circulates.

Coinage Metal	High-Point Color After Friction
Copper	Dark brown
Nickel	Dark gray
Silver	Dull gray
Gold	Dull, dark gold

It is simple to identify high-point wear. Look at the delightfully lustrous 1930 Standing Liberty quarter shown in Fig. 3–12. Pay particular attention to the knee, which is free of friction. The weakness in the shield is not wear, but rather a weakly struck area—an area on the coin which has a corresponding weak area on the die. Now look at the other Standing Liberty quarter (Fig. 3–13). Wear is evident on the knee and breast. Notice the difference in color between those high points and the rest of the coin. Even though this type of identification seems simple, people continue to buy coins like this About Uncirculated quarter as Mint State and for Mint State prices.

Let's examine another quarter which has high-point friction that is less prominent (Fig. 3–14). This 1815 Bust quarter is typical of the Bust material offered as MS-63. Genuine Mint State examples are exceedingly

Fig. 3–12.   MS-65 Standing Liberty quarter obverse. This lightly toned jewel is problem-free. (ANACS photograph)

Fig. 3–13.   AU-55 Standing Liberty quarter obverse. Look at light wear on the knee, indicated by the arrow. (Photograph by Bill Fivaz)

Fig. 3–14. AU-55/55 Bust quarter, obverse and reverse. The slightly lighter color of the high points is wear. (ANACS photograph)

difficult to locate. But if you are buying an A.U. coin, know it. Don't pay an MS-63 or even an MS-60 price. This example is nicely toned with wear evident on both sides. On the obverse, light wear is evident on the curl above the eye, the ear lobe, the curl above the ear, the nose, the tip of the ribbon, and sections of the hair. On the reverse, light wear is evident on the tips of the eagle's wings, the area above the eagle's eye, the eagle's claws, the eagle's feathers, and at the edges of the leaves.

Once you begin to realize that differentiating between About Uncirculated and Mint State is nothing more than training yourself to examine a coin's highest parts for wear, you will have overridden anyone's ability

Fig. 3–15. AU-55/55 Large cent, obverse and reverse. The high points are lighter than the rest of this coin and in this picture appear white. (ANACS photograph)

to sell you About Uncirculated coins as Mint State. Look at another A.U. coin (Fig. 3–15). This specimen is an 1838 Large cent. Have you spotted the wear? Many of the white high areas are what constitute the wear. Look at Ms. Liberty's nose and at the highest points of the portrait (hair, ear, etc.). On the reverse, check the edges of the leaves. If you're able to see the wear in these photos, you ought to be able to identify wear on the actual coins. It's just as simple.

Spotting Wear on Unusual Parts of a Coin

One of the most popularly overgraded coins is the Liberty Seated half-dollar. About Uncirculated specimens graded Mint State range from almost impossible to detect to incredibly easy. The easiest specimens to identify display a lighter, duller color on the high points than the rest of the coin. Those high points are (obverse) the knees, breast, and hair above the eye and (reverse) on the eagle's head, beak, and area above the eye.

Specimens that display wear on unconventional high points are more difficult to identify. I call these coins *conventional high-point deemphasis* pieces. In other words, the "conventional" points of wear or parts of a coin on which you are accustomed to spotting wear do not display wear because they are not the high points; they have been deemphasized. The high point or points exist on another area of the coin, perhaps the stars or the arm. Conventional high-point deemphasis occurs as a result of striking. If the striking pressure is not even or if one of the dies is slightly tilted, one side of the coin may be sharply struck, while the other side may be soft in its details. Thus, the highest points of a coin shift. You could use a microscope and look at Ms. Liberty's knees, breast, and hair above the eye for hours, but if the high points shifted as the result of an uneven strike, you would not find wear at those conventional points you studied. You might find the wear on the arm or even the stars. When looking for wear, look at the entire coin. Just because a grading guide or even your personal experience tells you that wear should always be on a certain place to be considered wear, don't necessarily believe it. That advice may be right 99.99 percent of the time. But that 0.01 percent error rate could mean the difference between money in your pocket or in some dealer's pocket. Wear is wear; it doesn't matter if it's on the arm or on the stars. If the coin is lightly circulated . . . well, you finish it (then it isn't Mint State). Photographs of this are beyond the scope of this book.

Spotting Wear on Coins with Beautiful Toning

Presented for your examination in Fig. 3–16 is a very deceptive coin, an AU-55 1878 Liberty Seated half-dollar. Yes, the wear is on the conven-

Fig. 3–16. AU-55/55 Liberty Seated half-dollar, obverse and reverse. This originally toned example has light, almost unnoticeable wear on its highest points. (ANACS photograph)

tional high points. But the coin is so beautifully toned that the wear is almost impossible to detect. The piece displays breathtaking original toning, with electric splashes of sky-blue, violet, and olive green. The overall color is cherry-gold, and this example is a warm, beautiful, and wholly original coin. But look closely; look very closely. First appearances may be deceiving. This half-dollar displays merely a hint of wear on Ms. Liberty's highest points (study where the arrows point on both obverse and reverse). This example proves that just because a coin displays original luster and has never been dipped, cleaned, or chemically enhanced does not give you a guarantee that the coin is Mint State.

Gold Coins That Look Mint State

Almost all gold coins look Mint State from a distance because gold coins retain some luster indefinitely. Often, though, gold coins that are not Mint State are lacking some luster, as well as displaying wear on the high points and having a different "feel" than their Mint State counterparts. The 1926 Saint-Gaudens $20 shown in Fig. 3–17 is an ANACS-graded MS-63/63. It's a truly stunning example, and a borderline MS-65, if not a real MS-65 that was undergraded. Look at the intense luster which emanates from the mark-free, spot-free surfaces. There are a few detractions not even worth mentioning. But of course you can see why this piece is Mint State. Now look at the 1913 Saint-Gaudens $20 featured in Fig. 3–18. That $20 gold piece is an ANACS-graded AU-55/55. But it resembles many "Saints" sold as Mint State (too many). On the obverse, wear is visible on the right breast and right knee (the left breast and left knee to Ms. Liberty).

Fig. 3–17 (above left).   MS-63 Saint-Gaudens double-eagle obverse. This coin exhibits full luster and has no wear. (ANACS photograph)

Fig. 3–18 (above right).   AU-55 Saint-Gaudens double-eagle obverse. This coin is lackluster and is lightly circulated, as indicated by the arrows. (ANACS photograph)

An area of trouble to both dealer and nondealer is the difficulty in recognizing wear on gold pieces which have partially incuse designs. The quarter eagle shown in Fig. 3–19 is such a coin. This 1911 2-½ graded AU-55/55 by ANACS appears at first glance to have no wear—or at least the wear isn't clearly visible. But upon close inspection, light signs of

Fig. 3–19.   AU-55/55 Indian head quarter eagle, obverse and reverse. The wear seems hidden but can be uncovered. (ANACS photograph)

circulation are visible throughout the obverse portrait on the cheekbone and ever so slightly on the headdress. On the reverse, inspect the shoulder of the eagle's right wing (left wing to her), as well as the breast and head.

When buying gold coins graded Mint State, pay particular attention to the lighting details explained in chapter 2.

The Rub

When it comes to differentiating between Mint State and About Uncirculated, nothing can be more difficult to find than a "rub." Rub is the term used to identify a small area on a coin, perhaps no larger than a thumb print, which is evidence of the coin having seen circulation. Rub is an appropriate term, for it represents a coin having been rubbed. A rub is slight friction—wear which results from a coin having circulated slightly. A rub, which lowers an otherwise Mint State coin to About Uncirculated, should not be confused with a fingerprint, which, in some cases, is acceptable on an MS-65. A fingerprint is a sharp imprint; a rub is a smear, an interruption of luster, the color that circulation on each respective coinage metal assumes, and difficult (if not sometimes impossible) to detect unless the coin is carefully tilted and rotated, as explained in chapter 1.

The reverse of the ANACS-graded MS-65 Indian cent reverse shown in Fig. 3–20 displays full, fiery-red luster—undisturbed. The reverse of the Indian head cent graded AU-55 by ANACS (Fig. 3–21) has a rub. Imagine a thumb full of perspiration touching that coin's reverse. You can see where the finger might have once touched by examining the darkened area (brown in color, while the rest of the coin is a blazing red). Examine the fields of both reverses around the words "One Cent." The

Fig. 3–20.   MS-65 Indian head cent reverse. Undisturbed luster. (ANACS photograph)

Fig. 3–21.   AU-55 Indian head cent reverse. The slightest "rub" of circulation, as indicated by the arrows, is all that keeps this coin from the Mint State category. (ANACS photograph)

Mint State field is lustrous; the About Uncirculated field displays a dullness and an interruption of the luster.

Dealers occasionally buy coins as Gems, only to later discover that the Gems have rubs. Dealers have learned the hard way to take the time to examine coins closely during the buying process. You're not the only one who asks, "What rub?" Dealers ask it too—and sometimes discover the answer when it's too late.

STRIKE

Strike refers to how much detail a coin exhibits the second it leaves the dies. A "poorly struck" Mint State coin was manufactured without the detail the Mint intended it to have.

Some professional numismatists might take issue with placing the subject of strike in the grading chapter. They would insist that strike is not a variable related to grade, but a separate category of study. That may be true, but so many dealers believe that strike affects the grade that including it in this chapter seemed necessary. *Strike does not affect the level of preservation; it affects the price.* As explained earlier, Mint-made imperfections do not detract from the numerical grade. They do, however, affect the value. It's the same with strike. This is not cut-and-dried and is being heavily debated by professionals. For an explanation of how the price guides consider strike, see chapter 7.

The term *weak strike* refers to insufficient striking pressure used to manufacture the coin. "Weakly struck" specimens exhibit a softening or loss of design on the example's high relief portions. This results from the

Fig. 3–22. Blowup of a weakly struck Morgan dollar obverse. The weakly struck area can be distinguished from wear because it has Mint luster. (Photograph by Bill Fivaz)

deepest areas of the die not filling adequately because of this lack of pressure. On the Morgan dollar shown in Fig. 3–22, look for this loss of design on the ear and on the hair above it. Planchet luster is visible on these areas, so you can be sure the piece is Mint State.

Worn dies refer to the areas of softening or loss of detail in the portions of low relief on the specimen (usually at the device's edges). On the Walking Liberty half-dollar shown in Fig. 3–23, you can spot the loss of design on the flag's end—the low relief part of this design. Another type of worn die strike is the "orange-peel" effect exhibited by the

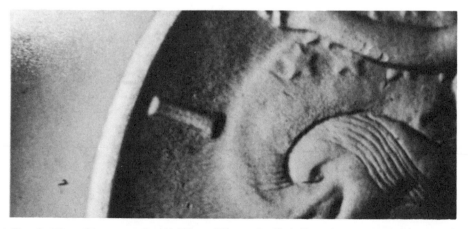

Fig. 3–23. Blowup of a Walking Liberty half-dollar obverse, weakly struck from worn dies. Detail is missing at the flag's tip, the coin's lowest area. (Photograph by Bill Fivaz)

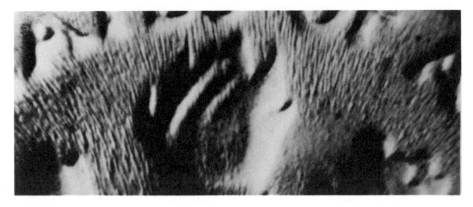

Fig. 3–24.   Blowup of a Roosevelt dime reverse weakly struck from worn dies. There is a distinct lack of detail. (Photograph by Bill Fivaz)

Roosevelt dime reverse in Fig. 3–24. Notice how the orange-peel effect radiates toward the rim and the letters appear soft in execution.

The terms *weak strike* and *worn dies* are often used in connection with each other. If weak strike is used alone, assume the simple definition for weak strike. If the description *weak strike from worn dies* is used, assume the second explanation.

The 1944-S Walking Liberty half-dollar in Fig. 3–25 is an example of a weakly struck coin. However, it is still an ANACS-graded MS-65/65. The weak strike would have to be mentioned in the description, but it would affect only the price, not the numerical grade. Notice the weakly

Fig. 3–25.   MS-65, weakly struck, Walking Liberty half-dollar obverse. Strike does not affect a coin's technical grade, just its price, according to the A.N.A. (ANACS photograph)

Fig. 3–26 (above left).   MS-65, weakly struck from worn dies, Buffalo nickel obverse. The luster is uninterrupted. (ANACS photograph)

Fig. 3–27 (above right).   AU-55 Buffalo nickel obverse. The luster is interrupted and, thus, the coin is not Mint State. (ANACS photograph)

struck areas, and realize that they possess planchet luster.

The 1935-D Buffalo nickel seen in Fig. 3–26 is an example of a coin weakly struck from worn dies. Notice that the weak areas are the areas of low relief. That Buffalo nickel was graded MS-65/65 by ANACS. Beside it (Fig. 3–27) is a 1913-D Variety II Buffalo nickel; this example was graded AU-55/55. It isn't weakly struck or weakly struck from worn dies. It has wear. Look at the lack of luster, the dullness, the high-point friction. Uncirculated coins that are weakly struck or weakly struck from worn dies have full luster. About Uncirculated coins have a diminution of that luster.

Valuable Striking Characteristics

Most coins have intricate designs, with small details in some areas. A number of people collect certain coins for the sharpness or detail in a certain small area. For this reason, a coin that exhibits some small detail may command a premium many times in excess of its counterpart that does not exhibit that small detail. The presence or absence of these details is a result of the strike.

Mercury Dime Bands.   One of the most heavily collected and traded coins for presence of a small detail is the Mercury dime. Look at the small details on the reverse of the one shown in Fig. 3–28. Some people will pay a higher price if the two small center bands are unbroken and separated. Examine the closeup of the reverse that has bands which are not split (Fig.

Fig. 3–28.   MS-65 Mercury dime reverse. The critical bands on the fasces are indicated by the arrow. (Photograph by Steven Ritter)

3–29). Now compare it to the Mercury dime reverse with "split bands" shown in Fig. 3–30. The split bands reverse displays full separation of the two bands. Compare the split bands reverse with the "full split bands" reverse shown in Fig. 3–31. The separation is full and complete on the full split bands reverse. If you purchase a Mercury dime as having "full split bands," make sure it looks like the coin in the picture. The reverse bands are sometimes tampered with to create this effect (through careful manipulation of a sharp knife, such as an X-acto®).

Fig. 3–29.   Blowup of non-split-bands Mercury dime. (Photograph by Bill Fivaz)

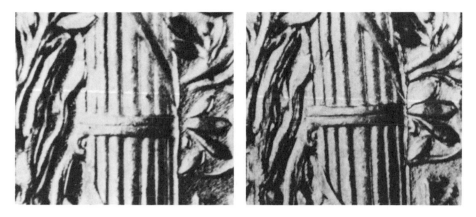

Fig. 3–30 (above left).   Blowup of split-bands Mercury dime. (Photograph by Bill Fivaz)

Fig. 3–31 (above right).   Blowup of full split-bands Mercury dime. This is what numismatists look for when the term "full split bands" is used. (Photograph by Bill Fivaz)

Jefferson Nickel Steps.   Jefferson nickels are also collected for clarity of a certain detail: the steps. You can see how small a detail it really is by examining the reverse of the Jefferson nickel shown in Fig. 3–32. The steps are classified as Type I and Type II. Type I (see Fig. 3–33) steps appear soft in detail. They are found on 1938 Jefferson nickels, some 1939 business strikes, most 1939 Proofs, and some (but not many) 1940 Proofs. There are six steps on Monticello, and coins which display these six steps

Fig. 3–32.   MS-65 Jefferson nickel reverse. The critical steps are indicated by the arrow. (Photograph by Steven Ritter)

Fig. 3–33. Blowup of steps of a Type I Jefferson nickel. The Type I steps are characteristically lacking in detail. (Photograph by Steven Ritter)

Fig. 3–34. Blowup of steps of a Type II five-step Jefferson nickel. (Photograph by Bill Fivaz)

are defined as "full step nickels." Now look at the Type II steps shown in Fig. 3–34. This example has five steps. Compare the five-step example with the six-step Type II example in Fig. 3–35. Once you compare for a few minutes, the difference should be clearly apparent. Interestingly, some Jefferson nickels are not available with six or even five steps!

Franklin Half Bell Lines. The Franklin half-dollar is becoming increasingly popular, and with that popularity comes attention to a small detail on its reverse: the bell lines on the bell's bottom portion, of which there can be seven lines. Take a look at a Franklin half's reverse to see what a small detail it is (Fig. 3–36). Now examine the bottom half of the bell, and count the seven recessed bell lines (Fig. 3–37). The lines must be complete and unbroken in order for the coin to be in the category of "full bell lines."

Fig. 3–35. Blowup of steps of a Type II six-step Jefferson nickel. This is what is required for the "full-step" title. (Photograph by Bill Fivaz)

Fig. 3–36. MS-67 Franklin half-dollar reverse. The critical bell lines are indicated by the arrows. (Photograph by Steven Ritter)

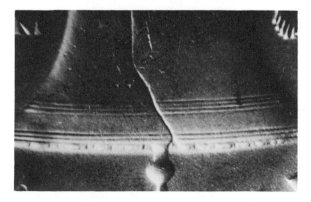

Fig. 3–37. Blowup of a seven-bell-line Franklin half. This is what it takes for "full bell lines." (Photograph by Bill Fivaz)

Fig. 3–38.   Blowup of a full head Type I Standing Liberty quarter. (Photo-graph by Bill Fivaz)

Standing Liberty Quarter Head.   Standing Liberty quarters have attracted the attention of the "collect-by-detail" crowd. The head on Ms. Liberty is what attracts attention. Type I (1916–1917) is common with full head (Fig. 3–38). Type II, however, is uncommon with that detail visible. In order for a Standing Liberty quarter to be considered a "full head," it has to display a complete three leaves on the headpiece, as well as an unbroken hairline from over the forehead to the ear and ear opening. Examine the close-up of the full head shown in Fig. 3–39 and compare it with the 75 percent fully struck head shown in Fig. 3–40.

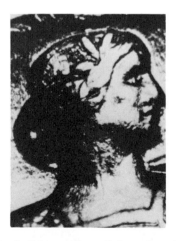

Fig. 3–39.   Blowup of a full head Type II Standing Liberty quarter. (Photo-graph by Bill Fivaz)

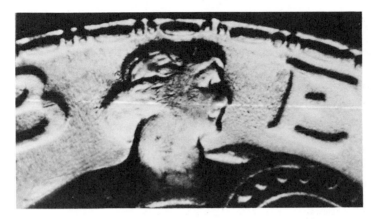

Fig. 3–40.   Blowup of a 75-percent full head Type II Standing Liberty quarter. (Photograph by Bill Fivaz)

Roosevelt Dime Torch.   Even Roosevelt dimes are collected for strike. Look at the reverse of a Roosevelt dime soft in detail on the torch (Fig. 3–41). Now look at its more clearly defined counterpart, as shown in Fig. 3–42. The bands display a clear separation.

Collectors pay attention to almost every small detail when it comes to buying coins. Even if a certain coin with every detail apparent is not collected only for that certain detail, chances are that some collector somewhere will pay a premium for it if it is difficult to find that particular coin with the detail.

Fig. 3–41.   Blowup of a non-fully struck torch line Roosevelt dime. (Photograph by Steven Ritter)

Fig. 3–42. Blowup of a fully struck torch line Roosevelt dime. (Photograph by Steven Ritter)

TONING

Toning refers to the slow and regular process by which a coin acquires color over months and years. Toning should be differentiated from tarnish, which is quick and irregular. Toning is a description of the intermediate process between a coin's period of full brilliance and full darkness. No matter how beautiful any toning may be, it represents an intermediate stage of the coin's progression to full darkening. This is a process that can take a hundred years. Certain types of toning affect the grade to a major extent, and other types of toning do not affect the grade at all. This section deals with natural toning. Artificially induced toning is discussed in chapter 12, and other aspects of toning are discussed throughout the book.

Toning ranges from breathtaking to unattractive; from even and consistent to odd and streaky; from exquisitely colorful and rich in hues to incredibly drab and dull in variety; from phenomenal to despicable; and from telling to deceptive. The variety of tones is both the numismatist's best friend and most threatening enemy. Toning can downgrade a Gem, upgrade a Select, and cause a lot of confusion.

What follows is a coinage metal chart, as well as a brief explanation of the type of toning that each respective metal encounters and a description of how that toning may affect grade and value. Beauty of toning is so subjective that any type of toning listed as subtracting from the price might actually add to it in some transactions.

Coinage Metal	Toning Description	Grade Impact	Value Impact
Copper	Cherry-red	—	—
	Purple-violet	—	—
	Brown and red	—	Lowers value
	Brown	—	Lowers value
	Black spots	Lowers grade	Lowers value
Nickel	Silver-gold	—	Adds value
	Silver-gray	—	—
	Black spots	Lowers grade	Lowers value
Silver	Even iridescence	—	May add
	Uneven iridescence	May lower	May add
	Concentric circles:		
	Golden center; violet periphery fading to blue and red	May add	Adds value
	Golden russet	—	May add
	Black spots	Lowers grade	Lowers value
Gold	Not applicable		

Beware of Heavy Toning That Covers Up Surface Imperfections

Some dealers never purchase heavily toned coins, for fear of there not being full luster underneath the toning. However, the brilliant-is-best mentality is dangerous. If you take this attitude, you'll end up with nothing except cleaned coins.

Toning is the most subjective part of coin evaluation. I may think a coin is ugly, but a dozen dealers could insist that it's the most attractive example they've ever seen.

WHY DEALERS OVERGRADE

Stupidity and ignorance play a major role in dealer overgrading. There are no licensing requirements for becoming a coin dealer, and many people sell coins who know little about them. Some dealers who overgrade bought overgraded coins themselves and actually stand to make a nominal profit off their overgraded offerings. Many of these dealers take tables at shows and overpay for their coins from hustler vest-pocket dealers strolling the aisles. If you think that these dealers who don't know any better are out to rip you off, you're wrong. Some of them are very honest, but they themselves have bought overgraded coins.

Greed also plays a role in overgrading, but a less important role than some believe. Dealers rely on repeat business. If they make a habit of taking advantage of customers, those customers will never return. Professional numismatists work together constantly to attract new people to the world of coin collecting. The greed of professional numismatists is the greed of attracting people involved in other fields to the coin hobby. Once they're attracted, though, the subconscious of some dealers can't help but take the attitude that "if it's mine, it's better than others like it being offered."

4

The Grade Survey

The ANACS is (an) *unbiased* grading opinion available to collectors and investors. However . . . the top grading experts in the world do not work for the ANACS. Most of these top experts own major rare coin dealerships. Unfortunately, though they are totally capable of grading coins correctly, some of these experts overgrade coins when selling to the public . . . 90% of all coins sold as Mint State through the mail and through auctions are overgraded by at least a half a grade . . . They (ANACS) will eventually offer a true solution to the overgrading problem.

—David Hall, Editor/Publisher
Inside View

Nothing is more frustrating to the collector than having a prized coin "talked down" by a dealer. It happens all the time to truly exceptional coins. A knowledgeable collector buys a Morgan dollar as Choice Mint State-65/65 from an honest and intelligent dealer. The coin is ANACS (American Numismatic Association Certification Service) grade confirmed. The collector asks the opinion of another dealer, not for appraisal purposes, but because he or she is so proud of the new acquisition. The other dealer says that the coin is an MS-63 because the feathers on the reverse are not sharply struck.

This may not be a case of a dealer trying to buy an MS-65 coin at an MS-63 price. As explained in the last chapter, many dealers believe that strike should be considered when grading a coin. Many dealers do millions of dollars in sales each year. They know what a coin has to look like in order to command the MS-65 market price. And some just don't care about "technical levels of preservation." They care about bucks. They reason that there is no need to call a coin MS-65 if they are going to sell it for below the MS-65 price.

Further proof of this is the growing number of dealers selling ANACS-grade-confirmed coins at grades below their certified grades.

These dealers take issue with the way ANACS grades coins; they have established their own methods of grading coins through the years, have established reputable businesses, and are respected for adhering to high ethical standards. They don't want to be told by a service which doesn't sell coins how coins should be graded.

These dealers have a valid gripe. Some may even view themselves, and rightly so, as small-scale institutions because of the volume they do and the hundreds or thousands of people who seek and respect their judgment. One large firm, with a large and loyal following, had every intention of adopting A.N.A.'s numerical scale when it was first introduced in 1977. But after they used it in printed offerings and in their store, their customers objected to the new way of grading by numbers. They much preferred the word-grades which had been successfully used for so many years. As a result, that firm switched back to grading by words. Other dealers had similar experiences with the A.N.A. grading system and have stuck with their own variation of it.

Interestingly, there is no sense in using numbers to grade coins. The numbers don't represent anything scientific. Words can be used to do the same thing the numbers do: describe the level of preservation. MS-60 is "Typical" Mint State; MS-63 is "Select" Mint State; MS-65 is "Choice" Mint State; MS-67 is "Gem" Mint State; and MS-70 is "Perfect" Mint State. Theoretically, if the numbers are deleted from the grade, you should be able to understand the grade being communicated. You should know that a coin described as Typical Mint State is an MS-60 and that a coin described as Select Mint State is an MS-63. But the numbers are used because not all dealers use the same words to describe the same numbers. For example, some dealers think that the MS-65 grade is Gem Mint State (it's Choice Mint State). And other dealers may be under the false impression that MS-63 is Choice Mint State (it's Select Mint State). The numbers are needed to promote uniformity and understanding.

ANACS GRADE SURVEY

An examination of the general dealer grade consensus as opposed to how ANACS would grade a coin should greatly aid your buying decisions by helping to prepare you for the ANACS result by demystifying the Service's thought process. Further, if you ever do buy coins that happen to be ANACS certified, you will be better prepared to understand the relationship between their marketability and technical grade.

No subject elicits more hostility and conversation in the coin industry than A.N.A. grading standards and ANACS grading. Some say that

ANACS standards are not consistent; that a number of individuals use the service, and in so doing, avoid learning how to grade; that grading is so subjective that a definitive grade can never be assigned; that ANACS just doesn't know how to grade; and that ANACS papers are worthless because a coin can deteriorate and not be in the same level of preservation it was when originally graded by the service.

In the survey that follows, an ample cross-section of individuals representing different factions of the hobby are surveyed regarding ANACS grading. The survey was designed to minimize debate over the mechanics of the survey, while maximizing debate over the issue of grading.

The survey covers thirty-two imaginary coins. (Of course, some of the individuals surveyed immediately started comparing my descriptions to real coins that they viewed.) Each description, which is listed by metallic category (silver, gold, etc.), starts out by stating whether the coin is a business strike or a Proof, followed by a general description of overall appearance or "feel." A description of strike, toning, high points, and luster is included in order to give you the best possible description.

The survey participants were informed that the descriptions given were beyond debate (or were told to assume that the descriptions were accurate). Each participant was asked to provide two grades: one, the grade that he would speculate the A.N.A. Certification Service would give the coin and the other the grade the participant would give the coin. It was stressed that since the coins in the survey are imaginary, participants should assign the coins ANACS grades based on how they think ANACS would grade the coins as a survey participant with survey in hand—*not* what ANACS would grade the coins if they were real coins submitted for a grade by the dealer participating in the survey. (Some didn't pay full attention to this.)

Strike is referred to in percentage form. For example, if you see 90 percent, that means that the coin is 90 percent fully struck. I did not state, however, whether a coin not 100 percent fully struck was not fully struck (having been manufactured by the Mint with all design details visible) because of weak or uneven striking pressure or worn dies. Participants were given the opportunity to add this information, for each participant was told that if he felt that the survey lacked any information necessary to arrive at a grade, he should add that information.

Toning is referred to by coloration and variation. If a coin was supposed to be imagined with spotting, that was stated. If a coin was supposed to be imagined untoned, "Brilliant" was listed.

Surfaces are referred to by Mint State grades of the A.N.A. grading system. For example, if Choice surfaces are listed, that means that the coin has surfaces which meet the A.N.A. grading system's standards for MS-65. There are no exceptions to this; the adjectives in this survey refer only to Mint State coin adjectives. Surfaces are extremely important because surface defects such as scratches can detract considerably from the grade. In every case, however, it's a matter of how severe the scratch or scratches is or are and the location of the imperfection(s). A nick on the cheek is more detracting than one on the reverse buried between two letters. In some cases, though, more than just the A.N.A. Mint State adjective is used (e.g., hairlines).

High points are where numismatists look for wear. In the survey, "circular luster" means no wear (see chapter 2 for an explanation) on business strikes. For Proofs, the term *unimpaired* is used, meaning there is no wear or friction. Sometimes the word *cameo* is used, meaning the devices are frosted and the fields are mirrorlike.

Luster refers to how a coin reflects light circularly. A coin can be toned dark and have original luster underneath. Wear interrupts luster, and dipping or cleaning lowers its quality. Again, the A.N.A. Mint State adjectives are used to describe a category. If the word *Gem* is used, for example, it means that the luster of the imaginary coin described rates MS-67. (For Proofs, this category also refers to the reflective quality, even though Proofs reflect light differently than business strikes.)

The format is as follows: the participant's name (e.g., SMITH), the prediction of the ANACS grade (e.g., MS-65/65), and personal grade (e.g., Gem BU MS67.08). The personal grade does not have to conform to the A.N.A. grading system. The bold-face ANACS grades are "probable" ANACS grades as prepared by the Service's staff, whose analysis immediately follows the survey. As you know, the ANACS grade is a split grade for obverse/reverse. MS-63/65 means an MS-63 obverse and an MS-65 reverse.

Sit back and read the survey. Or "participate" in the survey yourself! You have the same ability to "look" at the coins as the participants had. Then draw your own conclusions. Make sure to read the ANACS analysis, as well as Paul Taglione's analysis. Both are intriguing. But remember that there are no right or wrong answers. A lengthy conclusion seems unnecessary, since these results speak for themselves. Now meet the participants in the great grading debate.

Participants

ANACS. Thomas K. DeLorey, senior grader and authenticator for the Service (and based at the Service's Colorado Springs facility), played a key role in the ANACS response. Before joining ANACS, DeLorey was editor of *Coin World*'s "Collector's Clearinghouse" column.

Harry J. Forman, president, Forman Enterprises, Ltd. Forman is a noted Philadelphia dealer and author whose outspoken investment philosophy has brought him fame and fortune.

William P. Paul, chairman of the board, American Heritage Minting,

Inc. His firm is a driving force in the area of high-quality United States coins, and his company is the market maker for British coinage.

Robert S. Riemer, a mail-order dealer who specializes in lower-priced ANACS-graded coins.

Joseph H. Rose, president, Harmer, Rooke, Numismatists, Ltd. Rose is a founder of the numismatic department of the now half-billion-dollar-per-year business of Manfra, Tordella, and Brookes. He is a coeditor of Don Taxay's *Encyclopedia of U.S. Coins,* as well as being a counterfeit detection authority who received training with the United States Secret Service.

Maurice Rosen, editor/publisher, *The Rosen Numismatic Advisory,* and president, Numismatic Counseling, Inc. Rosen publishes a highly acclaimed and controversial consumer advocacy numismatic newsletter. He is the author of the first in-depth study concerning ANACS grading.

Anthony J. Swiatek, editor/publisher, *The Swiatek Numismatic Report.* Swiatek, an ANACS consultant, and the foremost United States commemorative coin expert, is one of the coin industry's most visible authorities. He is the sole author and formulator of A.N.A. grading standards for commemorative coins listed in the A.N.A. official grading guide. Swiatek's newsletter has one of the highest circulations of any coin newsletter published, and the commemorative encyclopedia he co-authored is as popular as ever. Swiatek has testified before Congress and recently completed a new book about Walking Liberty half-dollars.

Paul F. Taglione, president, New England Rare Coin Galleries, Inc. Taglione is credited by many with starting the ANACS-graded coin revolution. Before joining New England, Taglione authored a series of powerful display ads which extolled the virtues of buying only ANACS coins. Taglione has probably handled and studied more ANACS-graded coins than any other dealer. This, combined with his high level of thinking (he was a Harvard professor), is reason for you to take an extra close look at what he has to say. Taglione is the originator of Multi-Dimensional Grading, an innovative method of describing each coin's grade by separate characteristic grades and comments. Taglione's analysis of this survey is presented in its entirety.

Bob Wilhite, price guide editor, *Numismatic News, Coins* magazine, and *Coin Prices* magazine. Wilhite determines what coins receive what values in these publications. He's very important, but doesn't wield the power you would at first think he does. Prices are set by supply and demand, not by what Wilhite thinks they should be.

(*Note:* In the survey you will find some typographic inconsistencies, for example, "Proof-67" one time, "Proof 67" another, and "PF-67" still another—all for the same coin. Responses are spelled and punctuated exactly the way the participants wished them written with the exception of Wilhite's response: his single-number grades were changed to double-number grades [e.g., MS-65 changed to MS-65/65].)

Copper

1. Business strike. Wholly original.

> Strike: 100%
> Toning: Brilliant
> Surfaces: Choice
> High points: Circular luster
> Luster: Choice

ANACS:	**MS-65/65**
FORMAN:	MS-65/65; Choice B.U.
PAUL:	MS-65/65; Gem BU-67
RIEMER:	MS-65/65; MS-65/65
ROSE:	MS-65/65; MS-65
ROSEN:	MS-65/65; MS-63+
SWIATEK:	MS-65/65; MS-65
TAGLIONE:	MS-65/65; MS-64
WILHITE:	MS-67/67; MS-67/67

2. Business strike. A delicate patina somewhat subdues immaculate surfaces. Wholly original.

> Strike: 100%
> Toning: Red and brown
> Surfaces: Choice
> High points: Circular luster
> Luster: Choice (under tone)

ANACS:	**MS-65/65**
FORMAN:	MS-63/63; Choice B.U., toned
PAUL:	MS-63/63; Gem Unc. 65
RIEMER:	MS-63/63; MS-63/63
ROSE:	MS-65/65; MS-65
ROSEN:	MS-63/63; MS-63
SWIATEK:	MS-63/65; MS-63/65
TAGLIONE:	MS-63/63; MS-63
WILHITE:	MS-67/67; MS-67/67

3. Business strike. Wholly original.

> Strike: 50%
> Toning: Brilliant
> Surfaces: Choice
> High points: Circular luster
> Luster: Choice

ANACS: **MS-65/65, Weakly Struck**
FORMAN: MS-65/65; B.U., weak strike
PAUL: MS-63/63; Ch BU 63
RIEMER: MS-65/65, weak strike; MS-63/63
ROSE: MS-65/65, with qualifier; MS-65, with qualifier
ROSEN: MS-63/63; MS-60+
SWIATEK: MS-63/63; MS-63
TAGLIONE: MS-65/65, weakly struck; MS-63
WILHITE: MS-65/65; MS-65/65

4. Proof. Rather dingy. Particularly unattractive.

          Strike: 100%
          Toning: Brilliant
          Surfaces: Typical; dense hairlines
          High points: Unimpaired
          Luster: Typical; reflective devices

ANACS: **PF-60/60**
FORMAN: PF-60/60; Impaired Proof
PAUL: PF-55/55; Proof 60
RIEMER: PF-60/60; PF-60/60
ROSE: PF-60/60; PF-60
ROSEN: PF-60/60; Proof-55
SWIATEK: PF-60/60; PF-60
TAGLIONE: PF-63/63; Proof-60
WILHITE: PF-60/60; PF-60/60

5. Proof. Wholly original.

          Strike: 80%
          Toning: Carbon flecks
          Surfaces: Select
          High points: Unimpaired, but oxidized
          Luster: Cameo contrast; Choice

ANACS: **PF-63/63, Weakly Struck**
FORMAN: PF-63/63; Proof, weak strike
PAUL: PF-60/60; Proof 60
RIEMER: PF-63/63; PF-63/63
ROSE: PF-63/63, with qualifier; PF-60, Carbon flecks detract drastically
ROSEN: PF-63/63; Proof-60
SWIATEK: PF-63/65; PF-65
TAGLIONE: PF-63/63; Proof-63
WILHITE: PF-60/60; PF-60/60

6. Proof. Choice in all respects, but the color is not original. The coin has been recently dipped. However, the dipping could not be proven in a court of law.

> Strike: 100%
> Toning: Off-color (orange-white)
> Surfaces: Choice
> High points: Unimpaired
> Luster: Gem; cameo contrast

ANACS:	**Too difficult to answer**
FORMAN:	PF-60/63; Cleaned Proof
PAUL:	PF-55/55 to PF-65/65; Proof 63
RIEMER:	No grade; Not enough information
ROSE:	PF-63/63, qualified; PF-60, Recolor detracts fully
ROSEN:	PF-65/65; Proof-63
SWIATEK:	Who knows?!; PF-60
TAGLIONE:	PF-65/65; Proof-63, once dipped
WILHITE:	PF-60/60; PF-60/60

Copper-nickel

7. Business strike. Breathtaking! Dazzling reflective fields; frosted devices. Delightful streaks of golden-russet emanate from prooflike surfaces. Knife-edge rims. Easily mistaken for a Proof.

> Strike: 100%
> Toning: Golden-russet
> Surfaces: Gem
> High points: Circular luster
> Luster: Gem prooflike

ANACS:	**MS-67/67**
FORMAN:	MS-65/65; Gem BU 1st strike
PAUL:	MS-65/65; Gem BU 67
RIEMER:	MS-67/67; MS-67/67
ROSE:	MS-67/67; MS-67+
ROSEN:	MS-67/67; MS-65
SWIATEK:	MS-65/65; MS-67
TAGLIONE:	PF-65/65; MS-67
WILHITE:	MS-69/69; MS-69/69

8. Business strike. Particularly attractive. Beaming semi-prooflike surfaces. Weakly struck reverse.

Strike: 75%
Toning: Gray-tan
Surfaces: Select
High points: Circular luster
Luster: Choice; semi-prooflike

ANACS:	**MS-63/63, Weakly Struck**
FORMAN:	MS-65/63; B.U.
PAUL:	MS-65/65; Gem BU 65
RIEMER:	MS-63/63; MS-63/63
ROSE:	MS-63/63, qualified; MS-63, qualified
ROSEN:	MS-63/63; MS-60+
SWIATEK:	MS-65/63; MS-65/63
TAGLIONE:	MS-65/65, weakly struck reverse; MS-63
WILHITE:	MS-63/63; MS-63/63

9. Business strike. A few scattered toning spots. Original.

Strike: 75%
Toning: Gray-tan
Surfaces: Typical
High points: Circular luster
Luster: Select

ANACS:	**MS-60/60, Weakly Struck**
FORMAN:	MS-63/63; B.U.
PAUL:	AU-55/55 to MS-60/60; Unc 60
RIEMER:	MS-63/63; MS-63/63
ROSE:	MS-60/63; MS-60+
ROSEN:	MS-60/60; MS-60
SWIATEK:	MS-63/63; MS-63
TAGLIONE:	MS-63/63; MS-60
WILHITE:	MS-60/60; MS-60/60

10. Proof. Phenomenal! This specimen immediately captures the viewer's attention. Spectacular contrast between the mirror fields and frosted devices. A single patch of die polishing marks in the right obverse field. Perfect in all respects.

Strike: 100%
Toning: Golden-russet
Surfaces: Perfect
High points: Unimpaired
Luster: Perfect

ANACS: **PF-70/70**
FORMAN: PF-65/65; Gem Proof
PAUL: PF-65/65 or PF-67/67; Gem Proof 69—Nothing is
             perfect.
RIEMER: PF-67/67; PF-67/67
ROSE: PF-70/70; PF-67++++
ROSEN: PF-67/67; Proof-67
SWIATEK: PF-65/65; PF-67
TAGLIONE: PF-65/67; Proof-67
WILHITE: PF-69/69; PF-69/69

11. Proof. Ugly. Cleaned years ago.

Strike: 90%
Toning: Carbon flecks; abrasively cleaned
Surfaces: Typical
High points: Friction
Luster: Typical

ANACS: **PF-60/60, Cleaned**
FORMAN: PF-60/60; Impaired Proof
PAUL: PF-50/50; Proof 55
RIEMER: PF-55/55; PF-55/55, Cleaned
ROSE: PF-60/60, qualified; PF-60, qualified
ROSEN: PF-60/60; PF-50
SWIATEK: PF-60/60; PF-60
TAGLIONE: PF-60/60, Cleaned; Proof-58, Cleaned
WILHITE: PF-60/60; PF-60/60

12. Proof. The color and surfaces bespeak a Mint State Proof. But
    light wear is evident on the high points.

Strike: 100%
Toning: Golden-russet
Surfaces: Choice
High points: Wear
Luster: Choice

ANACS: **PF-55/55 or PF-60/60**
FORMAN: PF-55/55; Impaired Proof
PAUL: PF-55/55; Proof 55
RIEMER: PF-50/50; PF-50/50
ROSE: PF-55/55; PF-55++
ROSEN: PF-63/63; PF-60
SWIATEK: PF-55/55; PF-55
TAGLIONE: PF-63/63; Proof-58
WILHITE: PF-55/55; PF-55/55

Nickel

13. Business strike. Unusually weak strike.

> Strike: 25%
> Toning: Silver-gray
> Surfaces: Choice
> High points: Circular luster
> Luster: Gem

ANACS:	**MS-65/65** (Never seen one only 25% struck.)
FORMAN:	MS-63/63; BU Weakly Struck
PAUL:	EF-45/45 to MS-60/60; Unc 60
RIEMER:	MS-63/63 Weak; MS-63/63 Weak
ROSE:	MS-63/63, qualified; MS-63, qualified
ROSEN:	MS-63/63; MS-60+
SWIATEK:	MS-63/63; MS-63
TAGLIONE:	MS-63/63, Weakly struck; MS-60
WILHITE:	MS-60/60; MS-60/60

14. Business strike. Unusually strong strike.

> Strike: 100%
> Toning: Silver-gray
> Surfaces: Choice
> High points: Circular luster
> Luster: Gem

ANACS:	**MS-65/65**
FORMAN:	MS-65/65; Gem B.U.
PAUL:	MS-65/65; Gem BU 65
RIEMER:	MS-65/65; MS-65/65
ROSE:	MS-65/67; MS-65+
ROSEN:	MS-65/65; MS-63+
SWIATEK:	MS-65/65; MS-67
TAGLIONE:	MS-65/65; MS-64
WILHITE:	MS-65/65; MS-65/65

15. Business strike. Scattered die cracks.

> Strike: 70%
> Toning: Silver-gray
> Surfaces: Gem
> High points: Circular luster
> Luster: Gem

ANACS:	**MS-67/67, Weakly Struck**
FORMAN:	MS-63/63; BU

PAUL:	MS-65/65; Gem BU 65
RIEMER:	MS-67/67; MS-65/65
ROSE:	MS-65/65, qualified; MS-65, qualified
ROSEN:	MS-65/65; MS-63
SWIATEK:	MS-63/63 or MS-65/65; MS-63
TAGLIONE:	MS-65/65; MS-64
WILHITE:	MS-63/63; MS-63/63

16. Proof. A Type II Jefferson nickel.* Needle-sharp strike with full steps. Bold contrast between the snow-white devices and dazzling, reflective mirror fields. No detractions of any kind.

> Strike: 100%
> Toning: Brilliant
> Surfaces: Perfect
> High points: Unimpaired; cameo contrast
> Luster: Perfect

ANACS:	**PF-70/70**
FORMAN:	PF-67/67; Gem Proof
PAUL:	PF-65/65; Proof 67
RIEMER:	PF-67/67; PF-67/67
ROSE:	PF-70/70; PF-67+
ROSEN:	PF-67/67; PF-67
SWIATEK:	PF-67/67; PF-67
TAGLIONE:	PF-67/67; Proof-69
WILHITE:	PF-69/69; PF-69/69

17. Proof. Another Type II Jefferson nickel. Deep Proof surfaces.

> Strike: 100%
> Toning: Brilliant
> Surfaces: Perfect
> High points: Unimpaired
> Luster: Perfect

ANACS:	**PF-70/70**
FORMAN:	PF-65/65; Choice Proof
PAUL:	PF-65/65; Proof 67
RIEMER:	PF-67/67; PF-67/67
ROSE:	PF-70/70; PF-67+
ROSEN:	PF-67/67; PF-67
SWIATEK:	PF-67/67; PF-67

---

* 56% copper, 35% silver, 9% manganese

TAGLIONE: PF-67/67; Proof-69
WILHITE: PF-65/65; PF-65/65

18. Matte Proof. The epitome of originality. Spectacular knife-edge rims. Concentric circles of cherry-red and ocean-blue fade into silver-gray. No spots.

> Strike: 90%
> Toning: Red, blue, silver-gray
> Surfaces: Gem
> High points: Unimpaired
> Luster: Choice

ANACS: **PF-67/67**
FORMAN: PF-65/65; Choice Proof
PAUL: PF-65/65; Gem Matte Proof 67
RIEMER: PF-65/65; PF-65/65
ROSE: PF-67/67; PF-67+
ROSEN: PF-67/67; PF-67
SWIATEK: PF-65/65; PF-65+
TAGLIONE: PF-67/67; Proof-69
WILHITE: PF-65/65; PF-65/65

19. Proof. Shield type. Delightfully reflective surfaces. A few scattered hairlines. Attractive light golden toning.

> Strike: 95%
> Toning: Light golden
> Surfaces: Select; a few hairlines
> High points: Unimpaired
> Luster: Choice

ANACS: **PF-63/63**
FORMAN: PF-65/65; Choice Proof
PAUL: PF-63/63; Proof 65
RIEMER: PF-65/65; PF-63/63
ROSE: PF-63/63; PF-60+
ROSEN: PF-65/65; PF-60+
SWIATEK: PF-63/63; PF-63 or PF-65
TAGLIONE: PF-65/65; Proof-63
WILHITE: PF-63/63; PF-63/63

20. Proof. Liberty head type. A visual knockout! This little jewel transfixes the viewer's attention. Electric splashes of cherry-gold and sky-blue with a hint of russet. Radiant Proof surfaces with only a few hairlines and a single spot on Ms. Liberty's cheek.

Strike: 100%
Toning: Gold, blue, russet
Surfaces: Typical; a cheek carbon fleck; hairlines
High points: Unimpaired
Luster: Select

ANACS:	**PF-63/63**
FORMAN:	PF-63/63; Proof
PAUL:	PF-60/60; Proof 63, with spot on the face
RIEMER:	PF-65/65; PF-63/63
ROSE:	PF-63/63; PF-60+
ROSEN:	PF-65/65; PF-63
SWIATEK:	PF-65/65; PF-65
TAGLIONE:	PF-65/65; Proof-63
WILHITE:	PF-63/63; PF-63/63

Silver

21. Business strike. Rare date Liberty Seated half-dollar. Stunning! Possible condition census. Shades of violet, red, and green upon satinlike surfaces. Ms. Liberty's knee is completely free of even the most minute abrasion. Perfect, save for very slight obverse and reverse rim wear—which is almost unnoticeable. On perfection's threshold. An exquisite example of a date accorded much respect by the collector.

Strike: 100%
Toning: Violet, red, green
Surfaces: Perfect
High points: Circular luster (light rim wear)
Luster: Perfect

ANACS:	**MS-67/67**
FORMAN:	MS-65/65; B.U.
PAUL:	MS-65/65; Gem Toned 67
RIEMER:	MS-67/67; AU-55/55
ROSE:	AU-55/55; AU-59+, super slider
ROSEN:	MS-67/67; MS-67
SWIATEK:	MS-67/67; MS-67
TAGLIONE:	MS-67/67; MS-65
WILHITE:	MS-63/63; MS-63/63

22. Business strike. Common date Morgan dollar. Scattered scuff marks. Huge, obverse rim nick. Large scratch through eagle's breast.

Strike: 100%
Toning: Brilliant
Surfaces: Typical
High points: Circular luster; heavily scratched;
friction
Luster: Typical

ANACS:	**MS-60/60**
FORMAN:	AU-55/55; A.U.
PAUL:	AU-50/50 to AU-55/55; Unc 60
RIEMER:	MS-60/60; MS-60/60
ROSE:	MS-60/60; MS-60
ROSEN:	MS-60/60; AU-55
SWIATEK:	MS-60/60; MS-60
TAGLIONE:	MS-60/60; AU-55
WILHITE:	MS-63/63; MS-63/63

23. Business strike. Rare date Morgan dollar. Stunning! Euphoric
glimmer. Mark-free and highly desirable. Slight reverse softness
of strike.

Strike: 80%
Toning: Brilliant
Surfaces: Choice
High points: Circular luster
Luster: Choice

ANACS:	**MS-65/65**
FORMAN:	MS-65/63; B.U.
PAUL:	MS-65/65; Gem BU 65
RIEMER:	MS-65/65; MS-65/65
ROSE:	MS-63/63; MS-63+
ROSEN:	MS-65/65; MS-65
SWIATEK:	MS-65/65; MS-63+
TAGLIONE:	MS-65/65; MS-64
WILHITE:	MS-63/63; MS-63/63

24. Proof. Liberty Seated quarter. A crescent of silver-violet blends
into chestnut. Hairline free. Possibly dipped years ago, but could
not be proven in a court of law. Three obverse toning areas (not
darkly toned).

Strike: 100%
Toning: Silver-violet; chestnut; 3 watermarks
Surfaces: Select
High points: Unimpaired; cameo
Luster: Gem

ANACS:	**PF-63/63**
FORMAN:	PF-65/65; Choice Proof
PAUL:	PF-60/60; Ch Proof 65
RIEMER:	PF-65/65; PF-65/65
ROSE:	PF-63/63; PF-63+, qualified
ROSEN:	PF-65/65; PF-63
SWIATEK:	PF-65/65; PF-65
TAGLIONE:	PF-67/67; Proof-64
WILHITE:	PF-63/63; PF-63/63

25. Proof. Barber quarter. Wholly original with delicate polychromatic tone. A Gem in all respects with an unsightly obverse planchet depression.

> Strike: 100%
> Toning: Rainbow, iridescent
> Surfaces: Gem
> High points: Unimpaired; cameo
> Luster: Gem

ANACS:	**PF-67/67, Planchet flaw**
FORMAN:	PF-65/65; Impaired Proof
PAUL:	PF-60/60 to PF-65/65; Proof 63
RIEMER:	PF-67/67, Planchet defect; PF-65/65, Planchet defect
ROSE:	PF-67/67, qualified; PF-67, qualified
ROSEN:	PF-65/65; PF-63+
SWIATEK:	PF-63/63; PF-63
TAGLIONE:	PF-65/67; Proof-64
WILHITE:	PF-65/65; PF-65/65

26. Proof. Barber half. Gorgeous! Beautiful streaks of golden-russet upon hairline-free surfaces. A thin pin-scratch across Ms. Liberty's cheek is obscured by patches of blue and red.

> Strike: 100%
> Toning: Golden-russet; blue; red
> Surfaces: Gem
> High points: Unimpaired; cameo
> Luster: Gem

ANACS:	**PF-63/65**
FORMAN:	PF-60/60; Impaired Proof
PAUL:	PF-60/60; Proof 63
RIEMER:	PF-65/65; PF-65/65
ROSE:	PF-65/65; PF-63, qualified

ROSEN: PF-67/67; PF-63+
SWIATEK: PF-63/65 or PF-65/65; PF-65
TAGLIONE: PF-67/67; Proof-64
WILHITE: PF-63/63; PF-63/63

Gold

27. Business strike. Saint-Gaudens $20. A problem-free strong Choice, save for an obverse and reverse rim nick.

> Strike: 90%
> Toning: Brilliant
> Surfaces: Choice; 2 rim nicks
> High points: Circular luster
> Luster: Choice

ANACS: **MS-63/63**
FORMAN: MS-63/63; B.U.
PAUL: AU-55/55; Ch BU 63
RIEMER: MS-63/63; MS-63/63
ROSE: MS-65/65; MS-63
ROSEN: MS-63/63; MS-63
SWIATEK: MS-60/60; MS-60
TAGLIONE: MS-63/63; MS-63
WILHITE: MS-63/63; MS-63/63

28. Business strike. Rare date. Radiant luster upon immaculate surfaces. A Gem in all respects, save for light, almost unnoticeable wear on the obverse and reverse rims.

> Strike: 95%
> Toning: Brilliant
> Surfaces: Gem
> High points: Circular luster (light rim wear)
> Luster: Gem

ANACS: **MS-67/67**
FORMAN: MS-60/60; Unc
PAUL: MS-65/65; Gem BU 65
RIEMER: MS-65/65; AU-55/55
ROSE: AU-55/55; AU-59, super slider
ROSEN: MS-65/65; MS-65
SWIATEK: MS-67/67; MS-67
TAGLIONE: MS-63/63; MS-65
WILHITE: MS-63/63; MS-63/63

29. Business strike. Superb! Mark-free, spot-free surfaces. Fully struck.

Strike: 100%
Toning: Brilliant
Surfaces: Gem
High points: Circular luster
Luster: Choice

ANACS:	**MS-65/65**
FORMAN:	MS-65/65; Choice BU
PAUL:	MS-65/65; Gem BU 69
RIEMER:	MS-67/67; MS-65/65
ROSE:	MS-65/65; MS-65
ROSEN:	MS-65/65; MS-65
SWIATEK:	MS-65/65; MS-65
TAGLIONE:	AU-55/55; MS-65
WILHITE:	MS-69/69; MS-69/69

30. Proof. A problem coin. Lightly polished and impaired. No evidence of wear, but multiple contact marks and friction.

Strike: 100%
Toning: Green oven-baked color
Surfaces: Typical
High points: Impaired
Luster: Typical

ANACS:	**PF-50/50**
FORMAN:	PF-55/55; Impaired Proof
PAUL:	PF-50/50; Proof 55
RIEMER:	PF-55/55; PF-55/55, Polished
ROSE:	PF-60/60; PF-60, qualified
ROSEN:	PF-60/60; PF-50+
SWIATEK:	PF-55/55; PF-50
TAGLIONE:	PF-60/60; Proof-58, Polished
WILHITE:	PF-50/50; PF-50/50

31. Proof. At first glance, a breathtaking cameo. A closer look reveals acid-treated/artificially frosted devices. What a shame! A few hairlines.

Strike: ?
Toning: Brilliant
Surfaces: ? Select fields
High points: Impaired or cannot be determined
Luster: ? Select fields

ANACS:	**Returned as altered**
FORMAN:	PF-60/60; Impaired Proof

PAUL:	PF-50/50 to PF-55/55; Proof 55 or Proof 60
RIEMER:	PF-60/60, Whizzed; PF-55/55, Whizzed
ROSE:	Cannot be graded; No grade
ROSEN:	PF-60/60; PF-55
SWIATEK:	PF-50/50 or return with no grade; PF-50
TAGLIONE:	PF-70/70; Proof-60, Doctored
WILHITE:	PF-50/50; PF-50/50

32. Proof. Scattered hairlines. Small, reverse carbon fleck by rim at 4:00.

> Strike: 100%
> Toning: Brilliant
> Surfaces: Select; single spot
> High points: Unimpaired
> Luster: Select

ANACS:	**PF-63/63**
FORMAN:	PF-55/55; Impaired Proof
PAUL:	PF-55/55 to PF-60/60; Proof 60
RIEMER:	PF-63/63; PF-63/63
ROSE:	PF-63/63; PF-63, qualified
ROSEN:	PF-63/63; PF-60+
SWIATEK:	PF-63/63; PF-63
TAGLIONE:	PF-63/63; Proof-60+
WILHITE:	PF-63/63; PF-63/63

PLEASE NOTE: The ANACS grades presented in bold-face type are *my* assumption of the grades the Service would assign the coins based on its analysis, which follows. In cases in which the Service referred to "probable" grade, I listed that grade as the ANACS grade. In other cases, I used my discretion in listing ANACS's probable grade. In other words, the ANACS grades are compiled only from the analysis presented below, *not* a separate list.

ANACS RESPONSE TO GRADE SURVEY

By the ANACS Staff

1. Depends on contact marks. Normally cents and half cents are relatively free of contact marks due to the plain edges. If virtually none probably MS-67/67. If some light marks but nothing

obviously distracting probably MS-65/65. If any marks that bla-
tantly catch the eye, probably MS-63/63 or possibly MS-60/60.
Brilliant color (i.e., full original red) is an unlikely survivor on
early copper, however, so be sure to check carefully for signs of
dipping and/or recoloring.

2. Same comment on bagmarks as #1. Toning is the natural fate of
   early copper, and ANACS does not penalize a coin for it. Beware
   of coins dipped in a time when "brilliant" was fashionable and
   recolored in a time when tastes have changed.

3. Assuming a Mint error where literally 50% of the design was
   never struck up, grade the same as #1 and add "Weakly Struck"
   or "Very Weakly Struck" to the description of the coin. Remember that the unstruck areas of the planchet will show numerous
   contact marks typical for a planchet but normally squeezed
   closed during the strike. The value of the coin will probably be
   determined by the market value for Mint errors of this type.

4. If the hairlines are heavy enough to see with the naked eye, then
   probably a PF-60/60. If you need a magnifying glass to distinguish the hairlines as such, then the coin may go PF-63/63.

5. Any weakness of strike on a Proof coin should be mentioned in
   the description of the piece. It does not cause an automatic sub-
   traction of points from the numerical grade of the coin, although
   presumably it will decrease the value of it. The carbon flecks, if
   few and small, might still allow a PF-65/65. If numerous or large,
   the coin would probably be a PF-63/63. If numerous and large,
   the coin might grade a PF-60/60. The oxidation of the high
   points, if merely toning caused by contact with a paper envelope,
   would not in itself lower the grade. However, it might reduce the
   desirability somewhat, depending upon the pattern, and thus the
   price. If the oxidation has eaten through the luster on the high
   points, it would probably reduce an otherwise PF-67/67 to a PF-
   65/65 or a PF-65/65 to a PF-63/63. If severe it could reduce a PF-
   63/63 to a PF-60/60 though it would not reduce a PF-60/60 below
   that grade. A "Select" surface would normally refer to a PF-
   63/63.

6. Difficult to answer. Depends on the grader's experience with
   dipped and undipped coins and his ability to "know" that a coin
   has been dipped regardless of his ability to prove it. Then it
   depends upon the dipping itself. A single, carefully controlled
   dipping may not affect the grade at all. A too long or too strong
   dipping may lower an otherwise normal grade from 2 points to
   10 points within the same grade.

7. Probably MS-67/67, with a chance at MS-70/70 if there are *no*
   contact marks or hairlines. Remember that copper-nickel coins,

being struck on the hardest planchets, are most likely to retain traces of nicks and scratches that were on the planchet and that were not squeezed shut by the strike. Some tolerance must be allowed for these.

8. Probably MS-63/63, with "Weakly Struck" added to the description of the coin. However, it is very unlikely (though not impossible) for a coin to be weakly struck on one side only, so be sure to check for signs of a worn or grease-filled die.

9. Probably MS-60/60, with same comments as #8.

10. Probably PF-70/70, if exactly as made. The random die polishing marks need not be mentioned, though it should not hurt to do so and may help to avoid misunderstandings.

11. Probably PF-60/60. The description should include the word "cleaned." How bad is the "friction" on the high points?

12. Often a very difficult and controversial combination. If the "wear" consists of light, criss-crossed scratches from contact with other coins, then perhaps a grade of PF-55/55 or lower is justified on some coins. However, having seen original Proof sets where the coins have been stored loose together with resultant nicks, scratches and "wear," we can justify an "Impaired Proof-60/60" on others. If the "wear" consists of a light burnishing or polishing from contact with a coin cabinet or a holder, then again there can be good arguments for either a PF-55/55 or a PF-60/60. The judgment has to be made on a case-by-case basis.

13. Have never seen one only 25% struck. If it existed, it would be treated as a Mint error by most people and the grade would be relatively unimportant. From a theoretical standpoint the coin could still be graded as an MS-65/65.

14. MS-65/65. May command a premium price in the marketplace because of the strike.

15. Probably MS-67/67 with "Weakly Struck" added to the description. Would probably bring a discounted price because of the strike. Die cracks have no effect on grade, though they are usually found on coins struck from worn dies that impart indifferent luster.

16. PF-70/70 if absolutely no detractions; PF-67/67 if any. We do not mention "Cameo" proofs.

17. Same as #16.

18. PF-67/67, assuming a few trivial imperfections. Possibly PF-65/65 depending on luster. The weak strike should be mentioned.

19. Probably PF-63/63.

20. The description contradicts itself. A coin with Typical (PF-60) surfaces and Select (PF-63) luster is not likely to be the "knock-out" adjectivally described. PF-63/63 possible.

21. Probably MS-67/67, possible MS-65/65 depending on the rim wear.
22. MS-60/60.
23. Another contradictory hypothesis. Is the strike "slightly soft" or 20% missing? The coin would probably grade MS-65/65, and if severe enough the weakness would be mentioned in the description.
24. Depends on the surfaces. Probably PF-63/63, if the surfaces are indeed "Select." Possibly PF-65/65 if everything else is better than average.
25. PF-67/67, with the planchet flaw cited in the description. Will probably not bring a PF-67/67 price.
26. Probably PF-63/65, possibly PF-63/67. PF-65/65 or PF-67/67 remotely possible, depending on how well hidden the scratch is.
27. Probably MS-63/63, depending on the size and depth of the rim nicks. Possibly MS-65/65, if the nicks are minor and the luster is better than average Choice.
28. Probably MS-67/67, possibly MS-65/65 depending on the severity of the rim wear.
29. Probably MS-65/65, possibly MS-67/67 if the luster was a bit dull to begin with.
30. Probably PF-50/50, depending on the friction. Possibly PF-60/60. The impairments should be described.
31. Would probably be returned as Altered.
32. Probably PF-63/63, depending on the severity of the hairlines and the spot.

RESPONSE TO ANACS SURVEY

By Paul F. Taglione

NOTE: Paul Taglione's grade in capacity as professional numismatist followed by slash (/) followed by conjecture of ANACS assigned grade. Comments follow.

1. MS-64/   MS-65/65
   Fairly unproblematical. Choice denotes to me a coin better than 63 but less than 65. My experience with ANACS leads me to believe that the same distinction is not in force with their graders. There is an outside possibility that ANACS would grade the coin MS-63/63 or MS-63/65.

2. MS-63/ MS-63/63

   A red and brown copper coin cannot, in my schemata, be graded MS-65 and *never* commands an MS-65 market price. It was explained to me at Midyear ANA 1982 by three ANACS graders that a copper coin without full red would not be graded MS-65 by them; although I have seen many examples to the contrary, I would presume that their avowals are practiced. Hence, an MS-63/63.

3. MS-63/ MS-65/65, weakly struck

   A weakly struck coin never commands an MS-65 market price. The philosophy of ANACS allows for MS-65/65's which are weakly struck. Note that if the presumption that grading is the determination of the state of preservation is in force, then their conjectured assigned grade is justified. If grading is taken to be the state of quality relative to market, then my grade would be more appropriate.

4. Proof-60/ Proof-63/63

   Eye-appeal is a market grading factor, hence my 60. ANACS does not, in my experience, account for eye-appeal, thus their conjectured Proof-63/63.

5. Proof-63/ Proof-63/63

   Unproblematical but an outside chance that ANACS would grade Proof-65/65.

6. Proof-63, once dipped/ Proof-65/65

   Note that on my account, the coin would be worth a Proof-60+ wholesale price. In my experience, in less than blatant cases, ANACS has not properly distinguished original copper color from nonoriginal. This cuts both ways for I have seen more cases of ANACS terming a copper coin cleaned when it has not been than of cases where it had been cleaned but they failed to note it.

7. MS-67/ Proof-65/65

   As with (6), in my experience, the staff at ANACS has rarely properly distinguished Proof and business-strike copper-nickel coinage. For that matter, very few dealers or collectors are capable of making this distinction.

8. MS-63/ MS-65/65, weakly struck reverse

   Same comments as found in (3).

9. MS-60/ MS-63/63

   Toning and typical surfaces mandate my grade. Luster would, I reckon, lead ANACS to opine at MS-63/63.

10. Proof-67/ Proof-65/67

    Die polishing marks neither hinder market price nor downgrade coin to a 65. The visual difference would, my experience leads me to believe, result in ANACS split grade.

11. Proof-58, cleaned/   Proof-60/60, cleaned
    In my experience I have found ANACS to discount friction in
    grading Proofs. On more obvious wear, they do a suitable job.
12. Proof-58/   Proof-63/63
    Same comments as (11).
13. MS-60/   MS-63/63, weakly struck
    Again, some mention of market value must be considered. A
    nickel coin this weakly struck will never command better than
    an MS-60 value.
14. MS-64/   MS-65/65
    This coin meets the classic definition of an ANACS-65 and a
    "Commercial-65" but is not one which would command MS-65
    wholesale value (due to surfaces being less than Gem).
15. MS-64/   MS-65/65
    Same comments as (14) but justification for my grade is that
    nickel must be perfect and without striking eccentricities to
    command MS-65 price.
16. Proof-69/   Proof-67/67
    An obvious and unproblematical case. Sociologically, it is con-
    ventional and acceptable to grade a Jefferson Nickel Proof a 69.
    ANACS no longer grades anything MS-70 or Proof-70 (a wise
    choice, I have seen about 9 coins graded by them as perfect and 8
    were considerably less than perfect).
17. Proof-69/   Proof-67/67
    Same comments as (16).
18. Proof-65/   Proof-65/65
    It is about 35 percent probable that ANACS would grade this a
    business strike.
19. Proof-63/   Proof-65/65
    A hairlined Proof will not command wholesale Proof-65 value.
    From my experience, ANACS allows hairlines for Proof-65s;
    technically, a correct practice but market-wise, a blunder.
20. Proof-63/   Proof-65/65
    Similar comment as in (19).
21. MS-65/   MS-67/67
    By "rim wear," I am not sure what is meant but I would venture
    to claim that such wear was induced in shipping or bagging and
    cannot be considered "circulation wear." In the market sense, it
    would not count for much for it is irrevelant to the expectations
    from potential buyers (whereas knee wear is most consequen-
    tial). A highly speculative example which might not exist in
    actuality.
22. AU-55/   MS-60/60
    Wear is wear. On common Morgans, my experience with

ANACS leads me to conclude that a quite wide range of quality (from AU-53 to MS-64) is encompassed.

23. MS-64/ MS-65/65
No comment(s).

24. Proof-64/ Proof-67/67
I would quite possibly grade this a Proof-65 but the watermarks and uneven toning would seem to preclude it from obtaining a Proof-65 market value. Most assuredly, ANACS would grade this Proof-67/67; they have a long tradition of grading Proof Seated material most optimistically.

25. Proof-64/ Proof-65/67
Planchet depression would certainly preclude it from Proof-65 price levels. Same would not seem to alter ANACS grade insofar as it is Mint-incurred.

26. Proof-64/ Proof-67/67
Pinscratch would downgrade it. ANACS, in my experience, has not been adept at discerning hidden defects.

27. MS-63/ MS-63/63
Unproblematical, although I have seen ANACS grade Double-Eagles in the most unusual fashion (for example, one of the finest known 1900 Liberty's which they graded AU-55/55 and which sold to a knowledgeable dealer at $2200 in 1982 and a 1927 St-Gaudens graded 65/65 which was a commercial MS-60 fished from a Silvertowne roll). May I note that ANACS grading on Double-Eagles is, in my opinion, wildly inconsistent irrespective of period.

28. MS-65/ MS-63/63
Rim "wear" on this issue can only be shipping-incurred and is of no consequence.

29. MS-65/ AU-55/55
Most superb or Gem gold which I have seen is invariably graded A.U. by ANACS.

30. Proof-58, polished/ Proof-60/60, impaired and polished
Friction is wear, to my mind.

31. Proof-60, doctored/ Proof-70/70
From my experience with ANACS, I know of only one Gold Proof which even remotely fits this description and it was certified as a Proof-70/70. What else can I say?

32. Proof-60+/ Proof-63/63
Insofar as hairlines on Proof Gold tend to be most visible, I would suspect that, market-wise, the present hypothetical coin would command no more than a strong Proof-60 price. Technically, this coin is probably a 63, thus justifying the ANACS grade.

EXAMINING THE SURVEY RESULTS

Results of this survey pinpoint the healthy debate among professional numismatists. A similar debate would take place if actual coins had been used. The principles which these individuals use to arrive at their conclusions are the same they use in their day-to-day coin-market dealings. By studying the results, we know, for example, that ANACS claims not to take toning into consideration when grading copper coins, but that the majority of dealers responding feel that ANACS does. Coins 1 and 2 of the survey are described identically, with the exception of the red-and-brown toning on coin number 2. ANACS writes: "Toning is the natural fate of early copper, and ANACS does not penalize a coin for it." ANACS says the same grading criteria apply to both 1 and 2. Paul Taglione, however, writes: "It was explained to me at Midyear ANA 1982 by two ANACS graders that a copper coin without full red would not be graded MS-65 by them. . . ."

You'll also be able to confirm or deny the rumors you've heard about what ANACS places emphasis on. For example, if you've heard that an otherwise Choice MS-65 Saint-Gaudens $20 with a rim nick on the obverse and reverse would warrant the ANACS grade of MS-63/63, you'll know now that the rumor you heard might be correct (see no. 27).

Strike

Respondents tend to express a belief that strike affects the grade, not just the price. The academic definition of "strike" (see chapter 3) indicates that by A.N.A. grading standards, strike affects only the grade. It is apparent from this survey that numismatists have less disagreement assigning grades to fully struck coins. The survey coins which were not fully struck are (survey number followed by the percentage fully struck in parentheses): 3 (50 percent); 5 (80 percent); 8 (75 percent); 9 (75 percent); 11 (90 percent); 13 (25 percent); 15 (70 percent); 18 (90 percent); 19 (95 percent); 27 (90 percent); 28 (95 percent). This is not a scientific study, and therefore it would be impossible to state that dealers subscribe to one school of philosophy concerning strike and that ANACS subscribes to another. What is clear, however, is that a number of dealers subtract from a coin's grade if it isn't fully struck and that ANACS will go to extremes to make clear that it does not consider strike when grading a coin. However, mention should be made of an unusually strong or weak strike.

For example, coin number 13, stated to be 25-percent fully struck, is given the probable grade of MS-65/65. ANACS writes, "From a theoretical standpoint, the coin could still be graded as an MS-65/65." Every respondent to 13 anticipates the ANACS grade to be MS-63/63 or lower.

And every respondent to 14 (the same coin, but 100-percent struck) antic-ipates the ANACS grade to be MS-65/65 or higher. This response indi-cates that participants don't or won't accept the fact that ANACS does not care whether a coin is 100-percent struck or 25-percent struck when it assigns the numerical grade (although a coin particularly weakly struck would be described as such); strike does not affect the level of preserva-tion. It affects the price. In the personal grades of respondents, their strike prejudice is reflected. Every respondent gives a higher personal grade to the 100-percent fully struck specimen. Examine the results for yourself, and look at the survey results for other strike-sensitive survey coins. From this cross-section, it is evident that a respected segment of the numismatic fraternity believes that weak strike negatively affects the level of preservation. Further, this segment may not be aware of ANACS's strong stance, accounting for so many accusations that the service is unpredictable. "How can ANACS call this 100-percent fully struck beauty an MS-65 and also call this particularly weakly struck exam-ple an MS-65, too?" many would ask. The answer: *strike affects the price, not the grade, in the eyes of ANACS.*

Toning

The impact of toning a coin's level of preservation has been described in depth in chapters 3 and 12. ANACS's and Taglione's contrasting views concerning red and brown coppers have been included earlier in this analysis. Other than the copper debate discussed earlier, the respondents' attitudes toward toning is somewhat predictable. If a coin has universally attractive toning, ANACS may slightly upgrade the coin (see chapter 3). If the coin has universally ugly toning, ANACS may lower the grade. Re-spondents tend to be aware of ANACS's philosophy concerning toned coins, and respondents' personal grading philosophies tend to duplicate one another. In number 20, for example, ANACS chooses the PF-63 grade and gives the coin the benefit of the doubt because of the beautiful ton-ing. The respondents are pretty much aware that ANACS would go for the PF-63 grade. And the personal grades of the respondents don't differ, in general, from the ANACS grade, although there is a normal variation of opinion.

Mint-Made Imperfections Versus Acquired Ones

This proves to be another area of sharp debate, not between ANACS and the other respondents, but among most respondents. ANACS does not take Mint-made imperfections into consideration when assigning a grade.

Mint-made imperfections affect the price, not the technical grade. Some respondents disagree. In response to number 10, the coin perfect in all respects with the exception of the die-polishing marks in the right obverse field, Paul Taglione writes: "The visual difference would, my experience leads me to believe, result in ANACS split grade (Proof-65/67)." The response to number 25 was inconsistent. But it still reflects a sentiment that a Mint-made imperfection can subtract from the grade. ANACS, of course, doesn't take Mint-made imperfections into consideration when grading a coin, only when describing it (PF-67/67, *Planchet flaw*). Again, ANACS believes that the best way to describe a coin is to describe the technical level of preservation and any imperfection. Mint-made imperfections affect the price and attached description, not the numerical grade.

Never forget that grading is used to communicate what a coin looks like. If you describe a Fine-12 coin with an acquired scratch as VG-8, nobody except you knows that you're referring to a coin which has worn down to Fine-12 but has a scratch. So numismatists are supposed to have agreed that the grade refers to the degree of wear, with the imperfections described. When grading Mint State coins, however, since there is no wear, acquired imperfections subtract from the Mint State numerical grade (which cannot go below 60); and Mint-made imperfections are described, but don't subtract from the grade.

High Points

In general, respondents show little difficulty in differentiating between About Uncirculated and Mint State on the clearly stated example (12). But some difficulty arises in telling the difference between friction and wear (friction being from something other than circulation touching a coin; wear being from a coin having circulated and having been handled). Numbers 11, 22, and 30 are representative of coins with friction, not wear. However, 11 was abrasively cleaned, and 30 was polished. General agreement among respondents is that polishing might take an otherwise Mint State coin out of the Mint State category. In general, respondents are unsure whether number 22 should be graded Mint State or About Uncirculated. With the exception of two respondents, all know that ANACS would not downgrade a coin for having friction, not wear, on the high points.

Two survey descriptions (21 and 28) concerning the concept of rim wear are of particular interest to purists. The rim and edge alone don't count in determining whether a coin is Mint State or About Uncirculated. All respondents (with the exception of one) know that ANACS doesn't downgrade a Mint State coin to A.U. on this basis alone. But two respondents indicate that they would personally grade each of the two pieces as A.U. Rim wear might be a sign of *conventional high-point deemphasis.* So check the entire coin closely to make sure there is no wear in any other area. If it's only a little "rub" on the rim, it's still Mint State.

Surfaces Versus Luster

The prime determinants of grade assignment are surfaces and luster. The number and depth of scratches and nicks and particularly their *placement* may very well determine whether a coin grades MS-67 or MS-60. Numismatists throughout the world are in complete agreement on this point. Luster, however, is subject to debate. If a coin with Gem surfaces and Choice to Gem luster is examined, what grade should it be assigned? ANACS, according to the survey response, often opts for the Gem or MS-67 designation. ANACS views surfaces as more important than luster.

Examine the responses for yourself. The coins involved in the debate are 5, 6, 8, 9, 13, 14, 18, 19, 20, 24, and 29. Most of these descriptions receive a numerical grade from ANACS equal to the surface grade. The exceptions are made clear. For example, the gold coin with Gem surfaces and Choice luster (number 29) is graded Choice overall by ANACS, because gold coins usually have Gem luster to begin with. ANACS writes: "Possibly MS-67/67 if the luster was a bit dull to begin with." The Proof copper which is Choice in all respects but has been dipped (number 6) isn't graded by ANACS. The only coin left in this group of coins whose surface and luster grades are different is 20. This is the nickel with the phenomenal toning. In this case, the outstanding overall appearance might compensate for the Typical or MS-60 surfaces.

A topic related to surfaces and luster is contrast between the fields and the devices. Collectors of Morgan dollars place particular emphasis on this variable in arriving at values, and *coins of the same technical grade with varying degrees of contrast between fields and devices often bring radically different prices.* Collectors call coins which are not Proofs, but which have frosted devices and reflective fields, *Prooflike,* because these coins look like Proofs. Morgan dollars which are fully reflective—including devices—are called *semi-Prooflike.* The difference between the Prooflike and the semi-Prooflike is that the Prooflike has *frosted* devices, and the semi-Prooflike has *reflective* devices. Morgan dollars which have fields which are reflective to an unusual degree and devices which possess deep Mint frost are called *cameo Prooflike* because of the cameo contrast between the fields and the devices.

Similarly, coins which are in fact Brilliant Proofs display this cameo effect in varying degrees. If a Proof coin which is rarely found with a deep cameo contrast is located with a deep cameo contrast, it will probably command a hefty premium.

Much to the dismay of numismatists, ANACS makes no provisions for grading or mentioning whether or not a coin is Prooflike at all, even though dealers and collectors would like the Service to make note on its certificates of degrees of "Prooflikeness." The Service also doesn't make mention of how deep the cameo contrast is on Proof coins. Some dealers will actually lower the grade if a Proof coin usually found with frosted devices has reflective devices. Descriptions 16 and 17 illustrate this.

Chemically Altered Coins

Often, chemically altered coins cannot be graded because too little information is known about the characteristics needed to grade them. Description 31 is such an example. Only two participants (Joseph Rose and Anthony Swiatek) knew that ANACS might not have been able to grade this coin. As has been stressed throughout this book, coins which have problems when you buy them pose a big problem when you try to sell them.

Industry Uniformity

There is none. In order for uniform grading standards to prevail and be used with a moderate degree of success, there has to be agreement among experts as to what parameters should be used. In the coin industry, there is no agreement. Even today, several years after introduction of the A.N.A. grading guide, many dealers don't know that Choice means MS-65 and that Gem means MS-67. Many professional numismatists won't accept that the grade is used to communicate the level of preservation and that the added description should be used to describe the Mint-made imperfection or striking weakness.

The survey response of ANACS indicates that the Service feels great pressure placed on it by dealers who want the grade to reflect level of preservation and market value. For years, ANACS has been telling the collecting public that it will not comment on a coin's value. But in this survey, in which a number of coins with serious value detractors receive high grades, ANACS comments about the grade and its relation to market value. Perhaps in a few years when ANACS works out its differences with the numismatic community, uniform standards will be adopted which are agreeable to all. Until then, you're on your own. One dealer's Choice could be another dealer's Gem. And another dealer's Gem could be yet another dealer's MS-67++++++.

HOW TO PROTECT YOURSELF IF YOU BUY AN ANACS-GRADED COIN

- *Make sure the coin pictured on the certificate is the one you're buying.* As ridiculous as it may sound, some people have accidentally purchased coins with ANACS certificates, only to find later that the coin they bought was not the one pictured! Carefully compare the photograph with the coin before you buy.
- *Be certain the coin is in the same level of preservation as it was when examined.* Be especially cautious if the certificate is more than a year old. Coins deteriorate, are mishandled, and are subjected to contaminants. Just because the certificate says "MS-65/65" does not mean the coin is still in that grade. Dealers dip coins, clean coins, and artificially retone them.
- *Check for weakness of strike.* Don't buy an ANACS MS-65/65 if there is weakness of strike unless the price is low enough. Any dealer will tell you that practically any coin with striking weakness is worth considerably below its MS-65 price guide listings. ANACS doesn't take striking weakness into consideration when grading any coin except Standing Liberty quarters.
- *Look at the coin first.* Some people make the big mistake of deciding which coins they want to purchase by looking through stacks of ANACS certificates without looking at the actual coins! If you insist on buying ANACS-graded coins, at least look at the coins before you look at the certificates.
- *Remember that ANACS isn't perfect.* ANACS has made mistakes, and you don't want to buy one of them. If you're buying an ANACS grade-confirmed coin, examine it closely to make certain that it is in fact deserving of the grade ANACS assigned to it. Be suspicious of coins with heavy toning and coins called Proof which don't look Proof.
- *Don't deal with dealers who sell a lot of ANACS coins.* Some dealers who sell a lot of ANACS "certified" coins haggle with the Service over grades, as well as resubmit coins. If you insist on buying from a dealer who has a significant number of ANACS-graded coins, get a guarantee from him or her that if the coin is resubmitted to ANACS and doesn't come back with the same grade you will be given a refund of the purchase price.
- *If you submit coins to ANACS, take note of any imperfections the coins may possess.* You don't want to blame ANACS unfairly for scratching coins. When submitting coins to ANACS (P.O. Box

2366, Colorado Springs, CO 80901), photograph them first, mail them via Registered mail, insured for their full value, and wrapped securely. Of course, never place tape on the coins themselves. The most popular mailers for coins are manufactured by Safe-T-Mailer Company, Westport, CT 06880. The "Safe-T-Mailer" is an adhesive piece of cardboard which folds over to allow your coin to travel in its holder like an ordinary letter.

5

How to Tell Proof from Prooflike

These days even the neophyte with only the briefest acquaintance with American coins as collectors' items will sooner or later encounter proof coins, whether as offered to the general public by the San Francisco Mint, or as offered to collectors by coin dealers. And sooner or later . . . you will come across borderline cases, claims of extreme rarity, proofs not listed in the usual reference books, coins which present frank puzzles. . . . And though there is no way to become expert overnight in even so well explored a field as United States numismatics, there is a way to raise your own level of knowledge from that of neophyte and swindlers' mark to—at least—informed amateur.

—Walter Breen
Walter Breen's Encyclopedia of U.S.
and Colonial Proof Coins

The silver quarter-dollar labeled "Proof" glistened and glimmered in the dealer's showcase. How spectacular it was as its *devices* (the raised part on the coin, for example, the lettering and portrait) appeared ivory-white and its fields (the background on a coin which isn't raised) seemed like an antique mirror, complete with a light, even cloud of russet as testimony to its age. That coin was awesome in every respect and the epitome of originality. The cameo contrast between the fields and devices would convince almost any prospective buyer that the coin was unquestionably a Proof. But it wasn't a Proof; it was a *Prooflike business strike*.

Many people, including experts, often cannot tell whether a coin is a Proof or a business strike. The coin described above has some characteristics of a Brilliant Proof. (Many people have just as much trouble differentiating Matte Proof from coins which *look* like Matte Proofs—Proofs struck from sand-blasted dies which exhibit the same incredible detail but are granular instead of brilliant in appearance.)

85

A good deal of this confusion can be blamed on the Mint. During the late 1800s and early 1900s, the Mint would collect money from collectors who wanted to order Proof coins. The number of people ordering usually wouldn't exceed a couple of thousand during any given year. After the Mint made the special Proof dies and struck the few coins needed to fill the orders, *sometimes the Proof dies were saved to strike coins for circulation!* As explained in chapter 3, a Proof coin is struck *twice,* a business strike *once.* Some coins were made for circulation with the same dies used to strike the Proofs; and the only difference between a Proof and a business strike struck from Proof dies is that the business strike is struck once by the dies, and the Proof is struck twice by the dies. It almost goes without saying that some of the earliest coins made to spend from those Proof dies look just like Proof coins.

An outstanding work, *The Encyclopedia of U.S. and Colonial Proof Coins,* by Walter Breen, gives the characteristics of every Proof die made. However, useful though this book is in identifying Proof dies, if the Proof dies were used to strike coins for circulation, you really cannot determine whether a coin is a Proof or a Prooflike unless you know *how many times that coin was struck: once or twice.*

The Mint has been known on occasion to highly polish dies for coins struck for general circulation. A coin struck from these highly polished dies might look like a Proof to someone without years of experience. In this area, the Breen book is indispensable. Breen clearly identifies business strike dies. If a coin which looks like a Proof is struck from dies used to manufacture coins for circulation, then it isn't a Proof. Period.

Knowing whether a coin is a Proof or Prooflike is an area of infinite uncertainty. Beginners have no idea what a problem this is until they are no longer beginners and find out that a coin purchased as Proof is only a Prooflike and worth a mere fraction of what a real Proof would be worth. It can happen the other way around, too: real Proofs are sometimes sold as business strikes when the business strike value is higher than the Proof value!

It's so difficult to tell Proof from Prooflike for some coins that I've prepared a chart to illustrate the problems that even experts have with some issues. If you were to take Prooflike coins which look like Proofs to the country's coin dealers, these are the results you might get.

Category	Percentage of Dealers Sure	Percentage Unsure
Easy	100	0
Moderate	85	15
Difficult	25	75
Most difficult	1	99

HOW TO TELL PROOF FROM PROOFLIKE

- *Examine the overall appearance.* Make sure the alleged Proof is well defined and well struck in every detail. If it isn't, it may not be a Proof. Proofs are struck twice, and they should exhibit far more detail than their non-Proof counterparts. Look at the breadth of detail on the Proof quarter shown in Fig. 5–1. Compare it with the Mint State business strike in Fig. 5–2. The Proof is chromiumlike, with spectacular definition of detail. The business strike is not as defined, not chromiumlike, and exhibits no contrast between its fields and devices. The same rule applies to Matte Proofs, although they will not exhibit reflectivity, but a uniform graininess instead.

Fig. 5–1. Proof Liberty Seated quarter, obverse and reverse. Deep chromium Proof surfaces and a spectacular contrast between the fields and devices on this ANACS-graded Proof-65/65 make this a no-question Brilliant Proof.

Fig. 5–2. Mint State business strike Liberty Seated quarter, obverse and reverse. This coin possesses the slightly weakly struck right-side stars characteristic of a business strike.

- *Check the edge.* The edge is the part your fingers touch when you hold the coin. On Proofs, the edge usually appears perfectly reflective. On non-Proofs, the edge has what looks like many little parallel, vertical lines.
- *Check the rims.* The rims are the rings on both sides which encircle the coin. On Proofs, the rims usually are sharp, squared-off, "knife-edge," or well defined. On business strikes, the rims are often dull, rounded-off, and poorly defined (Fig. 5–3).
- *Check the reeding on reeded coins.* "Reeding" refers to vertical raised and indented lines on a coin's edge which have been manufactured there by the Mint, as shown in Figs. 5–4 and 5–5. On Proofs, the reeding is razor sharp and extends the height of the edge. On business strikes, the reeding extends *only* to the areas where the rims slope (Figs. 5–4 and 5–5).
- *Examine the depth of the reflectivity for Brilliant Proofs.* The term *reflectivity* refers to the depth of the mirrored surfaces. Always examine both sides to be certain a coin is a Proof. If a coin has every characteristic of being a Proof on one side and none on the other side, it isn't a Proof. If a coin has "patches" of Mint luster which interrupt highly reflective surfaces, it isn't a Proof. Is the reflectivity deep and chromiumlike with breathtaking depth or does it appear fragile and not very deep? Brilliant Proofs have deep reflective surfaces. Prooflikes have surfaces that possess less depth of reflectivity.
- *Look at small details.* Make sure the surfaces are reflective inside every small unfrosted area. Check around stars and letters. Does that same mirror surface extend to inside that shield or within details of each star? If it doesn't, the coin may not be a Brilliant Proof. Also, are there striations (lines created during the manufacturing process) throughout the coin? Striations might indicate that the coin is a business strike.
- *Become suspicious if the coin possesses many detracting marks.* Proof coins were made for collectors on specially selected planchets and were handled very carefully. Non-Proofs went into circulation. Therefore, the non-Proofs are far more likely to have big scratches and gouges than the Proofs are. Proofs are often mishandled, but infrequently have the same kinds of huge marks and detractions as coins made for circulation.
- *Check for evidence of double striking.* The dies come down twice on the planchet that is to become a Proof coin. Many Proofs exhibit a slight doubling of parts of the design, especially stars, as a result of this double striking. The doubling looks like a slight shadow and is only visible under a microscope.

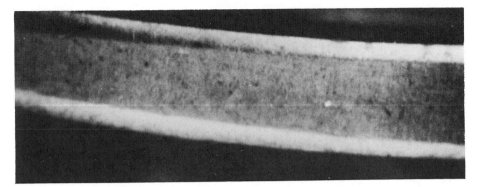

Fig. 5–3. Business strike edge. There is a prominent rounding. (Photograph by Bill Fivaz)

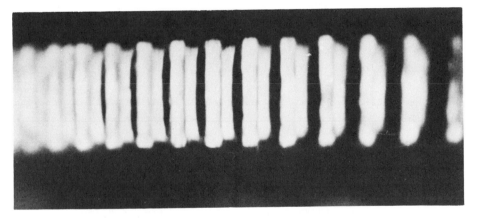

Fig. 5–4. Proof coin reeding. (Photograph by Bill Fivaz)

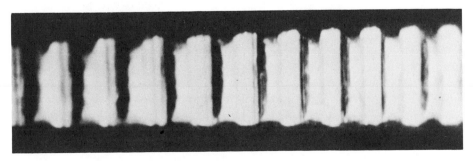

Fig. 5–5. Business strike reeding. (Photograph by Bill Fivaz)

THE MOST DIFFICULT COINS TO
CONFIRM PROOF STATUS OF

Business strike Buffalo nickels which look like Matte Proofs are among the most difficult to tell from the real thing. One clever trick is to know about the characteristic line across the rim. This line (Fig. 5–6) is found on every Matte Proof of 1914 and 1915, as well as on every 1913 Type II. However, some business strikes were struck using this reverse die. A real Matte Proof, though, possesses the characteristic Matte Proof edge, with very little slope or bevel (Fig. 5–7).

Look at the two attractive Trade dollars shown in Figs. 5–8 and 5–9. The 1880 specimen is a delightfully toned Proof, complete with a spectacular chromiumlike appearance and a cameo contrast between the fields and the devices. Pay attention to the incredible detail and the tiny unfrosted areas of the eagle's feathers which do not display luster but, rather, possess that chromiumlike Proof reflectivity. The 1876 is a Prooflike. It's a beautiful coin, but not a Proof. Although it's difficult to see from the photograph, areas of the reflective fields are shallow in reflectivity. This Prooflike displays patches of luster in areas, instead of

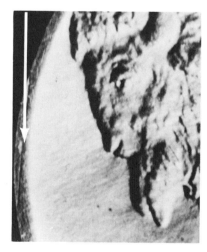 

Fig. 5–6 (above left).   Matte Proof Buffalo nickel rim indentation. This is found on 1913 Type II, 1914, and 1915, as well as a limited number of business strikes on which this reverse die was used. (Photograph by Bill Fivaz)

Fig. 5–7 (above right).   Matte Proof Buffalo nickel edge and rim. There is little rounding at the edge. (Photograph by Bill Fivaz)

Fig. 5–8. Proof Trade dollar, obverse and reverse.

the mirrorlike surfaces it's supposed to be sporting. Also, the rim is not fully squared off. If you were to look up the 1876 Trade dollar in Walter Breen's proof encyclopedia, you would read:

> (1150 reported) Type I. Berry under claw. Exceedingly rare. (1) 1975 GENA II: 1272. (2) Anomaly from the John Zug estate; obv. perfect proof, rev. uncirculated and frosty but with the striking qualities, borders and rims of a proof. It may have been made in error using a wrong reverse. —Type II. Without berry under claw. Most regular proofs seen to date of the 1876 Trade are of this type. I have not seen the copper or aluminum proofs, Judd 1476–77, AW 1480–81, but surmise that they too would be of this type. Certainly the pattern trade dollar showing motto in cartouche above date and no stars, with

Fig. 5–9. Prooflike Trade dollar, obverse and reverse.

reverse of regular issue, Judd 1474–75, AW 1492–93, has a Type II reverse. Minor positional varieties probable.

Your ability to tell the Proof from its business strike counterpart can only come from practical experience. Even those in business for many years and who have studied Proofs for many years are not always absolutely certain whether certain coins are Proofs or Prooflikes.

The two outstanding references which provide invaluable information and illustrations of how to tell Proof from Prooflike are *Walter Breen's Encyclopedia of U.S. and Colonial Proof Coins* (F.C.I. Press, 1977) and *The Encyclopedia of United States Silver & Gold Commemorative Coins 1892 to 1954*, by Anthony Swiatek and Walter Breen (Arco Publishing, 1981).

6

Altered and
Counterfeit Coins

The threat of your buying counterfeit rare coins is not nearly as real as
it is often perceived to be, for the ratio of counterfeit to genuine is
comparatively small. But *you* could be one of the few people who ends
up buying a fake. The time you spend learning about counterfeits
could account for the money you save in not buying one.

—Pedro Collazo-Oliver
National Collectors Laboratories
Former ANACS Authenticator, Grader, and
Seminar instructor

Altered and counterfeit coins have received a great deal of attention.
Both the numismatic press and dealers have cooperated in trying to rid
the coin industry of fakes. They have succeeded rather well. Probably
fewer fake coins are offered for sale in the coin market, relatively speak-
ing, than are fakes in other collectible fields. One reason might be the
coin industry's strict adherence to the Hobby Protection Act, which
makes selling counterfeit coins illegal. Big money, however, is not made
from selling fake coins but rather from overgrading. Some dealers offer to
refund your money plus pay a percentage per year compounded annually
if any coin you buy from them ever turns out to be a fake. And many
dealers with this guarantee have never had a coin returned for reasons of
inauthenticity. The American Numismatic Association Certification
Service (ANACS), the International Numismatic Society Authentication
Bureau, and National Collectors Laboratories are to be credited with outstanding records for spotting fakes and alerting the public to their existence.
    There are three basic types of inauthentic coins: altered, cast coun-
terfeit, and die-struck counterfeit. All will be explored and illustrated

with photographs taken by and reproduced here by courtesy of Pedro Collazo-Oliver, the man behind National Collectors Laboratories.

ALTERED COINS

An altered coin is a real coin that has been tampered with. For example, the 1856 Flying Eagle cent is a rare, valuable, sought-after coin in all grades. Even heavily circulated examples command phenomenal premiums. But the 1858 Flying Eagle cent, although somewhat scarce, is not a major rarity. Some 1858s have been found with altered dates to resemble 1856s. Look at the altered 1856 small cent illustrated in Fig. 6–1 and compare it with the real example shown in Fig. 6–2. The tooling marks on the altered example are readily apparent and might even be detected without a glass. The retooling of the "eight" to make it look like a "six" is obvious. Dates are altered by other ways too. Always look closely at the date if the coin is a date rarity.

Fig. 6–1.   Blowup of an 1858 Flying Eagle cent altered to look like an "1856." (Photograph courtesy National Collectors Laboratories)

Fig. 6–2.   Blowup of a genuine 1856 Flying Eagle cent. (Photograph courtesy National Collectors Laboratories)

Fig. 6–3.   Blowup of a genuine 1895 Proof Morgan dollar. (Photograph courtesy National Collectors Laboratories)

A coin sometimes found with either an altered date or removed Mint-mark is the "1895" Morgan dollar. Apparently, no examples of this coin are known to exist as business strikes, only as Proofs. But occasionally an "1895 business strike" Morgan is offered. The 1895 Proof is worth at least $25,000 as a Proof-65. The coins offered as business strikes probably have their dates altered or their Mint-marks removed (from an 1895-O or -S). Examine the date of the genuine 1895 shown in Fig. 6–3. Notice the obvious Proof rim and clear date. Now look at the altered coin in Fig. 6–4. It's a business strike. The date, in this case, has been altered. Possibly an 1885 was changed to an 1895. Always check for an altered date or removed Mint-mark on rare-date coins.

Fig. 6–4.   Blowup of a business strike with a numeral altered to resemble a 9. (Photograph courtesy National Collectors Laboratories)

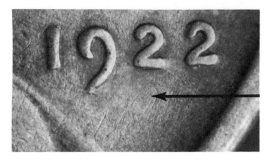

Fig. 6–5.   Blowup of a 1922-D altered by the Mint-mark having been re-moved to resemble a 1922-Plain. (Photograph courtesy National Collec-tors Laboratories)

The 1922-D Lincoln head cent's Mint-mark is commonly tampered with. It sometimes can be found with a removed "D" to mislead you into thinking it's a 1922-Plain Lincoln cent. In 1922, the Philadelphia Mint didn't manufacture any Lincoln cents. The reason that 1922 cents are found without an obvious Mint-mark is that the Mint-mark on the die filled in. Real 1922-Plain cents still have a trace of the Mint-mark. So look carefully at any Lincoln cents offered as 1922-Plain. The ones with removed Mint-marks are sometimes easily spotted because the removal marks are so obvious (see Fig. 6–5). Also, the genuine 1922-Plain tends not to be fully struck. If you see a phenomenally well-struck 1922 Lincoln cent offered as a 1922-Plain, beware.

In general, the coins you buy which have the highest risk of being altered (and even the highest risk isn't high) are coins with rare dates and Mint-marks in great demand. The 1909-S V.D.B. Lincoln cent is another example of a rare-date coin occasionally found altered. These alterations are usually in the form of an S Mint-mark added to a 1909-V.D.B. or V.D.B. added to a 1909-S. Rarely, two coins are sawed in half: a 1909-S and a 1909-V.D.B. The 1909-S obverse is then glued to the 1909-V.D.B. reverse. If you were to look at just the obverse and reverse you might be fooled. But from reading the first chapter, you know always to view the edge, which in this case would be a dead giveaway.

Look at the added S Mint-mark on the coin depicted in Fig. 6–6. The "S" just sits there and doesn't blend in with the coin. It appears out of place—and it is. Look at another added S Mint-mark (Fig. 6–7). In this example, the "S" has been carved out of the field. But so much concern has focused upon 1909-S V.D.B. cents turning out not to be real that collectors sometimes don't buy perfectly good ones because they are afraid the coins are altered! Collectors are often told never to buy coins which have a darkened area around the Mint-mark. This might be a good

Fig. 6–6. Blowup of a 1909 Lincoln cent with a fake "S" Mint-mark added. (Photograph courtesy National Collectors Laboratories)

Fig. 6–7. Blowup of a 1909 Lincoln cent with an "S" Mint-mark carved out of the field. (Photograph courtesy National Collectors Laboratories)

Fig. 6–8. Blowup of a genuine 1909-S V.D.B. Lincoln cent obverse. (Photograph courtesy National Collectors Laboratories)

general rule of thumb, but it isn't applicable in every case. For example, the 1909-S V.D.B. Lincoln cent illustrated in Fig. 6–8 is genuine. According to Pedro Collazo-Oliver, the darkening around the Mint-mark is "die-erosion radiating outwards from the center" which "is commonly encountered on this coin, making the field look scratched." On the real "S," an almost unnoticeable raised marking should be visible in the top loop of the "S."

Fig. 6–9.   Blowup of a genuine 1909-S V.D.B. Lincoln cent reverse. Note the slanted midsection of the "B," the most prominent distinction of the real V.D.B. (Photograph courtesy National Collectors Laboratories)

Fig. 6–10.   Blowup of a 1909-S Lincoln cent reverse with a fake V.D.B. added. Note the straight midsection. (Photograph courtesy National Collectors Laboratories)

Examine the real V.D.B. reverse in Fig. 6–9. Notice the slant on the midsection of the "B." Now examine an added V.D.B. (see Fig. 6–10). Pay particular attention to the straight midsection of the "B."

Sometimes, added Mint-marks are positioned well (see Fig. 6–11). These, as well as many other added Mint-marks, are spotted by looking at the coin under high power magnification or under a microscope and tilting the coin to spot a seam between the added Mint-mark and the coin's surface (see Fig. 6–12).

The 1914-D Lincoln is also found altered sometimes. Examine the real example shown in Fig. 6–13. Now look at its altered counterpart shown in Fig. 6–14. Observe the space between the "9" and the second "1." A 1944-D was altered to resemble a 1914-D!

 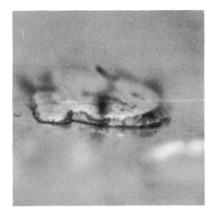

Fig. 6–11 (above left). Blowup of an 1893 Morgan dollar with a well-positioned but fake "S" Mint-mark added. (Photograph courtesy National Collectors Laboratories)

Fig. 6–12 (above right). Blowup of the added Mint-mark seam. You can tell when you tilt the coin and view it under magnification that the "S" is just resting there and is not part of the coin. (Photograph courtesy National Collectors Laboratories)

Fig. 6–13 (above left). Blowup of a genuine 1914-D Lincoln cent. (Photograph courtesy National Collectors Laboratories)

Fig. 6–14 (above right). Blowup of a 1944-D Lincoln cent altered to resemble a 1914-D. Look at the space between the 9 and the second 1. (Photograph courtesy National Collectors Laboratories)

Look at the Mint-mark of the 1916-D Mercury dime (a rare date) in Fig. 6–15. Pay attention to the doubling of the portions of the letter pointed to by the arrows. Now look at an added Mint-mark 1916 dime (Fig. 6–16). The "D" might look real to someone not knowing what real should look like.

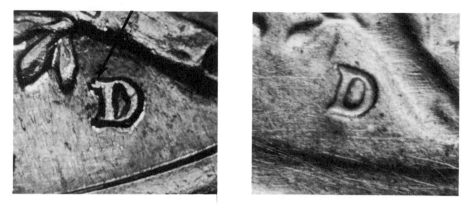

Fig. 6–15 (above left). Blowup of a genuine 1916-D Mercury dime reverse. The top tail of the "D" is doubled, a characteristic of the genuine. (Photograph courtesy National Collectors Laboratories)

Fig. 6–16 (above right). Blowup of a 1916 Mercury dime with a fake "D" added. (Photograph courtesy National Collectors Laboratories)

Distinguishing the real from the altered cannot be explained by listing a set of rules. It's practical experience that is the only solid teacher. Get out to coin conventions and look at lots of coins. By looking at the real coins and getting an idea of what they should look like, you can avoid buying an altered coin.

CAST COUNTERFEITS

Cast counterfeits refers to cast impressions of *copies* of the genuine coins. A cast counterfeit is, therefore, a copy of a copy. As I stress throughout this book, many survival strategies in coin buying involve gaining a "feel" for the right buy and a "feel" for the wrong buy. The ability to detect cast counterfeits is based on this feel, as well as an ability to really feel and determine certain characteristics. For example, a coin that feels slimy and oily might be a cast counterfeit. And if you hold it and it gets warm quickly, it might be a cast counterfeit. The less obvious "feel" is that a cast counterfeit—a copy of a copy—lacks much of the detail of its genuine, die-struck counterpart.

Detecting a cast counterfeit is easier than detecting a die-struck counterfeit, for certain tell-tale signs apply to many cast counterfeits. For example, if the coin lacks a reeded edge, a seam will be visible. This seam, though often disguised by the unscrupulous, is always there. On reeded

Fig. 6–17. Blowup of the surface of a cast counterfeit Barber half-dollar. (Photograph courtesy National Collectors Laboratories)

coins, that edge has no seam. But the reeding will be less uniform and even than on genuine coins. A dropped cast counterfeit won't ring true. Genuine coins have a delicate, warm ring when dropped.

Because a cast counterfeit is just that—a *cast* impression of a copy of a genuine coin—cast counterfeits are grainy and easily recognized for what they are. Many of the original cast counterfeits were made for circulation to fool local merchants, not astute coin collectors. The closeup of the cast Barber half-dollar (Fig. 6–17) points up the typical crude texture of a low-grade example made to pass off in circulation.

Examine Fig. 6–18 and Fig. 6–20, which show the sharp, genuine 1955 Doubled Die Lincoln cent, a valuable Mint error caused by the dies struck twice. Compare that genuine specimen's "LIBERTY" and date with those of the cast copy illustrated in Fig. 6–19 and Fig. 6–21. The cast copy is blurred and grainy; the genuine, sharp and clear. Cast counterfeits tend to have porous surfaces. The Gobrecht dollar in Figs. 6–22 and 6–23 has small holes throughout its uneven surfaces. Close examination reveals that these holes can be linked to the casting process, not circulation.

Electrotype counterfeits are similar to cast counterfeits; but whereas the cast is a copy of an impression made from a real coin, the electrotype is a direct copy of a real coin. The 1804 Large cent shown in Fig. 6–24 might look like a genuine example at first glance. But even if you can't tell by looking at these views of the coin, if you look at the edge (Fig. 6–25) you can see that the seam is more prominent in electrotypes than in any other type of cast counterfeit.

Fig. 6–18.   Blowup of the date of a genuine 1955 doubled-die Lincoln cent. (Photograph courtesy National Collectors Laboratories)

Fig. 6–19.   Blowup of the date of a cast counterfeit 1955 doubled-die Lincoln cent. The cast fake is blurry. (Photograph courtesy National Collectors Laboratories)

Fig. 6–20.   Blowup of the word "LIBERTY" on a genuine 1955 doubled-die Lincoln cent. (Photograph courtesy National Collectors Laboratories)

Fig. 6–21.   Blowup of the word "LIBERTY" on a cast counterfeit 1955 doubled-die Lincoln cent. The doubled letters are distorted and unclear, and the surface is of a low-grade texture. (Photograph courtesy National Collectors Laboratories)

Fig. 6–22.   Blowup of a cast counterfeit Gobrecht dollar obverse. (Photograph courtesy National Collectors Laboratories)

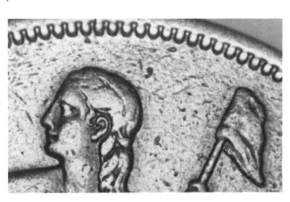

Fig. 6–23.   Blowup of the surface of the cast counterfeit Gobrecht dollar. The porous surface is characteristic of a cast counterfeit. (Photograph courtesy National Collectors Laboratories)

Fig. 6–24.   Blowup of an electrotype counterfeit Large cent, obverse and reverse. (Photograph courtesy National Collectors Laboratories)

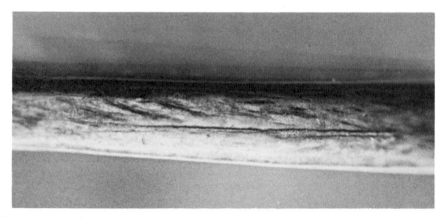

Fig. 6–25.   Blowup of the edge of the electrotype Large cent. The tell-tale seam characteristic of a fake is clearly visible. (Photograph courtesy National Collectors Laboratories)

DIE-STRUCK COUNTERFEITS

The die-struck counterfeit is the most difficult of all counterfeits to detect because it's struck with two dies—just like a genuine coin! Even some leading dealers are unable to distinguish every die-struck counterfeit that comes their way. Being able to detect a die-struck counterfeit

Fig. 6–26. Indian head $10 gold die-struck counterfeit, obverse and reverse. (Photograph courtesy National Collectors Laboratories)

requires many years of experience and study. Not only is it beyond the scope of this book to explain the intricacies of die-struck counterfeits, it's beyond the scope of any book to document and explain how to detect every die-struck counterfeit. And if there ever were such a book, as soon as the book were released, a new type of counterfeit would be released.

Two basic methods are used to teach people how to spot die-struck counterfeits. One involves showing pictures of the characteristics of real coins. The other involves showing photos of selected counterfeits. I've chosen the latter.

The ability to spot die-struck counterfeits has a lot to do with how good a memory you have for the hundreds of die varieties of die-struck counterfeits. If you had access to an information source which enabled you to spot a good number of die-struck counterfeits, the counterfeiter would use your source to his or her advantage. For example, the 1915-S $10 gold piece displayed in Fig. 6–26, die-struck counterfeit, was featured in the American Numismatic Association's official journal, with its diagnostic characteristics listed and photographically illustrated (Fig. 6–27). Two indentations are visible between the leaf and the "N" on the reverse. The counterfeiter read the article and altered his die so that those diagnostic characteristics would not be visible! (See Fig. 6–28.)

Counterfeiters do take pride in their work. One diagnostic characteristic that's evidence of this is the Omega initial. One counterfeiter placed the initial Omega on his die-struck counterfeit gold pieces. Look at the

Fig. 6–27 (above left).   Blowup of counterfeit die reverse diagnostic marks. (Photograph courtesy National Collectors Laboratories)

Fig. 6–28 (above right).   Blowup of counterfeit die reverse diagnostic marks, as filled in by counterfeiter. (Photograph courtesy National Collectors Laboratories)

beautiful but counterfeit 1907 Roman Numerals High Relief Saint-Gaudens $20 in Fig. 6–29. Inside the eagle's claw on the reverse (Fig. 6–30) is the Omega initial. If you spot this initial on any coin, don't buy the coin. The 1882 $3 gold piece shown in Fig. 6–31 is also an Omega counterfeit. The Omega initial is located on the obverse in the top loop of the "R" in the word "LIBERTY" (Fig. 6–32).

Fig. 6–29.   "Omega" counterfeit 1907 Roman numerals high-relief Saint-Gaudens double-eagle, obverse and reverse. The counterfeiter placed the Omega letter on the reverse and inside the claw, where the arrow points. (Photograph courtesy National Collectors Laboratories)

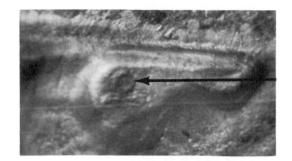

Fig. 6–30. Blowup of the claw where the Omega letter is located on the double eagle fake. (Photograph courtesy National Collectors Laboratories)

Fig. 6–31. "Omega" counterfeit $3 gold, obverse and reverse. The Omega letter is where the arrow is pointing, in the top loop of the "R." (Photograph courtesy National Collectors Laboratories)

Fig. 6–32. Blowup of the Omega letter on the $3 gold. (Photograph courtesy National Collectors Laboratories)

Almost every die-struck counterfeit has its own separate set of diagnostic characteristics. An example of a diagnostic characteristic is the broken "R" and weak die clash of the 1799 dollar shown in Fig. 6–33. A closeup is shown in Fig. 6–34.

The more familiar you become with what the real should look like and what the counterfeit does look like, the better you'll become at detecting counterfeits.

Fig. 6–33.   Die-struck counterfeit 1799 dollar. (Photograph courtesy National Collectors Laboratories)

Fig. 6–34.   Blowup of the tell-tale sign of the fake 1799 dollar. The "R" is broken. (Photograph courtesy National Collectors Laboratories)

FOR FURTHER ASSISTANCE

The following are the most recognized and highly acclaimed authentication services. For a small fee, they will authenticate coins submitted. They also publish educational material concerning how to spot counterfeits. (Dealers throughout the United States rely on the *Genuine Characteristics Reference* and *Counterfeit Analysis Reports* published by Pedro Collazo-Oliver of National Collectors Laboratories. They are available by subscription, but a limited number of past issues are available. I can't recommend them highly enough!)

  American Numismatic Association (A.N.A.) Certification Service
  P.O. Box 2366
  Colorado Springs, CO 80901
  1-303/632-2646

  International Numismatic Society Authentication Bureau
  P.O. Box 19386
  Washington, DC 20036
  1-202/223-4496

  National Collectors Laboratories
  P.O. Box 451, Radio City Station
  New York, NY 10101

The success rate of detecting counterfeits by these services is purported to be close to 100 percent. It's interesting that the two organizations besides A.N.A. have directors who were previously associated with A.N.A. Charles Hoskins, director of INSAB, was the former director of ANACS. And Pedro Collazo-Oliver was an ANACS authenticator, grader, and seminar instructor. All three services offer attractive photocertificates.

7

How to Get the Most Out of the Price Guides

The *Coin Dealer Newsletter* is an accurate reflection of values. You just have to know what the coins look like.

—James L. Halperin, Co-chairman of the Board
Heritage Capital Corporation

In a coin store, a casual coin buyer was looking for a circulated piece to complete his collection. He had a price guide from a popular coin publication. When he came across an example of the coin he wanted in the dealer's inventory—an accurately graded "Fine-12"—he looked up the "Fine-12" price for that coin in the price guide, which pegged its value at $35. But the price on the coin's holder was $50.

"But this price guide says a Fine-12 is worth $35," the casual coin buyer told the dealer.

"Write 'em a check, then," the dealer snapped back. "Our coin is $50."

"What do you mean 'write 'em a check'?" the casual coin buyer pressed. "It's only a guide to what the value is, not an offering of coins."

This is typical of what goes on every day in coin stores and at coin conventions throughout the country. Price guides say a coin is valued at one price, and dealers ask another price. This sort of discrepancy is a constant source of frustration to collectors, just as it is to dealers.

Price guides are imprecise listings of coin values. In most cases, the people writing the price guides don't know what the coins look like. The prices are compiled from confirmed sales between knowledgeable buyers. But as explained earlier, grading standards change as market conditions change. Further, price guides in magazines have to be compiled weeks—sometimes months!—in advance. For example, just because the month is July and the magazine you hold in your hands is dated August does not mean that its price guide has August prices. The prices were probably written in May, two months before release of the magazine. If prices increased between the time the price guide was written for the magazine and the time the magazine was released, the price guide would not reflect that increase. Hence, people go to buy coins with outdated price guides.

HOW THE PRICE GUIDES ARE COMPILED

Price guides are generally based on figures compiled from a variety of sources, which include, but are not limited to, teletype, mail-order offerings, and auctions.

The Teletype as a Reflection of Coin Values

The teletype is used by coin dealers to communicate and do business with one another. If a dealer wants the privilege of doing business this way, he or she has to subscribe to a coin dealer teletype network and pay a monthly fee. The teletype works like this: Dealer A offers a certain MS-63 coin and asks $100 for it (referred to as "the ask"). Dealer B is interested in dealer A's coin—but not at "the ask." So dealer B offers $75 for the coin ("the bid"). The actual selling price is usually somewhere in between.

Transactions like this occur all day and are monitored by the people who compile the price guides. Some price guides have columns for "bid" and "ask." Each column reflects an average of the amount of money dealers are offering to pay and the amount of money dealers are asking for their material. Sometimes, however, certain types of coins are not traded because of a period of disinterest. This is referred to as a "thin" market; and one or two transactions are responsible for the "bid" and "ask" in the popular price guides. Clearly, this invites unscrupulous individuals to manipulate the value guides. "Bid" and "ask" can be moved up or down artificially by dishonest dealers conducting phantom transactions over the teletype. If they own a large number of a certain coin, they might enter high "bids" and "asks" so that it will appear in the price guides that their coins are more valuable. If they know a certain area is about to experience a surge of interest, they might artificially depress prices in order to secure some really outstanding coins at giveaway prices.

Some time ago, a lot of publicity was given to an alleged manipulation of the teletype and, thus, the price guides. A few dealers were suspected of driving down prices of commemorative coins on the teletype. Anthony Swiatek, the recognized authority in the area, took such exception to this practice that in response he took out a public service advertisement in *Coin World*, the hobby's highest circulation weekly, in which he wrote an "Alert":

> The drastic price decline of U.S. silver and gold commemorative coinage is a farce, a fake, a sad plot, total humbug, a fraud, a sinister deception. It was created by a few dealers who are determined to depress this beautiful area of numismatics—which in all price history has never witnessed such a drastic "unnatural" rapid drop in price. Efforts by dealers looking to buy at current levels and slightly higher previous levels have experienced the following: A) Material is not available   B) Offerings are almost always overgraded. (The 63+ coin offered for the 65 coin.) Think for a moment. If many properly graded issues were not available at higher prices how can they be available now . . . Dealers can fight this negative numismatic move by using the teletype in a positive way.

Beware if you see a coin increase or decrease substantially during a short period of time with no apparent explanation. This increase or decrease could be the result of teletype manipulation.

Also, the people who monitor the teletype for the price guides have to go by the descriptions as set forth by the dealers composing them. If a coin is offered on the teletype and is described as MS-67 but is only an MS-60, nobody knows except the people who look at the coin.

Mail-Order Offerings as a Reflection of Coin Values

You can pick up a coin publication at any given time and find advertisements for coins termed exactly alike with prices very far apart. The only way mail-order offerings can be used as a guide is if you know the grading method of the company offering the coins. Nobody can categorize like this, price guide compilers included.

Public Auctions as a Reflection of Coin Values

Public auctions are the best indicators of a coin's value. As explained in chapter 11, though, the grades of coins at public auction listed in the catalogs are negotiated. Since public auctions reflect so accurately what the coins are really worth, go to public auctions and just look at the coins without the cataloged grades and descriptions; select coins which most resemble what you have. The prices these coins sell for will give you a rough estimate of what your coins are worth. This method is far more accurate than using any price guide. *But: price guides based only on auction prices are worthless, since coin grading in auctions is inconsistent.*

NUMISMATIC ECONOMICS

Three basic factors determine a coin's value: grade, quantity, and collector base.

How Grade Affects Value

Grade is a reflection of a coin's desirability. People want the best. Traditionally, the coins in the highest levels of preservation have appreciated at the fastest rates. Even for relatively common coins, fierce demand exists for coins as close to perfect as possible. The closer to MS-70, the rarer the coin, and the fiercer the demand.

How Quantity Affects Value

The quantity is the quantity available, not the number minted. Don't look up a coin's mintage figures and assume that something is common because a large number were minted. Mintage figures can be and often are very misleading. Coins can be melted or lost, and the mintage figures will not reflect this. This is especially true of silver coins, which both the government and private interests have melted for their silver content.

How Collector Base Affects Value

Collector base refers to the number of intelligent collectors who specialize in a particular series and need a particular coin to complete their collections. The coins needed to complete the sets are sometimes arbitrarily set by what spaces in coin folders and albums have been set aside for coins of a set.

The recent history of the 1866 No-motto dollar illustrates the impor-

Fig. 7–1. Valued at $1 million, this 1866 No-motto dollar was once considered the world's most valuable coin. (Photograph courtesy New England Rare Coin Galleries, Inc.)

tance of what *A Guide Book of United States Coins* says about a coin (Fig. 7–1). James Halperin, then chairman of New England Rare Coin Galleries, bought the coin for $48,000 from A-Mark Coin Company of California. He advertised it for resale at $97,500. The coin was considered to be a *pattern* (a design for a coin struck experimentally to see what it looks like as a real coin) because the *Guide Book* had listed it as a pattern for so many years. But Halperin convinced the *Guide Book*'s editor to change the listing to that of "transition-year" (struck one year before the official issue). The coin, with a mintage of two, became a million-dollar rarity overnight! Halperin sold it in 1982 in a private sale.

One coin listed as part of a set, but which is really a pattern, is the 1856 Flying Eagle cent (Fig. 7–2). Although the mintage is listed at 1,000,

Fig. 7–2. An 1856 Proof Flying Eagle cent, obverse and reverse, the most sought-after United States small cent.

Fig. 7–3.   1858 Indian head cent pattern, obverse and reverse. 1859 was the first official year that the Indian head cent was made. This 1858 was struck in a small quantity to see what the design would look like as a coin.

making it a very common pattern, it's a major rarity as part of the set of United States small cents—in fact, the rarest one. Demand persists for this coin; many show up at the same place and at the same time, and each one brings top dollar.

The 1858 Indian cent is also a pattern (and scarcer than the 1856 Flying Eagle cent), but it's in less demand because it isn't listed in the *Guide Book*, and there is no hole or space for it in coin folders and albums (Fig. 7–3). The first official year of the Indian cent was 1859.

Another coin with an album space for it is a mint error: the 1955 Doubled-die cent, valued at around $3,500 in MS-65 (Fig. 7–4). There is no sense in this coin being part of the series. But it, like other coins arbitrarily chosen for inclusion in the folders and albums, will continue to be popular, appreciate in value at mind-boggling rates, and be considered part of the series. The 1858 Indian cent is valued at considerably less than its less rare counterpart pattern, the 1856 Flying Eagle. Reason: the 1856 Flying Eagle is listed; the 1858 Indian isn't.

Fig. 7–4.   Popular 1955 doubled-die Lincoln cent valued at $3,500.

COMMERCIAL GRADING STANDARDS

The following chart lists what coins have to look like to be worth their price guide values. ANACS-certified coins meet these standards most of the time, except for strike.

Price Guide Grade	Scratches	Strike
MS-67	None	Needle-sharp
MS-65	Very few	Sharp
MS-63	Some, but not in a prominent area (e.g., face)	Slight weakness allowed
MS-60	Allowed	Weak strike allowed

THE PRICE GUIDES

A number of price guides are available, and a serious effort is made by their publishers to be as objective as possible. However, all price guides have inherent problems. Some of the best-known price guides are discussed in the following pages.

A Guide Book of United States Coins, by Richard S. Yeoman; yearly (Whitman Coin Products, division of Western Publishing Company, Racine WI 53404). The *Guide Book,* referred to as the "Red Book" because of its color, is relied upon by the numismatic fraternity for its reflection and documentation of coin market movement over years. Writers of investment charts often consult it for its accuracy. Further, its mintage figures are always cited; and no research in American coins can be conducted without the *Guide Book.* The *Guide Book* is so valuable as a research tool that past editions are in themselves valuable collectors' items. The first edition published in 1947 is valued at several hundred dollars.

As a reliable and up-to-date price guide, it falls short of being an accurate value listing. The coin market is just too volatile for you to be able to rely on a book released six months before its cover year: by the time each yearly edition is published, the values are outdated. It will, however, make your use of other value guides easier, for it clarifies all of the abbreviations and terms, which the other value listings don't do. Pick up a copy of this important work; just don't rely on its values.

Coins magazine's "Coins Value Guide"; monthly (Coins Magazine Krause Publications, Inc., Iola, WI 54945). This monthly retail guide is compiled months in advance and thus contains prices that are not up-to-date. The magazine itself, though, is excellent and well worth subscribing to for the superior quality of the articles. The price guide is a supplement or bonus to one of the coin field's best publications.

The Coin Dealer Newsletter (Fig. 7–5) and *Monthly Summary*; weekly and monthly, respectively (The Coin Dealer Newsletter, Inc., P.O. Box 2308, Hollywood, CA 90028). *The Coin Dealer Newsletter* (*CDN*), referred to as the "Gray sheet" because of its color, is a must for any serious collector or investor. Don't expect to glean any sound investment advice off its pages, though. *CDN* reports about coin market activity after the money has been made. In other words, *CDN* is slow to react, both to upswings and downturns. It's also susceptible to manipulation by unscrupulous individuals during thin markets, although recently it has started taking a number of safeguards to prevent this. Further, *CDN* is not an accurate indicator of coin market performance because most of its prices are based on teletype transactions, which fluctuate with coin-market conditions (loosen during booms and tighten during busts).

The key in using *CDN* is to go to coin shows and auctions and know what grading standards are acceptable in the marketplace. Concerning accuracy, *CDN* is the most accurate price guide available, as long as you know the state of the coin market and the quality of coin being referred to. *CDN* includes a weekly front-page analysis, as well as prices for the most popularly traded areas. The format is "bid" and "ask" and is, therefore, a "wholesale" listing price guide. A problem with *CDN* is that it refers to MS-63 as Choice and MS-65 as Gem. As I've stated over and over again, MS-63 is Select and MS-65 is Choice.

The Monthly Summary and Complete Series Pricing Guide, a *CDN* publication, is not a summary of the month's activities, as the title would lead you to believe. Rather, each issue includes some type of specialty article, as well as prices for coins on a date-by-date basis which are less frequently traded than coins in the weekly *CDN*. The format is "bid" and "ask."

The Summary is free to weekly *CDN* subscribers. Alone, *The Summary* is not that helpful. But when used to supplement the weekly *CDN*, it's quite powerful.

Coin Prices magazine; bimonthly (Coin Prices Magazine/Krause Publications, Inc., Iola, WI 54945). Don't let this authoritative-looking

the COIN DEALER newsletter

. . . a Monday morning report on the Coin Market

Vol. XXI No. 28 | July 15, 1983 | Single copy price: $2.50

SIX MONTHS REVIEW OF TYPE COIN MARKET

Coin Market Advances as Bullion Prices Move Higher

The Market in Depth

ALLEN HARRIMAN

Six months have passed since the current type coin market upswing began in earnest. True, it is now generally agreed that the "bottom" of the previous market cycle was reached sometime between the '82 A.N.A. Convention and the final months of last year. Cautious buying was evident at the convention itself—mostly by those scattered and venturesome dealers and investors who saw the proverbial "handwriting". At that early juncture, the more astute (and some of the more experienced) were well aware that the time was ripe to accumulate bargain priced material. But others (the majority) still had to be convinced that the "down market" of mid-'80 — mid '82 wasn't the "ultimate catastrophe". Slowly, over the months following the A.N.A., it dawned on more and more people that the coin market "had a future"—and, thus, the number of buyers began to multiply. Prices were still slipping a bit here and there. But those bargains which had seemed "plentiful"—and prices which had been "negotiable" for so long—were already becoming a thing of the past. Autumn auction prices also strengthened noticeably during this period. And the now regular complaint about the lack of gem material was heard more and more frequently as 1982 drew to a close. Those who bought while the majority was still waiting to be convinced were quite pleased with the early timing of their purchasing. By January, virtually everyone was aware that material which had been "so easy" to locate was long gone—and activity at the early '83 shows was a far cry from that which had been evident for about two years. Price levels, of course, were at a fraction of their record highs—a fact which created even more interest in the minds of the far-thinking.

Though various areas of the market "bottomed" and "rebounded" at different times (the commens, for instance, lagged until only a few weeks ago), the type coin market was definitely well "on its way" by the beginning of the year. Thus, a "six months review" of activity in this now very active segment of the market is particularly appropriate. The following charts compare the January 7th bid levels for both MS-65 and proof-65 specimens of all issues with those in effect at the beginning of July.

The average gain for the 122 issues covered below is 36%—and over half fall within ten percentage points of this average. There, of course, are a few "laggers" along with a few "high flyers". But, in general, the six month advances have been orderly and have been reflected by all issues. (It should be noted that the lower than average gains recorded for the gold issues might be somewhat misleading. Relatively major gains were already registered in this area during late '82 and thus are not included in this January-July recap).

The COPPERS (MS-65):	BID Jan. 7, 1983	BID July 8, 1983	% GAIN
Draped Bust half cents	$ 2,700	$ 4,150	54%
Classic Head half cents	1,700	2,200	29%
Braided Hair half cents	1,800	2,300	28%
Draped Bust large cents	8,500	11,000	29%
Classic Head large cents	15,000	17,500	17%
Coronet large cents	1,800	2,500	39%
Braided Hair large cents	1,500	2,100	40%
Flying Eagle cents	1,375	1,900	38%
Copper-nickel cents (1859)	1,375	1,900	38%
Copper-nickel cents (1860-64)	600	875	46%
Indian Head cents	240	300	25%
Two-cent pieces	900	1,200	33%
The NICKEL coinage (MS-65):			
Three-cent pieces	675	1,075	59%
Shield nickels (with rays)	2,000	2,500	25%
Shield Nickels	825	1,050	27%
Liberty Head nickels (no cents)	275	400	45%
Liberty Head nickels	625	775	24%
Buffalo nickels (type I)	120	180	50%
The SILVER coinage (MS-65):			
Three-cent pieces (type I)	1,500	2,000	33%
Three-cent pieces (type II)	2,200	3,250	48%
Three-cent pieces (type III)	1,500	2,000	33%
Flowing Hair half dimes	15,000	22,500	50%
Draped Bust half dimes (1796-97)	20,000	30,000	50%
Draped Bust half dimes (1800-05)	18,500	25,000	35%
Bust half dimes	2,600	3,600	38%
Seated Liberty half dimes (no stars)	2,700	3,300	22%
Seated Liberty half dimes (no drapery)	1,700	2,400	41%
Seated Liberty half dimes (stars obv.)	1,600	2,200	38%
Seated Liberty half dimes (arrows)	1,675	2,200	31%
Seated Liberty half dimes (legend obv.)	1,325	1,700	28%
Draped Bust dimes (1796-97)	18,000	25,000	39%
Draped Bust dimes (1798-1807)	13,500	17,500	30%
Bust dimes (large size)	5,250	8,000	52%
Bust dimes (reduced size)	4,150	5,800	40%
Seated Liberty dimes (no stars)	3,400	4,400	29%
Seated Liberty dimes (no drapery)	2,250	3,100	38%
Seated Liberty dimes (stars obv.)	1,900	2,700	42%
Seated Liberty dimes (arrows, 1853-55)	1,900	2,700	42%

The COPPERS (MS-65):	BID Jan. 7, 1983	BID July 8, 1983	% GAIN
Seated Liberty dimes (legend obv.)	950	1,350	42%
Seated Liberty dimes (arrows, 1873-74)	4,750	5,400	14%
Barber dimes	750	950	27%
Twenty-cent pieces	3,600	5,000	39%
Draped Bust quarters (1796)	32,500	42,000	29%
Draped Bust quarters (1804-07)	20,000	28,500	43%
Bust quarters (large size)	6,750	10,000	48%
Bust quarters (reduced size)	5,450	8,000	47%
Seated Liberty quarters (no drapery)	7,500	9,500	27%
Seated Liberty quarters (no motto)	1,825	2,800	53%
Seated Liberty quarters (arrows & rays)	4,250	5,600	32%
Seated Liberty quarters (arrows, 1854-55)	3,100	4,000	29%
Seated Liberty quarters (with motto)	1,550	2,200	42%
Seated Liberty quarters (arrows, 1873-74)	2,750	3,500	27%
Barber quarters	1,200	1.800	50%
Standing Liberty quarters (I; full head)	775	875	13%
Standing Liberty quarters (II)	290	330	14%
Standing Liberty quarters (II; full head)	825	950	15%
Flowing Hair halves	35,000	42,500	21%
Draped Bust halves	16,000	20,000	25%
Bust halves	3,300	4,500	36%
Bust halves (reeded edge)	4,500	5,600	24%
Seated Liberty halves (no drapery)	12,500	16,500	32%
Seated Liberty halves (no motto)	2,350	3,100	32%
Seated Liberty halves (arrows & rays)	7,000	11,500	64%
Seated Liberty halves (arrows, 1854-55)	3,500	4,650	33%
Seated Liberty halves (with motto)	2,000	2,900	45%
Seated Liberty halves (arrows, 1873-74)	3,700	4,900	32%
Barber halves	2,000	3,100	55%
Draped Bust dollars (1795-98)	35,000	40,000	14%
Draped Bust dollars (1798-1803)	24,000	28,000	17%
Seated Liberty dollars (no motto)	3,500	5,100	46%
Seated Liberty dollars (with motto)	3,800	5,500	45%
Trade dollars	2,650	3,800	43%
The GOLD coinage (MS-65):			
One dollar (type I)	3,800	4,400	16%
One dollar (type II)	12,500	14,500	16%
One dollar (type III)	3,250	3,900	20%
$2½ Liberty	1,525	2,100	38%
$2½ Indian	1,650	2,250	36%
Three dollars	7,500	9,000	20%
$5 Liberty (no motto)	6,750	7,500	11%
$5 Liberty (with motto)	2,350	3,200	36%
$5 Indian	3,000	3,800	27%
$10 Liberty (no motto)	11,500	13,000	13%
$10 Liberty (with motto)	2,600	3,200	23%
$10 Indian	2,850	3,400	19%
$20 Liberty (type I)	8,500	10,000	18%
$20 Liberty (type II)	3,000	5,750	92%
$20 Liberty (type III)	1,900	2,250	18%
$20 St. Gaudens	1,300	1,600	23%
The PROOFS (Pr-65):			
Flying Eagle cents	3,750	5,250	40%
Copper-nickel cents (1860-64)	1,450	2,200	52%
Indian Head cents	800	1,200	50%
Two-cent pieces	1,450	1,950	34%
Three-cent pieces (nickel)	675	1,150	70%
Three-cent pieces (silver; type II)	3,600	4,900	36%
Three-cent pieces (silver; type III)	1,600	2,050	28%
Shield nickels	1,000	1,600	60%
Liberty Head nickels (no cents)	1,200	1,550	29%
Liberty Head nickels	800	975	22%
Buffalo nickels (1936-37)	1,100	1,800	64%
Jefferson nickels (wartime)	210	250	19%
Seated Liberty half dimes (stars obv.)	2,700	4,000	48%
Seated Liberty half dimes (legend obv.)	1,450	1,900	31%
Seated Liberty dimes (stars obv.)	3,250	4,650	43%
Seated Liberty dimes (legend obv.)	1,250	1,700	36%
Seated Liberty dimes (arrows, 1873-74)	2,700	3,650	35%
Barber dimes	1,250	1,700	36%
Mercury dimes	220	300	36%
Twenty-cent pieces	3,600	5,200	44%
Seated Liberty quarters (no motto)	1,675	2,500	49%
Seated Liberty quarters (with motto)	1,550	2,200	42%
Seated Liberty quarters (arrows, 1873-74)	3,500	4,700	34%
Barber quarters	1,500	2,200	47%
Seated Liberty halves (no motto)	2,275	3,300	45%
Seated Liberty halves (with motto)	2,050	3,100	51%
Seated Liberty halves (arrows, 1873-74)	4,000	5,400	35%
Barber halves	2,400	3,300	38%
Walking Liberty halves	450	600	33%
Seated Liberty dollars (no motto)	3,500	5,600	60%
Seated Liberty dollars (with motto)	3,500	5,400	54%
Morgan dollars	2,600	4,000	54%
Trade dollars	3,250	5,000	54%
Gobrecht dollars	11,500	15,000	30%

U.S. GOLD: (Prices are for the most common date of each type.) Bullion related gold coins in this issue are figured on a basis of gold at $430.30 per ounce.

	VF		XF		AU		MS-60		MS-63		MS-65	
	BID	ASK	BID	ASK	BID	ASK	BID	ASK	BID	ASK	BID	ASK
$1.00 (I)	190.00 +	205.00	210.00	230.00	245.00 +	265.00	600.00	650.00	1100.00	1200.00	5400.00 +	4950.00
$1.00 (II)	275.00	300.00	425.00	465.00	750.00	815.00	2000.00	2175.00	5500.00	6000.00	14,500.00	---
$1.00 (III)	180.00 +	195.00	200.00 +	216.50	240.00 +	260.00	585.00 +	635.00	1025.00	1125.00	4000.00	4450.00
$2½ Lib	194.00 +	211.50	224.00 +	244.00	259.00 +	279.00	575.00 +	625.00	800.00	70.00	2250.00 +	2475.00
$2½ Ind	172.00 +	184.00	180.00 +	193.00	190.00 +	205.00	265.00 +	287.50	600.00	650.00	2350.00 +	2575.00
$3.00	475.00	520.00	690.00 +	750.00	950.00 +	102.50	2000.00	2175.00	3750.00	4100.00	9000.00	10,000.00
$5 Lib/nm	192.00	207.00	217.00	237.00	300.00	325.00	800.00	870.00	2500.00	2725.00	7500.00	---
$5 Lib/wm	181.00	193.50	189.00	202.00	201.00	218.50	245.00	265.00	575.00	625.00	3400.00 +	3750.00
$5 Ind	222.00	239.00	250.00 +	270.00	295.00 +	320.00	795.00	860.00	1250.00	1350.00	4000.00	4450.00
$10 Lib/nm	268.00	285.00	305.00	330.00	400.00	435.00	1100.00	1200.00	3750.00	4100.00	13,000.00	---
$10 Lib/wm	258.00	274.00	266.00	286.00	280.00	305.00	310.00	335.00	675.00	735.00	3400.00 +	3750.00
$10 Ind	420.00 +	445.00	445.00 +	475.00	470.00 +	492.00	540.00 +	590.00	975.00	1050.00	3500.00 +	3850.00
$20 Lib (I)	542.00 +	572.00	591.00 +	631.00	675.00	735.00	1250.00	1350.00	3200.00	3500.00	10,000.00	---
$20 Lib (II)	522.00 +	550.00	549.00 +	579.00	591.00 +	631.00	700.00	760.00	1650.00	1800.00	6000.00 +	6750.00
$20 Lib (III)	514.00 ·	539.00	524.00 +	549.00	566.00 +	591.00	615.00 +	645.00	875.00 +	950.00	2300.00 +	2550.00
$20 St. G.	644.00 +	669.00	654.00 +	679.00	679.00 +	704.00	700.00 +	730.00	825.00 +	895.00	1650.00 +	1825.00

FOREIGN GOLD: (Usually traded in quantity in AU/BU condition.)

	BID	ASK		BID	ASK
Austria 1 Du.	45.35 +	47.10	1/4 K'rand	115.10 +	117.60
4 Du.	189.50 +	194.00	1/10 K'rand	47.05 +	48.55
10 Cr.	42.15 +	43.65	Mex. 50 Pesos	527.00 +	537.00
20 Cr.	82.35 +	84.85	20 Pesos	208.55 +	213.05
100 Cr.	418.75 +	425.25	10 Pesos	102.20 +	104.70
Belgium 20 Fr.	80.35 +	84.35	5 Pesos	52.40 +	54.15
Canada M'leaf	443.50 +	450.00	2½ Pesos	26.95 +	28.20
Colombia 5 Pesos	98.25 +	102.25	2 Pesos	21.55 +	22.55
France 20 Fr. (Roos)	87.25 +	91.25	N.E. Indies 1 Du.	47.70 +	49.95
England Sovs.	103.25 +	107.25	Nether. 10 Gu.	82.25 +	86.25
Hungary 100 Kr.	416.75 +	420.75	Russia 5 Rubles	56.50 +	59.00
Krugerrand	443.00 +	449.50	Chev. 10 Rubles	104.00 +	108.00
1/2 K'rand	227.00 +	230.50	Swiss 20 Fr.	87.75 +	91.75

CIRCULATED SILVER BAGS ARE BID: (Approximate "melt" value)

U.S. 90%	$ 8,665 - $ 8,775	($ 8,810)
U.S. 40%	$ 3,455 - $ 3,515	($ 3,645)
Wartime 5¢	$ 2,250 - $ 2,300	($ 2,400)
Canadian 80%	$ 6,675 - $ 6,775	($ 7,330)

Bullion-related material figured at spot silver price of $12.30.

Fig. 7–5. Sample front page of The Coin Dealer Newsletter, *the buy-and-sell guide used by almost every dealer in the country.* (*Courtesy* The Coin Dealer Newsletter)

and comprehensive magazine lure you into believing that the prices (retail) contained within its pages are up-to-date. They are compiled many
months in advance. The magazine does contain some grading information in each issue, much of which is repeated issue after issue or available
elsewhere in clearer form. Nevertheless, this magazine serves an important need: it brings in new collectors by being readily available at news-
stands throughout the country.

Coin World "Trends"; weekly (Coin World/Amos Press, Inc., P.O.
Box 150, Sidney, OH 45367). *Coin World* is the clear leader in numismatic publications, and its "Trends" reinforces that image. However,
only retail prices are given; and half of the prices are given each week, so
that it takes two weeks to have a listing for every United States coin.
Coin World employs an intelligent coin-market analyst and former professional numismatist to write sensible advice about market activity.
Often, economic variables are considered.

Every collector should subscribe to *Coin World,* the newspaper in
which this price guide appears. The regular reading of the newspaper
itself is the best way of gaining a sense of market pulse and is the best
source of information about every area of the hobby—bar none! If you're
considering subscribing to just one coin publication, this should be it.

Numismatic News "Coin Market"; weekly (Numismatic News/
Krause Publications, Inc., Iola, WI 54945). Here is a truly superior price
guide. The "Coin Market" section of *Numismatic News* is the most
comprehensive price guide anywhere. Some believe it even surpasses *The
Coin Dealer Newsletter.* The complete objectivity of the compiler and
his enthusiastic attentiveness and quick response to market movement
make this guide well worth having.

"Buy" and "bid" are listed, and a third column, called "sell," for
retail prices is given. All of the frequently graded coins are listed, and
every four weeks a comprehensive market guide is issued.

The compilers of this price guide will not be fooled by the unethical
dealers who send messages on the teletype circuit to mislead price guide
writers; and "Coin Market" often states so! Whenever other guides show
artificial increases, the *Numismatic News* "Coin Market" column is the
first to report this. Further, the compiler of this column can often be
found at coin shows looking over dealers' offerings and talking to market
makers in order to report the most accurate prices.

United States Pattern, Experimental and Trial Pieces, by J. Hewitt
Judd; new edition every three to five years (Whitman Coin Products,
division of Western Publishing Company, Racine, WI 53404). This book
is essential to every collector of United States coins. It lists descriptions

and prices for patterns. Although the prices are always outdated, the listed numbers can be multiplied by a certain number to find the current value. This is because the pattern market usually moves as a whole. Ask a reputable dealer what number should be used with this book in order to arrive at rough estimates for the listings. This book uses a commonly referred to rarity rating scale:

Estimate of Number Struck

Unique	1
R-8	2 or 3
R-7, high	4–6
R-7, low	7–12
R-6, high	13–20
R-6, low	21–30
R-5	31–75
R-4	76–200
R-3	201–500
R-2	501–1250
R-1	1250+

CALCULATING PRICES FOR BEAUTIFULLY TONED COINS AND SPLIT-GRADE COINS

Determining the value of a beautifully toned coin which grades, say, MS-65, is difficult. Do you pay an MS-67 price or just a little more than MS-65, or nothing above the MS-65 price? Always buy a coin for the lowest price. If you can't secure it at the MS-65 price or a little above, do stretch to the MS-67 price if the coin is truly original and phenomenal. Don't get carried away and pay over the MS-67 price. The 67 price is often required to secure coins such as the one shown in Fig. 7–6, which displays the most breathtaking concentric circle toning imaginable: cherry-golden centers fade to peripheral rings of rich-red, olive-green, and sky-blue.

It's even more difficult to determine the value of split-grade coins. Do you pay the price of the higher grade, lower grade, or in between? Pay the lower grade price or in between. The 1906 Proof-65/67 Barber half-dollar shown in Fig. 7–7 illustrates the problem. Don't pay more than 1 percent or 2 percent more than the obverse grade's price; it's the obverse which sells the coin. Similarly, the 1862 Proof-65/63 Liberty Seated quarter shown in Fig. 7–8 commands closer to the 65 price than to the 63 price.

Fig. 7–6.   1864 Proof-65 Liberty Seated half-dollar, obverse, with awesome toning. Collectors and dealers alike have difficulty figuring out how much more than the 65 price should be paid for coins with unparalleled eye-appeal, such as this one.

Fig. 7–7.   1906 Proof-65/67 Barber half-dollar, obverse and reverse. Numismatists are always puzzled about how much to pay for coins which have a better reverse than obverse, such as this one.

TIPS ON MAKING A LOT OF MONEY IN RARE COINS

Collectors of coins should follow the same rules in completing their collections that successful investors follow in making money with rare coins.

- *Don't let the price guides decide your price.* Unless you're familiar with the coin-grading methods referred to by the guides, the guides

Fig. 7–8.   1862 Proof-65/63 Liberty Seated quarter, obverse and reverse.
Little reverse spots prevent this coin from being a full Proof-65/65. What
should you pay between the 63 and 65 price?

are not very effective. Buy the coin, not a grade and matching price-
guide price. And remember, the price guides are just that: *guides.*

- *Buy the highest quality.* Traditionally, the coins in the highest
levels of preservation have appreciated at the fastest rates. Coins
that are not in high grades appreciate, but not as rapidly. Buy the
absolute highest grade you can; don't skimp. If it means saving for
the higher-grade coin, then save. Try to buy only high-grade Mint
State business strike or Proof coins. This rule applies to everything, from Lincoln cents to Kennedy halves—everything.

- *Don't be shy about paying several hundred percent more for
"wonder" coins.* Coins that are truly rare and in unusually high
grades are priceless. Time after time, they bring unbelievable
prices at auction. I've seen coins which graded MS-67 sell between
knowledgeable dealers for close to $2,000—when the MS-65 price
was only close to $200! (For example, at a big auction called "Auc-
tion '83," an 1880-S Morgan dollar, MS-67, sold for $1,650. Its MS-
65 price: $130.) There's almost no such thing as overpaying for rare
coins which fall into the "wonder" coin category. Conversely, if
you're selling, don't be ashamed to ask an equally high price for
wonder coins. If you limit your purchases only to wonder coins and
will pay almost anything to secure them, you will be well rewarded when the time comes to sell.

- *Don't follow everyone else.* When everyone else is buying, sell.
When everyone else is selling, buy. The coin market moves in
cycles. Coins that are not increasing in value now probably will in
the near future. Coins going down in value should reverse themselves sooner or later and go back up.

- *Don't wait for magic numbers.* Don't wait for a certain coin on a downward trend to reach an even number. If you are waiting for a coin priced at $52.50 or $5,250 to go down to the near round number ($50 or $5,000, respectively), buy it now. Chances are, if it's on a downward trend, it's available at the lower rate without you having to wait for a price guide to reflect it. A lot of people wait for "magic" numbers which never arrive. This is true for all investments and particularly so for bullion.

- *Diversify*. No more than 25 percent of your total holdings should be invested in your coin collection. The strongest overall financial portfolios are those which consist of different types of assets or those portfolios which are well balanced. Similarly, the financially strongest rare coin holdings are those that consist of different kinds of coins. If you are completing a set, your holdings will still be diversified, for you will be acquiring different dates and Mint-marks.
- *Get friendly with your dealer*. You'd be surprised at the preferential treatment you'll receive if you are friendly with your dealer. You're far more likely to get a good deal and special advice if the dealer knows you than if you make a purchase in a cold, business-like manner. If your dealer doesn't want to talk to you except to know which coins you want so he or she can write up your invoice, don't deal with that dealer.

INFORMATION SOURCES FOR COIN VALUES

Besides the coin publications listed previously, the following magazine and newsletters offer superior advice about which coins are and aren't good values, as well as market reports and anti-ripoff advice. These publications will allow you to develop your own perspective on how to decide what is and isn't a good value.

COINage Magazine
17337 Ventura Boulevard
Encino, CA 91406

The Forecaster
19623 Ventura Boulevard
Tarzana, CA 91356

The Fortune-Teller
P.O. Box 36
Midland Park, NJ 07432

Inside View
P.O. Box 8521
Newport Beach, CA 72660

Investment Bulletin of
Investment Advisors, Inc.
50 Stockbridge Road
Great Barrington, MA 01230
(includes review of coins regularly)

Marketwise
P.O. Box 1316
Claremont, CA 91711

The Rare Coin Investor Newsletter Digest
P.O. Box 324
Lawrence, NY 11559

The Rosen Numismatic Advisory
P.O. Box 231
East Meadow, NY 11554

The Swiatek Numismatic Report
P.O. Box 343
Kew Gardens, NY 11415

8

The Coin Dealer

In a sparsely populated western town just north of Cheyenne, a retired policeman and his wife decided to open a small coin shop. The policeman was very familiar with coins; when he was on the force, he supplemented his income by serving as a vest-pocket dealer at coin shows. His wife knew how to manage money; for years, she co-owned the town's general store. The couple had been prepared to enter the coin business. The mortgage on the house was paid. Their children were off and raising families of their own. (The daughter became a big-city nurse; the son became a pilot and joined the Air Force in Colorado.) The wife sold her interest in the general store and pooled her money with the rest of their savings to open the coin shop. Within six months, they were doing a brisk business.

Not only were they selling coins, but they gained a good reputation among the townspeople. The children would ride their bicycles to the shop anytime they found a coin in change that looked interesting. And the shop owners were always patient enough to sit down and explain the value (or lack of it) of the children's coins. People on their way to and from work would stop by the shop and look at the window displays. Some would stop in to pick up a copy of a weekly coin newspaper. Folks would travel from miles around to sell their pre-1965 halves, quarters, and dimes for bullion value to the couple.

Earl had a filling station a few blocks away and a penchant for Lincoln cents. Over the years, he developed a close relationship with the retired policeman turned coin dealer. Earl set a goal of completing a 1909–1940 collection of Lincoln cents. He never relied upon himself; he listened to everything the dealer said. As the retired policeman and his wife grew older, the structure of their business changed. The wife dropped out of the enterprise for health reasons. And the retired policeman's eyesight was quickly deteriorating, although he refused to admit it. But Earl kept on spending money and buying Lincoln cents until he thought his collection was complete.

Several years later, Earl moved to a bustling metropolis. One afternoon, with his Lincoln cent collection in hand, he entered the headquarters of a large, established numismatic firm. He placed his collection, which was housed in a cardboard folder, on a velvet tray, carefully removing each coin for the professional numismatist to examine. The coin company executive, clothed in suit and tie, summoned two of his immaculately attired associates. The three scrutinized the coins, looked at each other, and convened a two-minute meeting out of Earl's sight. When they returned, they announced this verdict: 1909-S V.D.B.—counterfeit; 1914-D—added Mint-mark; 1922 Plain—removed Mint-mark. The three men insisted that the coins Earl believed to be Mint State were About Uncirculated.

"Counterfeit! Altered! Worn!" Earl exclaimed. The three well-dressed men were very convincing. Earl was thoroughly persuaded that the 1909-S V.D.B. cent was counterfeit and that the 1914-D had an added Mint-mark. But he wasn't sure that the '22 Plain really had a removed Mint-mark, or that all of the cents he believed to be Mint State were not. The three men claimed that since a trace of the "D" was visible on the '22 Plain, it was obvious that the "D" was removed. They pointed to a darker color on the high points on some of the cents, insisting that it was wear.

EARL'S COINS

As explained in an earlier chapter, a trace of the "D" indicates that the '22 Plain has *not* been altered. The coin which Earl presented was an authentic example! Further, many of the cents which the three men insisted weren't Uncirculated were. The coins were stored in paper envelopes for an extended period of time and had moved while in the envelopes, thus causing light oxidation on the high points, not wear. But some were About Uncirculated, as the men had insisted. Interestingly, the 1909-S V.D.B. was counterfeit, and the 1914-D had an added Mint-mark—just as the three men indicated.

EARL'S MISTAKES

Earl made three basic mistakes. First, he relied on somebody else's judgment when he bought the coins. Second, he didn't know enough about coins to know when the three men were wrong. Third, he didn't tell the three men why he was seeking their opinion. (Those of you who are extremely astute will find a fourth mistake: the Uncirculated coins were stored improperly.) With proper training, practice, and a little healthy skepticism, the Earls of this world can avoid misfortune.

We see a collector who was not extremely knowledgeable and a mom-and-pop rare-coin dealership that had apparently unknowingly sold misrepresented coins. We later see a large city coin company criticize the coins and evaluate several incorrectly. What we don't see is a deliberate intent to overgrade or defraud on the part of the mom and pop dealer.

You wonder whether the retired policeman knew that some of the coins weren't what he said they were or if he made consistent errors. And you must be wondering if the three men made a habit of making negative comments about coins brought in for appraisal.

You don't need to know what a dealer's motives are, just what motives exist and what actions are performed. All you need is to be alert, as well as educated about what can and does happen in the coin market. Most dealers are indeed ethical professionals.

Once you know what opportunities exist for a dealer to make money, you can save yourself from numismatic misfortune. Again, this is not to say that any dealer will deliberately and consistently engage in dubious practices in order to line his or her wallet. Opportunities exist for dealers to profit from overgrading, overpricing, undergrading, and underpaying. Capital is derived from these practices in multiple ways.

Overgrading, as discussed in chapter 4, is describing a coin as being in a higher level of preservation than is the case. A lot of money is lost to the "white collar overgraders," those individuals who would call, let's say, MS-63 coin X, valued at $100, an MS-67—and charge $1,000! But grading is a subjective process of evaluation: opinion. And if the coin is yours, it's difficult to be objective. Some dealers are unable to be objective and believe that their overgraded coins are of the grade they claim they are. Other dealers are able to be objective, but they can't resist the extra money from pushing the grade (or assigning their coins higher grades than are justified). In the past, a few dealers consistently grossly overgraded to the point of fraud. They went to jail.

Overpricing is pricing a coin considerably higher than the competitive retail price. A number of factors have caused generally honest dealers to overprice, and these factors are based on the dealer having paid too high a price for a coin. The most obvious factor which might cause a dealer to overprice is when he or she has bought an overgraded or overpriced coin. Another factor is a falling market. If the dealer pays $1,000 for a coin, and the retail market value drops to $700—below what he or she paid for it—the dealer might be reluctant to take a loss and sell it at the new level. Experienced professionals know that it is best for their businesses to take a loss, reestablish a cash flow, and repurchase coins at the new lower level in order to sell for a profit. Thus, many dealers are willing to take a loss and sell at the competitive market price, for they do not want money in coins which they can't sell. Overpricing was especially prevalent duing the severe market downturn of 1981–82, for many coins lost value on a weekly, sometimes daily, basis. However, a dealer may overprice an accurately graded or undergraded coin to increase his or her profit margin. So it is important for you to know values.

Undergrading is the act of describing a coin as being in a lower level of preservation than is the case. A dealer may undergrade for a few reasons.

Ignorance of grading is the usual reason for undergrading. Few dealers know how to correctly grade every series. When undergrading is a result of ignorance, it is often subtle: a Gem coin called Choice or a Choice coin graded Typical. This author has seen cases of Mint State coins graded About Uncirculated, but this is the exception, not the rule. The usual reason for this mistake is die wear being confused with circulation wear, as explained in chapter 4. Never underestimate your dealer's ability to know basic grading, though.

Your dealer also may undergrade for novices who are not familiar with price guides or don't pay attention to them while buying. Many nonknowledgeable coin buyers have acquired undergraded coins without seeking the use of a price guide, only to find later that the coin was grossly overpriced. This is not a very common practice.

A common practice is *underpaying*. This is usually done by a dealer convincing the seller that the coins are of a lower quality than the seller believes them to be. The dealer may undergrade them or claim them to be counterfeit or altered. Heirs attempting to liquidate numismatic estates should beware of this practice. In the same category as underpaying is *miscounting*. If you are buying or selling coins of uniform quality in quantity, always count the pieces. A dealer might undercount the pieces you are selling or buying from him or her. If you are buying rolls of coins, pay particular attention to the number of coins. Coins of the same series are not all the exact same size. Therefore, the plastic roll holders could appear full yet be short a coin or two. Paying attention to all of the above will help to prevent you from becoming an Earl.

Now that you know what a dealer can do to make money, you should acquaint yourself with basic negotiation strategy.

HOW TO NEGOTIATE
WITH A COIN DEALER

- *Maintain a poker face.* Your ability to hide your feelings, and to show them when you feel it is appropriate, is a prime determinant of your success at negotiations. If you're offered a coin at well

Fig. 8–1. Professional numismatists at a reputable coin firm examine some of their displayed specimens.

below its value, don't react favorably and get excited. If you're offered a coin well above its market value, express disapproval.

- *If you're making a buy offer, start low.* There's practically no such thing as too low (unless you offer under bullion!). If you start much too low, however, the dealer may refuse to discuss that coin with you anymore.
- *If you're making a sell offer, start high.* Remember, if you're too high, the dealer will probably shake his or her head in disbelief and not want to discuss the matter further.
- *Talk price, not grade.* Dealers have very strong opinions concerning grading. If a dealer is selling you a coin marked MS-65, with an obverse scrape which obliterates Ms. Liberty and nearly travels through to the reverse, the chances are that he or she has noticed it. There is no need to scream, "Are you a half-wit? Don't ever expect me to believe that this is an MS-65, dummy!" Don't have coins labeled with grades if you're presenting them to a dealer for sale. Often, dealers think of two things when buying coins: how low they can convince you that the grade is, and how high a grade they can reasonably pass off the coin as, when they sell it.
- *If you're selling, don't deny the existence of an imperfection.* If it's brought to your attention, you might want to just agree that the

imperfection exists or casually mention that it doesn't bother you. Many collectors ask why it's acceptable for dealers to make a big fuss about imperfections of coins brought to dealers, but not to accept such a fuss from people who go to them to buy coins. The answer is that when you go to a dealer's place of business (whether store or coin show), your criticism of his or her coins is not tolerated because you are going *to* the dealer. When you bring your coins to a dealer's place of business, his or her criticism of your coins *is* tolerated.

- *Know the market.* Your knowledge of the market and values is the most important negotiation aid. Knowing the real market value means that you'll know what the dealer's "real bottom line" is. It also means that you'll know how much to hold out for if you're selling.
- *Counteroffer well below the dealer's price.* For example, if a dealer is offering a coin for $1,250 and you make an offer of $1,225, do you think you would get the coin? Probably not. The dealer would know that you want that coin and would hold out until you gave him or her the extra $25.

Use the information given about negotiations only as a guide. Use judgment and discretion, for there are no rules for negotiating. There might be cases in which none of the aforementioned is applicable. But know that just because a coin is listed in a dealer's catalog for a certain price doesn't mean that the price is not negotiable.

TYPES OF COIN DEALERS

The local dealer runs a mom-and-pop organization similar to the one run by the retired policeman and his wife. The regional dealer has a large following from several nearby states and a hefty local following. The national dealer may have a strong local following, combined with a mail-order following throughout the country, as well as a strong following from attending coin shows. The national dealer may even have locations in more than one state. The international dealer has several departments, as well as a following throughout the world. This type of dealership might have one or more overseas offices, a strong mail-order following, and a heavy travel schedule.

The coin industry is one of boom and bust. During the booms, the number of dealers in all categories grows, but many dealerships themselves grow and advance to the next category. For example, during a boom, many regional dealers will become national dealers. But during the bust, dealers will exit the industry, and a number of expanded dealerships will shrink. The regulative structure of the field—none—allows dealers to enter and exit at will.

Establishing a relationship with a dealer in your locale is very important, for this dealer will serve as your central source of information. You'll buy your coin books there, your newspapers there, your magazines there, and, perhaps, some of your coins there. You'll hear market reports there, discuss your collecting needs there, and learn a great deal about buying and selling coins there—if not from the wisdom of a professional numismatist, then from your own mistakes.

Dealers acquire coins through collectors, investors, estates, auctions, coin shows, teletype, and any other source with coins for sale. In many cases, they are competing with you to buy coins. Dealers sell coins through their stores and offices to other dealers, collectors, and investors. Their other outlets include the bid board, auction, mail order, and teletype.

Establishing a relationship with a dealer might also save you money when you want a coin that another dealer possesses. For example, let's say that you establish a relationship with dealer A. One day, you discover that dealer X is offering just the coin you need to complete your collection. The coin is listed in dealer X's catalog for $3,000. You don't know how much the coin is worth because you haven't seen it. Dealer X only extends approval credit to known dealers and is hundreds of miles away. If you're a good customer, dealer A might order the coin on approval, get a wholesale price of $2,500, and sell the coin to you for $2,700, $300 less than dealer X's asking price.

The dealer you establish a relationship with might even represent you at an out-of-town auction for a minimal fee. For a 5-percent or 10-percent fee, you don't have to pay the transportation and lodging costs. However, this percentage fee adds up to a substantial sum of money if your auction spending is considerable. Use your judgment. If you attend yourself, it might be less expensive in the end if you know values and are self-disciplined.

Always beware of bargains. Remember, if something seems too good to be true, it probably is. Even if a coin is genuine, unaltered, and accurately graded, there could be trouble. It could be stolen. If you buy a stolen coin, you might be asked to return it. (Even if you're not, the coin is still not legally yours.) However, dealers who care about their reputations will refund your money. If you pay too low a price, you could face criminal penalties, depending upon what state you reside in or what states are involved.

If you encounter a dealer in whom you have implicit faith who treats you fairly and with respect, embrace him; and don't let him go. He or she will be your best numismatic friend, next to your coins, of course. Just gain an education about how the rare coin market works. Follow this advice, and you'll never be an Earl.

9

Guarantees and Mail-Order Coin Buying

A while ago we had the occasion to seriously question the values offered by an *enormously successful* firm. A deliberate selection of 20 or so coins were ordered from their hefty, profusely illustrated catalog where they *proudly displayed* their prestigious reputations and repeated insistence to satisfy customers. We were *shocked* by some of their coins! Their wonderful *"BU, light rubbing"* 2¢ piece was an *EF*; their *BU* Bust Dime was a sharp AU-50 adorned with *deep scratches*, too *trivial* to mention; their *Unc.* Trade Dollar was a *polished EF*; and on and on!

—Maurice Rosen
The Rosen Numismatic Advisory

It sounds so easy, so simple, so attractive. You get a coin offering in the mail. You read about a coin which sounds like the perfect addition to your collection. So you send off a check, hoping to get exactly what's advertised. If you order from a reputable dealer, you'll probably get what you pay for, since reputable dealers have integrity and have to maintain the respect of their customers. But if you unwittingly order from a fly-by-night dealer, you could get ripped off.

The coin market is easy to enter and easy to exit. There are no federal, state, or local laws regulating who may or may not be a coin dealer. You could get an offering in the mail from some dealer who started doing business yesterday, has no intention of really sending out the coin or coins you order, but who calls himself or herself "one of the most expert and honest dealers in the universe." And the dealer could leave the coin business just as rapidly as he or she entered it—leaving you high and dry.

HOW TO IDENTIFY A
DISREPUTABLE
MAIL-ORDER DEALER

Spotting a disreputable dealer isn't easy, for there are so many honest and ethical ones. However, there are a few things you should know before ordering from a dealer. Even if the answers to your inquiry turn out to be unfavorable, this does not mean that the dealer is a crook. It may mean, however, that you should inquire some more.

Membership in professional organizations in and of itself is no guarantee that a dealer is respected and honest, but make sure your dealer belongs to the American Numismatic Association (A.N.A.), which expels members who violate its code of ethics. Membership in this organization is not a guarantee that a dealer is honest, but nonmembership might be reason enough for you to further investigate a dealer. If your dealer has been expelled from an organization (such as A.N.A.), this may be reason to ask more questions. However, all it takes to become a member of many numismatic organizations is payment of nominal yearly dues. So don't be impressed by a dealer with a long list of memberships.

Advertising in respected numismatic publications such as *Coin World, Numismatic News, COINage,* and *Coins* is also not an absolute guarantee of a dealer's integrity. But these types of publications closely monitor the activities of their advertisers. If a fly-by-night or disreputable dealer is identified by one of the publication's consumer protection spotters, out that dealer goes. Make sure to read each publication's advertising policy before ordering. That way you'll know, for example, how long a dealer's return privilege is, even if it isn't stated in the advertisement.

Adherence to a standardized grading system is one of the most important dealer policies to check out. Some years ago, as I mentioned in the grading chapter, the absence of a "single, official standard for grading coins" caused a federal administrative law judge in Washington, D.C., to rule in favor of a San Antonio, Texas, dealer accused of selling "whizzed" and overgraded coins. According to the January 4, 1978, edition of *Coin World:*

> Judge Quentin E. Grant found the respondents, the Security National Rare Coin Corp. and Riverside Coin Co. innocent (not guilty) of allegations made by the United States Postal Service, after determining that the complainant had "failed to sustain the burden of proving the falsity of the representations alleged." . . . Among the judge's conclusions was one that "there are various, similar guides for the grading of United States coins, some of them widely accepted, but there is no single, official standard for grading accepted by, and binding on, all

dealers and collectors . . ." The respondent, Judge Grant found, used "its own unique system of grading, and so stated in its Riverside Coin Co. catalog"; the complainant, furthermore, "has not proved that respondent was bound, legally or morally, to use any other system." . . . The judge's opinion on "whizzing" or polishing coins was that it "is considered by some collectors to degrade a coin. For others it enhances the desirability of a coin," he found, adding: "There is nothing illegal about "whizzing" or polishing. There is no unanimity of opinion as to the effect of such procedures on the grading of coins, although increasing experience in collecting may tend to cause a collector to shun "whizzed" or polished coins . . . Therefore, I find no misrepresentation involved in respondent's practice of "whizzing" or polishing coins."

Legally, a dealer may not be bound to conform to specific grading parameters if he or she does not state that he or she uses a specific system to grade coins, such as *Official A.N.A. Grading Standards for United States Coins* (which was introduced shortly after the court case just mentioned in order to provide a basis for the "elimination of variations in grading on a national basis"). Although many numismatic publications may require their advertisers to conform to a specific set of grading standards, *if a dealer specifically states that his coins are graded by his own system of grading, you're on your own.*

But just because a dealer refuses to use the A.N.A.'s grading standards doesn't mean that he or she is dishonest. If you're buying circulated coins, for example, conformity to *Photograde* should be acceptable. Still, beware of dealers who say "all coins graded by our own unique grading system."

Bargains which seem too good to be true often are. If you see an offering from a dealer for coins at considerably below market value—no matter how respected the publication he or she is advertising in—the coins are probably below the advertised grade or else the price is probably a mistake.

A convicted felon testifying before the Senate Subcommittee on Civil Service, Post Office and General Services, pointed out that greed made his coin schemes work. According to the July 7, 1982, *Coin World*, "the scheme spelled out by the convict had to do with offering counterfeit rare coins to unsuspecting buyers by mail auction." The article recapped part of the testimony:

> "I would buy a coin for $100 that looks like a 1799 silver dollar. If it were genuine, it would be worth about $5,000 . . . I played on people's greed. There were any number of people who thought they would send in a low bid 'just in case' to see if they might get a windfall." In the case of the 1799 dollar, the bids received ranged from

$3,500 to $4,100, he recalled. The highest offer would be accepted and an invoice would be sent. "Those who received my invoices could not send me their money fast enough. They thought they were getting a real bargain and they wanted to push through their end of the deal before I changed my mind or something. When I received the cashier's check for $4,100 I sent the coin," recounted the convicted con man. The coin looked authentic; so the buyer was apparently satisfied with the "bargain," he indicated. Obviously, at the time, the swindler was happy with the deal, too, since he netted $4,000.

Guarantees offering the impossible often are. It's unlikely that you'll find a mail-order offering of this type in a respected numismatic publication. But you might receive a direct-mail offering guaranteeing you, perhaps, a yearly performance percentage, such as 25 percent per year. This percentage guarantee is a gray area as far as the law is concerned, but the general consensus among hobby leaders is that the Securities and Exchange Commission (SEC) has deemed percentage guarantees to be against the law.

Deletion of a coin's major imperfection in the description is a good reason for you not to order from a particular dealer again, provided you know that he or she has seen the imperfection. If you receive a coin graded, say, VG-8, with a large, unmentioned obverse scratch, telephone the dealer and tell him or her that you spotted the imperfection. If the dealer tells you to return the coin for a prompt refund and apologizes for not having seen the scratch, you might want to give him or her another chance. But if the dealer says that you're too fussy, tells you off, refuses to take back the coin, and insists that the scratch isn't important, you might think twice about buying from that dealer again.

Several years ago, some attention was given to a variation of grading which would lower a circulated coin's grade as a result of an imperfection. This system was not adopted, so don't expect a dealer to downgrade a coin as a result of an imperfection. Circulated coins are graded according to how worn they are, with the imperfection(s) mentioned separately. This system was adopted because a lot of collectors would rather buy a worn "Fine" without imperfections than a "Very Fine" with, say, a large scratch.

Dealers offer coins which they don't have in stock far more commonly than you would think. If your order seems unreasonably slow in being filled, the dealer may be looking to buy what you ordered. This shouldn't concern you. What should concern you is a dealer who offers the same date, denomination, and Mint-mark coin cataloged five different ways and with five different prices, leading you to believe that he or she has five different coins for sale, when in actuality there is only one. If you order, say, a Very Fine Buffalo nickel and return it with more money because you've decided you want the Extremely Fine example (a higher-grade coin) advertised, but receive the same piece back in a different holder with the higher-grade description, you have a right to return the coin and not deal with that dealer again.

MAIL-ORDER COIN GUARANTEES

A number of dealers offer a variety of guarantees. Some are valuable, others worthless. But it all comes down to one thing: a guarantee is only as good as the company which issues it.

Don't deal with mail-order dealers whose stated policy is "all sales final." Although such a dealer may be perfectly honest, you need time to verify the value of your purchase: grading variations are common. Frequently, dealers have a return privilege; five or ten days is reasonable. Members of the Professional Numismatists Guild, a dealer organization, offer a thirty-day return privilege, a more than ample amount of time. Many nonmember dealers also have such policies.

Many dealers are very concerned about the possibility of selling you a counterfeit and offer a virtually unlimited return period should a coin they sell you prove to be counterfeit. Many dealers have stories to tell about coins which turned out to be counterfeit which they bought back five and ten years after they were sold. Auction houses, too, are concerned about counterfeits. And if there is ever a question about the authenticity of a potential consignment, that consignment is often turned down. The auction company could sell a coin; give a consignor a check for the amount realized less the reasonable commission; then later have to give the successful bidder a refund if the coin turned out to be fake—when meanwhile the consignor has the money and doesn't have to give it back!

Some firms offer not only to refund your money, but to pay you interest on the money you spent should any coins you purchase from them prove to be counterfeit. Clearly, this is a guarantee you should request *in writing*.

Most grading guarantees are not binding on the dealer. The guarantee of a dealer who promises to buy back your coins at a price commensurate with the market value is a fair guarantee but not an iron-clad one. Who determines what "the market" is? Who determines which price guide is used? Similarly, the guarantee of a dealer who promises to buy your coins back at the same grade at which they were purchased is also a fair guarantee but one which isn't iron-clad. What if the dealer says, "Yes, these are MS-63s, but we don't need any right now and can only offer you an MS-60 price." Again, it's not the guarantee, but the dealer who offers it. Reputable dealers who offer these guarantees will bend over backwards to protect their image and be sure that you are satisfied—even if it means paying the MS-63 price for coins they sold as MS-63s but don't currently need.

A few dealers offer variations of the guarantee, promising you conformity with ANACS grading standards. But even if you receive the coins graded by ANACS, this is no assurance of a good value, as explained in chapter 3.

Some firms guarantee that they will auction coins at the same grade at which they sold them to you via mail order. This is most helpful if you go the auction route, for you know how your coins will be cataloged, but an auction catalog grade is not a guarantee that the coin will realize a price commensurate with that grade. However, this guarantee from a top dealer is quite meaningful, for the quality of the cataloging causes bidders to become fiercely competitive and bid liberally, using the catalog description and grade as a guide. And top dealers have loyal followings.

Professional Numismatists Guild members have the option of offering customers an organizational certificate which pledges the dealer's description of the coin. If the coin turns out not to be what the dealer says it is, the dealer is liable to be brought before the board of that organization. The certificate consists of a signed statement and photograph or description. Members of that organization are subject to legally binding arbitration in cases in which disgruntled customers request it.

As explained earlier, just because a company sells a lot of coins doesn't mean it's reputable. Reprinted here is an interview that Maurice Rosen of *The Rosen Numismatic Advisory* conducted with a former employee of a coin firm. I think you'll find it most enlightening. "Bob" is a pseudonym. In any industry, employees have isolated horror stories to tell. This is one such story.

CONFESSION OF A RIP-OFF COIN SALESMAN*

Rosen: *Bob, can you tell me something about the firm you worked for?*
Bob: It was an unusual place, as all the coins that were shipped were not at all what they were supposed to be. In the beginning, I did not realize this. At first, I was so overjoyed that all of my clients were getting a product that continually went up in price. However, I didn't realize that even though according to the Gray Sheet (*Coin Dealer Newsletter*) the product went up, my clients were not participating at all.

---

* Copyright © 1981, Numismatic Counseling, Inc.

Rosen: *Why are you now exposing the rip-off practices of this firm?*
Bob: I left the firm because I realized my clients not only weren't getting the profit appreciation they thought, but, in fact, were losing tremendously, even though the market was going up. And you reach the point where it is impossible to sell to people. I had one client, a Scottish lady, who invested virtually all of her savings through me. If she had tried to liquidate her portfolio, she would lose over 75%.
Rosen: *What kind of numismatic experience do the account executives have?*
Bob: The owners of the firm hope they have no numismatic experience at all.
Rosen: *Why?*
Bob: Because they want someone to give a prepared talk and not know at all what they're saying. Then you have total confidence in what you're saying. But as soon as you learn anything about the numismatic market, you lose your confidence in that firm.
Rosen: *Was it claimed, however, that each of the account executives was an expert who would manage the account?*
Bob: Of course. And in all the mailings it said: "Please call our toll-free number and speak to one of our numismatic experts." That may have meant that it would be someone who had been on the phone for two days and just found out what a coin is!
Rosen: *What is the mark-up of that firm on their average investor sale?*
Bob: Recently, I sent out one coin for $15,000. We settled for $7,000, and I made 8% on the coin. By and large, they would add approximately 70% to the Gray Sheet "ask" price for every coin they sold. This is based on the MS-65 "ask." They bought coins as About Uncirculated (AU) and sold them as MS-65. So their mark-up is in the hundreds of percent! We also had the option of coming "all the way" down to 20% over "ask." And if a client was really good, we could go to 10% over "ask." But that had to be a super client. Still, they were doubling or tripling up at the very least.
Rosen: *Were coins cleaned to make them appear to be in a higher grade?*
Bob: I think that it was unusual for us to send out a coin that wasn't cleaned. It was a standard practice to be cleaning coins in a silver dip and baking soda. Then we'd send them out as Choice BU regardless of the condition of the coins.
Rosen: *Have coins ever been sent back to that firm for sale, and if so, how were the people treated when they wanted to "reap their profits"?*
Bob: . . . If a customer wanted to sell coins back to us, we would say anything to change his mind. We always wanted to maintain the "cover" that the customer made a wise investment. We'd stress . . . the probability of much higher prices soon, even make false statements of apprecia-

tion in their portfolio. This would usually suffice for awhile. If that failed, we'd try to back out by telling them we didn't need their coins at the moment. Finally, we'd make an offer which was more than we paid, but still less than the customer's cost—and it would be paid over 6 to 12 months. Incidentally, those repurchased coins were sent out again at the "usual" multiple mark-up. . . . If they knew enough about our company . . . to see what we were paying for Choice BU or MS-65 coins, and they pushed, then they would get away with it if they threatened us. But situations like this were very rare.

Rosen: *How and from what sources does Firm X buy its coins?*

Bob: I would say at least 90% of the coins are acquired through ads . . . They receive on average 20–25 packages a day. They review the coins, call the sender, and make offers. If the sender knows he has good coins and wants a legitimate price, then the firm doesn't buy the coins.

Rosen: *The prices that this firm advertises to pay are related to the true market prices as you can see from the Gray Sheet. However, are you saying that they bought them for considerably less?*

Bob: Definitely! Occasionally, they got really nice coins in packages. Still, the sender was told that the coins were overgraded and worth much less than the advertised buy prices. I guess the impressiveness of the ads and the smooth-talking of the buyer convinced a lot of people to sell their coins way below what they were really worth.

Rosen: *How did your firm describe the true Choice BU coins that it bought when sent out in investment packages?*

Bob: If someone sent them a coin that was truly a Choice BU, every attempt would be made to buy it as a Choice AU or an AU. Then it will be sold as a MS-68 or 69 at a phenomenal premium. Understand that they were routinely sending out washed-up AU's as Choice BU. Can you imagine how an honest-to-goodness Choice BU would be priced?

Rosen: *How large is this company?*

Bob: The average salesman was making about $1,000 a week. They were working on 8% commission. That would be about $12,500 a week in sales or over a half-million dollars a year per salesperson. When I left, there were 20 salespeople. They were also very big on trades, buying silver at a terribly reduced price, and trading it in for other coins at an exaggerated price.

Rosen: *How would that work?*

Bob: I'm going back to early 1980 when a bag of silver was in the $30,000 range. We would buy it for $26,000 (an additional $4,000 right there because of an unwary customer) then sell him a $26,000 portfolio which in fact really cost $6,000–$10,000 . . .

Rosen: *. . . I am assuming that all the other salespeople at that firm realized that their customers were being ripped-off by the unfair pricing* *and grading policies of the firm. Yet how could each of these salespeople, yourself included, have spoken to the people and told them about the advantages of buying rare coins and the alleged integrity of your firm, knowing that the customers were going to be ripped-off? How could this have been justified?*

Bob: Each of the salespeople there justified it in their own mind by the amount of money they were making. That doesn't make it right. But it happens. Here's a good example: I asked one of the best salespeople there a question about coins after I was there a short time. His answer to me was, "How the heck do I know? I don't want to know anything about coins. If I learn anything about them, I would not be as good a salesman."

Rosen: *Were you ever in contact with other dealers in the coin business to know how they operated and treated their customers?*

Bob: I never had much contact with other coin dealers until I started going to local coin shows. And if I made reference to the firm that I worked for, it normally evoked a lot of laughs. Most of the people at the coin shows had a small clientele with whom they worked closely, as opposed to the situation that I had. If I showed them some of the coins that I was sending out, they would be absolutely amazed that anyone bought them.

Rosen: *Would you personally buy rare coins for investment?*

Bob: Absolutely, but not from the firm I worked for!

Rosen: *How would you go about buying coins? What procedure would you use?*

Bob: Based upon my experience, I think I know what firms and individuals are reliable—who will sell a coin at a specific grade and buy it back at a specific grade. I would go to those people.

YOUR RIGHTS AS A MAIL-ORDER
COIN BUYER

In a two-page flier, the Federal Trade Commission (FTC) outlines the mail-order merchandise rule as adopted by the Commission in October 1975. The FTC states:

- You must receive the merchandise when the seller says you will.
- If you are not promised delivery within a certain time period, the seller must ship the merchandise no later than 30 days after your order is received.
- If you don't receive your merchandise shortly after that 30-day period, you have the right to cancel your order and get a refund.

The Commission states, in part:

> The seller must tell you if the promised delivery date (or the 30-day limit) can't be met and what the new shipping date will be. Then the seller must give you the option to either cancel the order for a full refund or agree to the new shipping date. The seller also must provide a free way to reply, such as a stamped envelope or a postage-paid postcard. If you don't answer, it means you agree to the delay. If you do not agree to the delay, the seller must return your money by the end of the first 30-day delay. If you cancel a prepaid order, the seller must mail you the refund within seven business days. Where there is a credit sale, the seller must adjust your account within one billing cycle. . . . The rule does not apply to . . . C.O.D. orders or to credit orders in which your account is not charged before the merchandise is mailed.

HOW TO COMPLAIN AND GET RESULTS

You can pursue a number of courses of action if you think you've been ripped off by mail. You can write to the dealer or to the publication where the dealer's advertisement appeared, contact a professional organization the dealer is a member of, tell your documented story to a consumer action group, alert the United States Postal Service, complain to a government agency, or—as an absolute last resort—sue.

Write to the dealer by Certified or Registered mail, return receipt requested. Don't get mad in the letter and tell the dealer he or she is a good-for-nothing crook. Instead, be businesslike and professional. State the facts. If it's a coin you're returning within the stated return privilege, enclose the coin and request the refund politely. If it's an order you didn't receive, tell the dealer how long ago you sent your order, and, if possible, send a photocopy of the canceled check. You'd be surprised how many dealers fill their orders immediately and mail them via Insured mail (up to $400), only for the package to be lost. Insured mail travels with uninsured mail and can get lost. Registered mail, however, is deemed to be extremely safe with only a small percentage lost. (In fact, the Hope diamond was mailed and insured via Registered mail.) If the package was lost in the mail, ask the dealer to file the proper insurance form with the Post Office in order for your money to be refunded. If the piece, for some reason, was not insured and didn't reach you, the dealer is responsible. If the dealer refuses to cooperate after you've handled the matter as described above, you might need to take one of the following steps.

- Complain to the publication that carried the advertisement. In this case, too, be concise and factual. Don't make accusations which you can't back up. The most popular publications are:

    Coin World/Amos Press, Inc.
    P.O. Box 150
    Sidney, OH 45367
    Attention: Customer Service Manager

    Krause Publications
    (Numismatic News, Coins magazine, Coin Prices,
    World Coin News)
    700 East State Street
    Iola, WI 54990
    Attention: Advertising Manager

    Miller Magazines, Inc.
    (COINage magazine, Coin Collector's Yearbook, Rarities)
    17337 Ventura Boulevard
    Encino, CA 91316
    Attention: Advertising Director

    Dealers don't like being complained about to the publications in which they advertise because each legitimate complaint is held against them. At Krause Publications, for example, where advertisers vie for that company's Customer Service Award, which is awarded to several advertisers every year, a dealer receiving three or more legitimate complaints over a year is ineligible for the award. Dealers given the award are allowed to display a logo in their advertisements which indicates that they received the award and the year in which they received it.

    When writing to a publication, send copies of any correspondence you had with the dealer in question. Keep copies of any correspondence you have with the publications. Send the dealer copies of any letters of complaint you send to magazines.
- Write to numismatic organizations the dealer belongs to, following the advice stated above. Some organizations to contact are:

    American Numismatic Association
    P.O. Box 2366
    Colorado Springs, CO 80901
    Attention: Executive Vice President

    Professional Numismatists Guild, Inc.
    P.O. Box 430
    Van Nuys, CA 91408
    Attention: Executive Director

Retail Coin Dealers Association
P.O. Box 536
Denison, TX 75020
Attention: Executive Director

The American Numismatic Association only responds to inquiries from members. I strongly recommend that you join. The Professional Numismatists Guild offers legally binding arbitration.

- Contact consumer action groups, such as your local chapter of the Better Business Bureau, or a television station or newspaper. Such organizations and individuals have no legal authority but can serve as useful intermediaries in disputes and can wield considerable power, especially in the case of the media. Sometimes consumer action groups will contact the necessary government authorities so that necessary action will be taken. Send copies of pertinent documentation.
- Complain to the Inspector in Charge of the United States Postal Service office from which your order was supposed to have been sent. The U.S.P.S. usually investigates only when a pattern of allegedly suspicious dealings seems clear.
- Contact government organizations. Sometimes, just one letter from such an organization to an errant dealer helps. Again, make absolutely certain that your gripe is warranted and well documented. Make no false statements. A few places to try are your State Attorney General, your city's consumer affairs department, or the FTC's Bureau of Consumer Protection. The FTC is also responsible for enforcing the Hobby Protection Act of 1973, which makes the sale of counterfeit coins *illegal,* as opposed to unethical, and places restrictions on the selling of replicas (requiring the manufacturer to imprint on the replica that it isn't genuine).
- Sue the dealer. Use this option only as a last resort. Always consult an attorney. Even if you're suing, be open to any reasonable settlement; it might be better than continuing your legal battle. The following information is not intended to substitute for legal counsel.

Allen Kamp, Associate Professor of Law at John Marshall College of Law, Chicago, writing in the Fall-Winter 1981 edition of the no longer published *Review of Numismatics and the Law,* states:

> The sale of coins with numismatic value is governed by the provisions of Article II of the Uniform Commercial Code (UCC) . . . . a statute that has been enacted into law in every state except Louisiana . . . When a buyer receives a coin that has been stated to be of a certain grade and it appears not to meet that standard, he has several rights and remedies under the UCC. Basically, he can either send the goods

back to the seller and sue for damages, or keep the goods and sue for damages. *Both alternatives assume that he has been unable to achieve satisfaction without suing.* [author's emphasis] He has these rights because the seller has breached his contract to the buyer. The Code provides that statements of fact about the goods such as "this is a 1979 car," and "this is of 'mint' quality" are express warranties. The goods must conform to these warranties or there is breach of contract. . . . What a certain grade means and whether or not the coins are of that grade are questions of fact that, if disputed, will have to be established in court. . . . Upon receiving the coins, the buyer should inspect them to determine if they conform to the grading warranties. The inspection must be done promptly or the buyer may lose his rights. . . . The Code allows one to accept or reject "any commercial unit." . . . Upon rejection, the coins should be kept for the seller to pick up, or sent back if the seller so requests. (Of course, if returned they should be sent Registered Mail and properly insured, with all receipts retained.) . . . It should be noted that the seller may contend that the coins did meet the grading standards and that, therefore, the rejection is wrongful . . . Upon rejection, the buyer still can sue the seller for damages. The buyer can "cover," that is buy the coins elsewhere and recover the difference between the cover price and the contract price. He may also sue for the difference between the market price of the coins at the time he learned of the breach and the contract price. This is especially important if the coin in the grade ordered has appreciated significantly. If the buyer were to resell the coins, he could recover his expected lost profits, unless he were able to obtain the coins elsewhere. He may also collect his incidental damages, for such expenses as inspection, certification and storage of the rejected goods, and any commission in connection with his "cover." . . . No one should return coins claiming a breach of grading warranty just because the market has fallen. . . . These legal rights may well depend on retaining a lawyer and filing lawsuits, which are costly and risky propositions.

These basic legal rights as outlined by Kamp may appear straightforward, but they are really far more theoretical than their presentation suggests. Kamp himself admits that there is no precedent for the rights he discusses. The explanation for that might be that there are so many loopholes for the seller that no buyer could press a case. What proof is there that the coins you have in your possession are indeed the coins the dealer sold you? What proof do you have that the coins are in the precise level of preservation they were when sold? What proof do you have that the coins aren't as described if the dealer claims to grade by his or her own "unique system?" It's no wonder that no precedent exists!

Les Fox, who published *Review of Numismatics and the Law*, says his firm will send you a courtesy copy of his newsletter, *The Fortune Teller*, if you send a self-addressed, stamped envelope to P.O. Box 36, Midland Park, NJ 07432.

10

The Role of the Coin Convention

It was 9:15 AM. The security guard rubbed his mustache, scratched his forehead, and took his typical stroll around the exhibit area of the national coin convention. "Not much to do," he muttered to himself. There were five aisles of educational exhibits, each display having been painstakingly prepared by numismatists—advanced, intermediate, and junior. The area, along with the adjoining bourse room (the convention area where dealers gather to sell rare coins), was later to be opened to the public. But before the visitors arrived, the guard was looking at the educational displays and absorbing information.

There was one exhibit at which he stopped and stared. It consisted of small, silver coins spread out upon black velvet. It was as if the guard was transformed to the evening of his first date when he stood with his girl in the backyard under the moonlight, as they both looked at the stars. Like the gleaming stars upon a pitch-black, but moonlit, summer nighttime sky, the silver coins glowed with an effervescent magic. The simplicity of the exhibit provided for an inherent beauty which aided in holding the attention even of a noncollector.

Meanwhile, in the room next door, dealers were preparing for the influx of people by stapling holders, setting up coins in showcases, getting checkbooks in order, and counting hundred-dollar bills. Yet it was more like a social club than a room of cutthroat competitors. Dealers confided in one another about problems at home and at work, and they bragged to each other about sales made in days and weeks past. In fact, if an outsider had entered to buy coins at this point, he or she would have felt like an intruder.

Upstairs, lecturers were preparing for their educational forums, and organization leaders were setting up for specialty meetings of their groups.

Fig. 10–1.   The scene at a national coin convention.

This was the scene of a national coin convention. It could have been any national coin convention. But whether the convention is international, national, regional, or local, it can serve many of the same purposes for you: social, educative, buying and selling, auctioning, and exhibiting. The basic types of coin shows include, but are not limited to, local club meetings, local club shows, regional, state or seminational conventions, national conventions, and international conventions.

LOCAL CLUB MEETINGS

Although local club meetings are the most fundamental type of numismatic gathering, they aren't always open to everyone. Many local clubs take pride in their selectivity, even though they are primarily composed of intermediate collectors. A number of local clubs require each non-member to be accompanied by a member when attending a meeting of the club. If you have a friend who belongs to one of these clubs, you might want to attend a meeting. If you were to attend one of these meetings, you would have the opportunity to converse with other collectors and, perhaps, look at coins they want to sell. You might be given the opportunity to trade your coins for other coins, as well as to participate in the club's auction. The auction might consist of coins consigned by members, along with coins donated to the club. The type of individual who attends local club meetings is, in general, the person who lives within a ten-mile radius of the meeting place and who is categorized as an "intermediate" collector. But there can be really expert numismatists at these meetings.

If you educate yourself in buying and selling before the meeting and view it as a social and historically educative affair, you'll enjoy yourself immensely. Interested coin collectors can go on talking for hours. Just remember that you have to go to work the next morning!

LOCAL CLUB SHOWS

Watch out. Some dealers at local club shows are part-time hobbyists. Some of these nonprofessionals are not as concerned about reputation as their professional counterparts. This author is not claiming that all part-time dealers are not ethical; in fact, many are more ethical than some of their professional counterparts. But a part-time weekend dealer might not know all the rules of the game, might be ignorant of coin-market conditions, and might be very unhappy about your trying to return a coin. Yes, there *are* good deals available from part-time dealers. But a good part of the time, the material is of inferior quality and overgraded.

The cost to the dealer of renting a table at a local club show can range from $50 to $100. And often, the dealers at these shows have more to sell than coins: jewelry, watches, political campaign buttons, and baseball cards. (A variation of the local club show is the local show sponsored by a commercial organization, but composed of the same type of dealers.)

SEMINATIONAL CONVENTIONS: REGIONAL AND STATE

The seminational convention is where the action is. It is the backbone of the rare-coin industry, the place where values are determined and dealer inventory replenished. It is the place where the neophyte is educated, where the advanced collector exhibits, and where the professional numismatist wheels and deals. It is also the place where great sums of money are lost by the unknowledgeable. When you attend a seminational convention, don't hesitate to have this book at your disposal.

The seminational convention is sponsored by either a nonprofit or commercial numismatic organization. When the show is sponsored by the former, you have the opportunity of placing an educational exhibit. When the show is sponsored by the latter, you do not. Although the main attraction of this type of show is the dealers who form the bourse (between seventy-five and two hundred), the seminational convention offers an impressive array of invaluable educational activities—from organized youth forums to advanced educational seminars of the highest caliber. And there is usually an important auction held in conjunction with the show.

During the 1979–1980 boom, there was almost no distinction between the seminational show and the national convention, for dealers from across the country would attend most coin shows; there was always a lot of business. But as market activity became less hectic, the fine line became more identifiable. During the boom, there were numerous complaints from the professionals about there not being enough shows. Today, the number of shows seems enough.

Conventional wisdom says that the best place for the beginning collector is the local club show. But I suggest that the beginning collector

Fig. 10–2. Dealers do business at conventions on rented tables and sell coins from the boxes they bring with them.

should attend the educational forums of the seminational conventions, but refrain from buying during the early learning stages. You don't get the same feel for the hobby by only reading books before you buy. Do both; read books, and attend the seminational.

NATIONAL CONVENTIONS

The national coin convention is composed of a multiplicity of numismatic events conducted on every level. But it's also a place that might overwhelm you. Many beginners are actually scared when they look at a national coin convention, for they don't know what to do first. There are usually several hundred dealers, dozens of educational exhibits, scores of educational activities, and a huge auction.

Beginners might find the national convention unmanageable. For these individuals, it is advisable to obtain a copy of the convention program and study it in a quiet place. But beginners should refrain from buying *anything* until they have attended several national conventions. National conventions offer the young (the under-18 crowd) a thorough education through a series of innovative programs.

The pace of national conventions is so brisk that even an experienced dealer occasionally is a victim of intense activity. A friend and colleague of mine walked into an auction session of a major numismatic company during a national coin convention. He was so preoccupied with other convention events that he bid $9,000 (plus a 10-percent buyer's fee)—on the wrong coin! Two lots later, he informed the auctioneer of the error. But the auctioneer, also the company's president, refused to honor the request to reopen bidding on the piece. When the "successful" bidder offered the coin for sale to the underbidder, the underbidder admitted to getting caught up in the bidding and was no longer interested in the coin. The story had a happy ending, for the auction company later decided to put the coin into its next auction and not force a sale. But the lesson is that everyone, even the experienced professional, has to be careful at a national convention.

INTERNATIONAL CONVENTIONS

Although this book is primarily concerned with United States coins, a discussion of the role of the coin convention would not be complete without mention of international conventions. The size of these coin shows is between the seminational and national categories discussed earlier.

For the United States resident, there are two basic types of international shows: those held in the United States and those held overseas. The international convention differs from the seminational and national in that only foreign material is allowed during international shows held in the United States, whereas there are no restrictions during regular United States shows. There are many U.S. dealers; even the overseas dealers speak English, and American money is readily accepted.

But before anyone buys coins from any coin show or convention, it is necessary to become familiar with the unwritten rules of the bourse.

BOURSE ROOM ETIQUETTE

The following are don'ts for the rare-coin enthusiast:

1. *Don't loudmouth* a dealer for overgrading, and don't select pieces from his or her inventory and remark how ugly they are. If you don't like the way a coin is graded or looks, don't buy it.
2. *Don't deter a dealer's customer* who is interested in buying the same type of material you have to sell. If a prospective buyer is engaged in conversation with a dealer, don't interrupt. This is for your own protection, for many dealers become violent when this happens. If you want to sell your coins on the bourse floor, offer them to dealers who have tables. Or rent your own.
3. *Don't interrupt a potential transaction by offering a higher price* to purchase a coin than the dealer it is being offered to. In fact, don't make any offer, even if the dealer acts disinterested. Disinterest is a clever negotiation tactic. And if you interfere, the dealer might get very angry. If you want to be offered coins in this manner, rent a table.
4. *Don't remove the dealer's coin from the holder without first asking permission.* If you are given permission to remove it, make sure to hold it over a velvet tray or fabric with thumb and forefinger (explained further in chapter 1).
5. *Don't remove the dealer's coin from the holder if your hands are dirty.* Wash your hands before you enter a bourse room. Even if a dealer doesn't mind if you hold coins with dirty hands, you should mind. If you buy a coin which you've mishandled, its value could decrease markedly at a later date.
6. *Don't make a purchase offer if you don't mean it.* On the dealer-to-dealer level, purchase offers are considered binding, and deal-

ers are rarely offered a return privilege. Even for nondealers, however, offers are often considered binding. In general, dealers don't like to take back coins purchased at conventions. If pressed, most will accept returns, but they will refuse to deal with you again.

7. *Don't get mad at a dealer for asking a ridiculously high price* for the piece you have been desperately searching for. If the dealer senses your desire, he or she will put pressure on you to buy it. Remember, never allow yourself to be coerced into buying something. There is nothing wrong with asking, "What is your real bottom line?" If the dealer still won't lower the price, just say "we're too far apart." If he or she persists, tell the dealer what you're willing to pay. If you get that far, be ready to visit another table, for you might no longer be a welcome visitor. But you might get lucky and have your offer accepted.

8. *Don't ask for an appraisal within listening distance* of the dealer whose coin you are having appraised. In fact, if the coin is in a flip, remove the insert bearing the dealer's name when asking another dealer's opinion. If you return the coin, don't reveal whose opinions you sought.

9. *Don't fidget with price guides* during an auction presale viewing session. There are limited hours and many people waiting to view. Look at the coins first, and later determine what you want to pay—after you've finished viewing. The pros don't even bother with price guides on the bourse floor, except for an occasional, "What's bid?" Similarly, if you are offering coins for sale, know what prices you want before you offer them.

10. *Don't try to force your way into a crowded table.* If a dealer is busy, stroll the bourse floor. Not only is it best to deal on a one-to-one basis, but dealers get nervous when there are a lot of people around, for fear of losing a coin.

Convention goers should take adequate security measures to help insure their protection. For your convenience, a security checklist follows.

SECURITY TIPS FOR THE CONVENTION GOER

- Take off your convention badge after you leave the bourse floor.
- Don't wear the official convention medal. If you want one, buy it, and put it away. Only collectors wear the medals, and collectors often carry coins with them.

- Dress casually, and don't carry a bag if possible. During the summer months, attend in shirt sleeves, and don't wear a jacket.
- Avoid feeling your pocket where you know coins are; this alerts people to where your coins are located. Walk with your arms loosely at your side.
- Do not boast about the coins you just bought. Store your coins in a bank safe-deposit box, and if you ever discuss your numismatic holdings, remark about them being there.
- If you place an educational exhibit, be accompanied by someone upon placement and removal. Have that person accompany you with the coins back to the safe-deposit box or vault. If this is not feasible, consider not exhibiting.
- Take out insurance on collections valued above $2,500.

EDUCATIONAL FORUMS

The educational forum is the main reason for individuals to attend coin conventions. In order to maximize your benefits from attending one of these forums, you should do some preforum planning.

First, ascertain which forum is best to attend. For example, if you enjoy exploring commemorative coinage and have decided to build a collection, a lecture by Anthony Swiatek, the world's foremost commemorative authority, would be a far better choice than a lecture concerning political campaign buttons given by George Hatie, a former president of the American Numismatic Association (A.N.A.). Second, after you decide which forum to attend, read up on the topic to be discussed. Many lecturers have written books on the subject on which they lecture, and it is a good idea to obtain copies when possible. A.N.A. members may borrow books from the A.N.A. library at no charge except for postage. Third, prepare a list of questions before you attend the forum. If any remain unanswered after the lecture, speak up. Ask the lecturer the unanswered question(s). It is only by going through this process repeatedly that you will be able to obtain a top-notch education.

If you like the educational forum as a means of obtaining a numismatic education, there are two organizations which offer organized seminar programs at nominal fees: the American Numismatic Association and the Institute of Numismatic and Philatelic Studies at Adelphi University (INPS). Information is obtainable from both groups. The A.N.A.'s address can be found elsewhere in this book. The INPS can be contacted by writing (or calling) to Adelphi University, Garden City, New York 11530. Both organizations hold programs at their headquarters and elsewhere.

This author has been honored to have served on the board of governors of INPS. At a board meeting in New Orleans, this author posed the question, "Why can't INPS merge its educational interests and work with A.N.A.?" Edward Rochette, A.N.A. executive vice president, responded by explaining the basic policy differences between INPS and A.N.A. For example, A.N.A. does not teach seminar participants to grade using a microscope, but INPS does.

When attending any of these seminars or forums, take notes. You may find them very useful to refer to at a later date, but there are no rules. If you believe that you will gain a better education by just sitting back and listening, do that.

YOUTH PROGRAMS

This country's youth program saw its beginnings in 1971 when Michigan's Florence Schook set up a program for young collectors in conjunction with a coin convention. Young numismatists (YNs) from that state and others flocked to the meeting. The attraction was simple—motivational, participatory education. Young collectors, some of whom were not collectors but were attending the meeting with a relative or friend, were motivated to pursue numismatics by being given gifts and participating in activities of the meeting. What a success it was. By May 1974, the program was introduced at the Greater New York Coin Convention in New York City and met with more success. Dealers were willing to donate coins to be given free of charge, as well as sponsoring luncheons. The convention organizations were so ecstatic about the number of people the programs attracted that they encouraged having YN programs and advertised their existence. Within a year, Florence's programs were national in scope and gained a character and momentum all their own. The programs are now famous for the numismatic spelling bee (with impressive trophies given to the winners), exhibit contests (with expert judging), young persons' presentations and coin club updates (with valuable prizes given to every speaker), and play money auction (with play money given to every YN in attendance to buy real coins). The programs were so well received and represented in the press that numismatic luminaries from across the country jumped at the opportunity of being able to address the YNs. These programs, designed to maximize participation, present an ideal opportunity for YNs to broaden their numismatic knowledge and sharpen their collecting skills. Florence also administers a summer seminar scholarship program and an awards program. These programs have become fiercely competitive.

There are no requirements for young people who want to attend these programs in their locale, except that they be under 18, have an interest in, but not necessarily any knowledge of, numismatics, and be well behaved. For further information or for placement on Mrs. Schook's mailing list, write: Florence M. Schook, A.N.A. Governor and YN Program Chairperson, P.O. Box 2014, Livonia, MI 48154. It's too bad that there isn't a program as superior as Florence Schook's for adult beginning collectors; the closest to it is the educational forum held in conjunction with A.N.A.'s annual convention and sponsored by the A.N.A. YNs. It is geared to YNs, but adults are welcome (another Florence Schook creation).

HOW TO DESIGN A WINNING EXHIBIT

There is romance between coin collectors and their collections. So it follows that collectors like to prepare displays of their collections. Some displays get more attention than others. But although exhibits interest the noncollector, such as the type of exhibit described at the beginning of this chapter, they should be designed to please the exhibit judges.

Collectors involved on convention committees like to believe that exhibits are the main attraction of any convention. To some degree, this is true. The judging of numismatic exhibits has evolved into a fine art, much like horse- and dog-show judging. But many persons, even the most experienced exhibitors, often wonder why judges consistently select one type of exhibit over another to win first place or best of show.

One of the country's leading exhibit judges points out that in preparing the exhibit, one must adhere to the rules prepared by the exhibit committee. Most rules are modeled after those of the A.N.A.:

Subject	Number of Points
Information	35
Arrangement, aesthetic appeal	30
Completeness	15
Condition	10
Rarity	10

The method used by the convention you display at (display case, specification, etc.) is usually outlined in their exhibit rules. But there are certain tips, aside from the stock information, that will help you to win a prize. You should make sure the title is complete as it relates to the coins displayed. If you are displaying coins which do not constitute a complete set, design your title to reflect what you're displaying. Try to have the coins stand apart from the background by placing each one on a small platform or even a small pillow. Include adequate background information, and include an example of the coin's reverse. Do not use a background color that may bother a judge, such as red. Small items can make the difference between winning and losing because neatness counts. If your exhibit is pasted on a board which is too small for the case, place a piece of matching velvet or cloth underneath.

The exhibit judge says that the first place award is the easiest to determine because that display stands out in all respects. The second is also not a difficult choice. But the third is most difficult because most displays left after the selection of first and second place have an equal number of faults.

HOW TO COMPLAIN

"The dealer's risk is as great in taking your check as your risk is in taking his coin," a dealer acquaintance of mine once remarked. Every collector should make a note of this comment, for it focuses importance on the fact that every sale is a two-way street. Not only does the dealer hold a responsibility, but the collector does too. The collector should closely follow bourse-room etiquette. If a time ever arises when a collector feels that he or she has bought a misrepresented coin (whether overgraded, counterfeit, or other), he or she should not go back and tell off the dealer. Instead, the collector should quietly bring the matter to the dealer's attention. If the dealer still will not satisfactorily settle the matter, the collector may take action through the channels discussed elsewhere in this book (A.N.A. complaint, PNG arbitration, etc.). But when at a coin convention, it is best to take immediate action.

In few other industries do large transactions take place in so few seconds as they do in the rare-coin industry. If you are deciding whether or not to buy a coin, it might be bought by someone else while you are taking a walk around the bourse room to make up your mind. You can't tell a dealer that you might buy a certain coin from him or her next month, for that coin could be sold tomorrow. This pressure has caused many people to buy coins, only to regret it later.

If you buy a misrepresented coin at a convention or show, dealers and organization officials agree that the best way of handling it, if talking to the dealer fails, is by contacting a high official with the show and asking his or her assistance. Dealers usually cooperate when a complaint reaches this level.

Remember, the coin industry is an easy-entry one, assumed to be self-governing. Just because a dealer has a table at a show is no assurance of high ethical standards. The shows don't police their dealers. That's up to you. The best way to complain is not to have to in the first place. Prevention is the best cure. Educate yourself so that you can never be ripped off.

Despite all the attempts at education (through organizational meetings, seminars, and exhibits), coin conventions exist for one reason only—the bourse. Just don't get the reason they *exist* confused with the *purpose* they can serve for you. The bourse is the nucleus of virtually every coin gathering. Regardless of how much planning is done by the sponsoring organization, whether profit or nonprofit, to attract top-notch speakers or have other meritorious activities, it remains an inescapable fact that were it not for the bourse, there wouldn't be a coin convention. This is obvious to even the beginning collector who wonders why so many people flock to the bourse compared to the few who attend the educational forums and meetings. Attractions other than the bourse exist at coin shows to lure people to the bourse. There is an analogous relationship in commercial television. Television programs exist only as a lure to get people to watch the commercials. A.N.A. has been stepping up its educational programs, along with trying to attract more educational exhibitors to its conventions, in order to retain its tax-exempt status.

11

How to Sell
Your Coins

There is absolutely no correlation between the grade a coin is assigned and the price which that coin realizes at public auction.

—Paul F. Taglione, President
New England Rare Coin Galleries

Albert had degrees from Princeton and Yale, was a senior partner with one of the United States's largest law firms, and had an income well into six figures—and he was no dummy. He had a cooperative apartment on New York City's Park Avenue, a beach-front house in East Hampton, and a private Lear Jet.

Albert always seemed to make good investments. Not only did his real estate increase in value, but his stock holdings increased too. He bought IBM and Xerox at bargain basement levels in the early 1960s, only to strike it rich a decade later.

In 1979, Albert began to explore investing in coins to hedge against double-digit inflation. He read a study by the prestigious firm of Salomon Brothers on the performance of rare coins and was favorably impressed. He then visited a moderate-size coin company, where the vice president of sales told him everything he wanted to hear about rare-coin investment: low downside, high upside, convenience of storage and transport, and ease of liquidation. Albert didn't have time (or want to make time) to ask more questions or investigate his dealer more closely.

He was in the surroundings he had become accustomed to. There were plush leather chairs, sumptuous wall-to-wall carpet, black velvet-lined cases, and courteous employees. He popped out his favorite credit card and charged his $20,000 coin purchase.

Last year, Albert tried to sell those coins. He attempted to sell them back to the dealer from whom he acquired them. Much to his dismay, the company had gone out of business. He proceeded to show the coins to several reputable dealers. Not one wanted to buy the coins at any price; they claimed the coins were misrepresented—overgraded—when Albert bought them.

Albert found that hard to believe. But he was familiar with the art market and knew that auction was one of the best ways of liquidating one's holdings. So he contacted a small numismatic auction company. The auction company, in need of consignments, gladly accepted Albert's coins and assured him that his coins would be cataloged at the same grade at which he purchased them. Albert was ecstatic. He thought that this was his assurance of realizing the prices that the price guides indicated for those grades. Albert made sure that the auction contract specified that he retained title to the coins while they were in the possession of the auction house (in case the auction company went out of business). And he made sure that the coins were fully insured while in the auction firm's possession. He signed the contract and thought that his auction consignment was as good as money in the bank. The auction was scheduled for November, two months after the coins were consigned.

Albert attended the auction in person. He participated in the presale viewing to confirm that the coins being sold were indeed his. They were. There were close to twenty active bidders present on the auction floor. If Albert's coins had realized prices commensurate with their auction grades, they would have brought close to $10,000, about half of the purchase price. According to the price guides, his coins had decreased in value by 50 percent.

He waited patiently for the sale of his first consigned coin, lot 100. Lots 98, 99, and 101 were cataloged identically to Albert's coin. Lot 98 realized $600; lot 99, $700; *lot 100, $325;* and lot 101, $775. Albert was aghast! He thought it might have been a freak and anxiously awaited his next consigned coin, lot 149. Lot 148 was cataloged identically to Albert's coin. Lot 148 realized $150; *lot 149 realized $40.* This was not a freak, for this was the trend which dominated Albert's consignment. The total price realized for his coin holdings was $5,000, half of the value guide listing for coins of the cataloged grades and one quarter of the original purchase price. (And don't forget the auction company's commission, usually 5 to 20 percent.) How could everything go so wrong for someone who did everything so right?

Albert didn't do everything right. He bought his rare coins at high prices during the boom cycle; and he sold them during the bust cycle. Further, he didn't realize that buying coins isn't like buying stocks or bonds or real estate. There is no regulation of the rare-coin industry by any level of government (as has been repeatedly stressed throughout this book). An individual who is numismatically ignorant *can* buy coins for investment and not be ripped off. He or she just should have those coins examined by someone who is knowledgeable in order to confirm the grade, authenticity, and value, or should buy from a dealer who can be trusted implicitly. A helpful adage in the coin field is: "If you don't know your coins, know your dealer." Many people never realize the true value of their coins until the time comes to sell. This is true of both collectors and investors. Many collectors buy coins for their aesthetic value, only to realize years later that many of their coins are of considerably lower grades than they had believed them to be.

But when the time comes to sell—and sooner or later every coin buyer considers liquidation—the question arises, "How should I sell my coins?" The conventional sale means are public auction, private sale, public sale, and consignment to a dealer for over-the-counter sale.

PUBLIC AUCTION

Albert didn't realize that the price a coin realizes at public auction sometimes bears no correlation to its cataloged grade. This is because auction coins are not always cataloged with consistency. Auction sales often reflect deals made between consignor and auction house. For example, if a prospective consignor approaches an auction company with a rarity

Fig. 11–1.   Public auctions are the best vehicle to use to sell your coins.

valued at $50,000 and a collection of About Uncirculated quarters, the auction house might want the prestige of having the valuable rarity in its sale so much that it would catalog the A.U. quarters as Mint State! The auction company probably would not voluntarily offer to overgrade the quarters. But if faced with losing a rarity to a competitor, it might concede to calling A.U. coins "Mint State." Some small companies, such as the one Albert consigned his coins to, need consignments so badly that they will grade coins practically any way the consignor requests—as long as it means getting more coins in its auction.

Generally, auction companies like to grade very conservatively. In fact, given a free hand, many will undergrade. Undergrading is common in estate sales. Heirs who are not numismatically knowledgeable often present their inherited coins to the auction company with complete faith that the numismatists employed by the firm are experts who will act in the best interest of the consignor. They may be experts but they don't always act in the consignor's best interest. Undergrading is in the auction firm's best interest, for no dealer wants to have a reputation as a consistent overgrader. Undergrading creates action on the auction floor and impresses potential consignors who don't see the coins, just the impressive prices realized. It also makes the market appear strong, even if it isn't. Coins consigned by heirs could actually be Mint State, but be cataloged as About Uncirculated.

The auction catalogue, therefore, could consist of A.U. coins graded Mint State, Mint State coins graded A.U., and other grading inconsistencies. Of course, a respectable percentage of lots will be graded correctly. To further confuse things, mixed with the consigned coins are pieces owned by the dealer conducting the sale. But as a rule of thumb, auction houses view consignors, not bidders, as their primary clients.

Paul F. Taglione, President of New England Rare Coin Galleries, the world's largest rare coin dealer, says, "All auction houses favor consignors; but some do more than others. At New England, we favor consignors by about 60 percent." Taglione believes strongly that you should not sell outright if you're not numismatically knowledgeable. And he was candid and open about the effectiveness of public auctions: "In a strong market, it is a tremendously good method of disposal. In a weak market, it is an uneven method." *An auction is the best liquidation method for high-quality coins if the dealer from whom you purchased the coins will not buy them back.* Taglione, who works out of New England's world headquarters in Boston, suggests that you compare rates, services, etc., of at least three competing auction houses which are not in proximity to one another. The best time to sell is in the fall, preferably November, or in the spring, preferably March. Keep away from climatic extremes—summer and winter. Avoid auctions which conclude during the early morning, such as 3:00 AM. Also avoid small auctions, which attract too few bid-

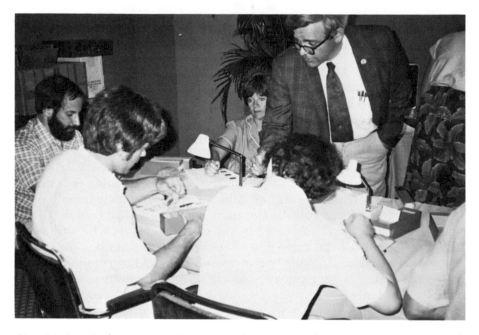

Fig. 11–2.   Before an auction, people interested in buying the coins of-fered for sale get a chance to look at them. This is called an auction presale viewing session.

ders. Sometimes, big auctions can be overwhelming. If the sale contains more than 2,500 lots, consider not consigning. It's difficult for bidders to view all of the coins. And remember that an auction house's estimate of what your coins will realize may not be 100 percent accurate.

If you're afraid that your coins will be switched for less valuable ones, photograph them before the sale, and have the auction firm initial the photos. This fear is probably unfounded, but photographs might help you prove that an auction firm damaged your coins if it did. Damage to coins is far more likely than switching. I've never heard of any case involving switched auction coins.

Some questions to ask the auction house include, but are not limited to, the following:

- How experienced are you at conducting numismatic auctions?
- Have you ever conducted an official American Numismatic Association convention auction?
- Are my coins insured while in your possession?
- May I retain title to the coins until they are sold?
- How will you grade my coins?

- How will you catalog my coins?
- What are the qualifications of the numismatist(s) who will grade and catalog my coins?
- How many lots will the auction consist of?
- What time of day will my coins be auctioned during?
- How many catalogs will be distributed?
- How are your catalogs organized: by consignment or by denomination and date?
- How many of my coins, if any, will be photographed in black-and-white or in color?
- How will you display my coins before the auction to prospective bidders?
- Will you describe my coins over the telephone to inquiring mail bidders?
- What precautions are taken to prevent collusion?
- How much of an advance on prices realized will I receive, and what will the interest charges on it be?
- What is your percentage fee?
- Are successful bidders assessed a buyer's fee?
- How soon after the auction will I be paid?
- What payment plans do you offer? (Check, cash, gold, etc.)
- What are the provisions governing "protective bids" I might want to place on some or all of my consigned coins?
- How can I get my coins to you? (Some auction firms offer bonded couriers who will pick your coins up and deliver them to the firm if a considerable holding is involved.)
- Will the auction contract specify all of the points we've discussed?

Only you can decide what answers are satisfactory.

PRIVATE SALE

Private sale can be the most treacherous route of disposal for the non-knowledgeable or unskeptical. When a dealer makes an offer on a collection, quite often it is for a fraction of the collection's true value. Dealers buy numismatic estates and count on their share of opportunities to buy collections below market value. One particular example of a large dealer buying a valuable collection for far below its market value occurred during the 1981 New Orleans A.N.A. convention. A collection had to be liquidated, and two coin companies were invited to submit competitive bids. Each company knew of its rival's invitation. One firm, which we'll call firm A, was huge; the other, which we'll call firm B, was quite large.

Both dealerships were (and are) considered highly reputable. Firm A has maintained a reputation of making offers which are not only "lowball," but laughably low. Firm B was aware of Firm A making low offers and bid low also. One source in firm B told me that his firm's offer was so low that he was certain that firm A would end up buying the collection, no matter how low its offer was. But A's offer was so low that firm B was the successful bidder! Firm B was delighted to have been the winning bidder but was genuinely disturbed that any firm could have bid lower than it did.

   This example points out the shortcomings of private sale. No matter how clever you may believe your sale strategy to be, dealers tend to pay very low prices for coins they are offered and can't immediately sell.

- Become knowledgeable about the marketability of your collection and each coin which composes it.
- Find out which dealers need the coins you have.
- Approach several dealers for offers at a national coin convention. Competition is the main ingredient which will help you get the most money for your collection.
- Know the real value and grades of your coins; and don't let a dealer "talk your coins down."
- Private sale might be required for those whose holdings fall below $2,000—the usual minimum dollar cutoff of the larger auction houses—and who don't want to consign to a small auction firm.
- Make your asking price on the high side and bargain if a dealer insists that you tell him how much you want for your coins. Try to get the dealer to make an offer instead of your telling him what your asking price is.
- To get a fair appraisal of your coins, tell the dealer that under no circumstances will you consider selling or buying coins from him or her. Offer to pay for the appraisal. This approach may only be theoretically sensible. Any dealer you show coins to, no matter what you tell him or her, knows that he or she has a chance of buying them.
- Be aware of the "percentage or sell appraisal" game. Heirs to numismatic estates sometimes fall prey to this tactic. This scheme is employed by a firm whose principals examine a collection and tell newly widowed people, orphaned children, or other bereaved people that they must pay a hefty percentage of the appraised value in appraisal fees—or sell the collection to the appraisers at their appraised value. The heirs are told this after the appraisal, and pressure is placed upon them to pay or sell.
- Beware of bad checks.

PUBLIC SALE

Public sale requires a great deal of work on your part, for you will be acting as the dealer. For those who have never been a dealer, it can be a devastating experience. But for those who are used to vest-pocket dealing and having bourse tables at coin shows, it might prove profitable.

I strongly urge you not to pursue this method of disposal unless you have been or are a professional numismatist. There are too many risks, including theft, switching, and bad checks. However, public sale is one way of using competition to your advantage. If you run ads in the numismatic press, you might be able to deal directly with the people who might attend an auction or buy from the dealer you would sell your coins to.

One of the most popular direct sale methods employed by collectors is the classified section of the numismatic publications. *Coin World*, *Numismatic News*, *Coins* magazine, *Coin Prices*, and *World Coin News* offer classified advertising at very reasonable rates. You won't even have to collect sales tax if it's your personal collection, for sale of tangible, personal property is exempt in most states. Before filling anyone's order, make sure the check clears. Also, your asking price should be between wholesale and retail, and your grading should be as accurate as possible.

CONSIGNMENT TO A DEALER FOR OVER-THE-COUNTER SALE

Dealers who have sold you coins that you want to sell back to them often suggest that you consign the coins to them. But consignment to a dealer for over-the-counter sale is a less viable means of disposal than the other methods described in this chapter. Unless you consign your coins to a scrupulously honest dealer, you can't be sure what price the coins were really sold for.

In certain cases this method may be a good strategy, for some dealers might place your coins within a few weeks. With other dealers, this might be a stall, the only way the dealer can give himself or herself more time to think about what you should do with your coins. If the dealer has grossly overgraded your coins, no auction house may accept them. And even when your holdings are considerable, when the quality is inferior (low circulated grades) and the dates aren't rare, it would be almost impossible to find any auction firm willing to accept your consignment.

Don't accept stalls. Give a deadline. When you consign to a dealer and don't get any coins sold by the deadline, insist that your coins be sold through a viable means, such as public auction. And in all cases, avoid consigning coins to a dealer for over-the-counter sale. As Paul F. Taglione says: "It's a method with a lot of potential and no real track record."

IRAS AND KEOGHS

Many Alberts will find out that they were ripped off, and dealers know this. In fact, after the Economic Recovery Tax Act of 1981 eliminated addition of tangible assets to self-directed retirement plans, I submitted the following question to the *Paul Revere Letter* (an utterly ingenious newsletter which compiles dealers' questions and reports the dealers' statistical responses or answers). The question, a multifaceted one, and the dealers' response to it as published follows, with minor editing:

> If investors were encouraged or required by legislation to liquidate coins now in their tangible retirement plans (IRA or Keogh), what do you anticipate would happen to the coin market in the next three years? (Please answer each of the following questions.)
> - The market would strengthen, and high-quality coins from retirement plans would be welcomed. Yes_____; No_____.
> - Nothing. Retirement plans don't constitute a big percentage of coin market business, and the coins would be quickly absorbed. Yes_____; No_____.
> - Chaos! Dealers who built their empires on the exploitation of nonknowledgeable investors would be exposed, and the coin industry would suffer for years. Yes_____; No_____.

Dealers answered as follows:

The market would strengthen, etc.: *Yes*—35; *No*—178; *NA*—17. Nothing, etc.: *Yes*—85; *No*—121; *NA*—24. Chaos!, etc.: *Yes*—128; *No*—21; *NA*—11.

The answers given by dealers are intriguing and deserve your close attention. . . . The answers to the third part of this question (Chaos!) indicate that the majority of dealers (over 55 percent) believe that many nonknowledgeable investors have been victimized by unscrupulous dealers and that this would become apparent *if* such investors were required to liquidate their holdings. Again, while such legislation is *not* imminent, it is interesting to note that the majority of dealers feel that the unregulated coin industry would suffer for years if such regulation were passed.

CAPITAL GAINS TAX

According to Philip Gottesman, a New York City attorney and certified public accountant, coin owners fall into one of two distinct classifications: collector/investor or dealer. The collector/investor is subject to long- and short-term capital gains tax. But the dealer is taxed on gains or profits as ordinary income. The line can be fine between collector/investor and dealer.

Coins held for less than one year and one day and sold for a profit are subject to short-term capital gains tax, which as of this writing does not exceed 50 percent of the gain. Coins held for one year and one day, or longer, are subject to long-term capital gains tax, which as of this writing does not exceed 20 percent. Gottesman points out that although individuals are subject to capital gains tax somewhat proportionate to the gain, people who lose money investing in coins are allowed no more than $3,000 as a capital loss—no matter how much more was lost. Gottesman advises refraining from liquidating for one year and one day in order to realize long-term capital gains.

Keogh and IRA liquidated coins are taxed as ordinary income. Coins are no longer approved for these retirement plans, but many individuals who have placed coins in them in the past will have to liquidate by age 59 1/2. Even if a loss is realized, the proceeds from self-directed retirement plans are taxed as ordinary income during the year the coin(s) is/are liquidated.

Many variables are involved in paying taxes. And there are provisions beyond the scope of this book. Like-for-like exchanges, which are not taxable, and charitable donations are just two other areas you might want to explore. Consult a competent tax accountant before you enter into any transaction.

The capital gains tax status of coins is being threatened. The Industry Council for Tangible Assets (ICTA) is putting its time and energy into making sure coins retain favorable tax treatment.

12

Cleaning Coins

Some mild types of coin cleaning under some circumstances might improve a coin's appearance. Other types of coin cleaning could destroy a Mint State coin's premium value. All coin cleaning has to be done with care; coins are delicate and susceptible to damage if mishandled in the least. My advice is to leave coin cleaning of any kind to the experts, unless you have or can become competent at cleaning by practicing on non-premium-value coins.

There are two types of coin cleaning: *abrasive* and *nonabrasive.*

ABRASIVE CLEANING

This is the most harmful type of coin cleaning. A coin's grade is based primarily on how much wear it has if it's a circulated coin and how well it has been preserved and looks if it is a Mint State coin. *Abrasive cleaning removes part of the coin and thus lowers the grade.* Further, abrasive cleaning activates the metal's oxidation process. Even if a coin is shining brightly one day, the next day it could turn black from its metal being activated.

The very definition of *abrasive* indicates it is something you would not want to subject your valuable coins to. Abrasive cleaning removes the top layer of metal of a coin. Using abrasive cleaning is like subjecting a coin to circulation! From the friction or rubbing on the coin's surface from cleaning, part of the coin's design is worn away.

Any process is abrasive which requires that you use a wire brush to clean your coins. Also, any process that involves treating coins with acid is abrasive. The same effect can be achieved chemically that a wire brush achieves. *Under no circumstances should you clean any coin abrasively.* *

   "But the products designed for abrasive cleaning seem so tempting . . ."

Don't listen to what the label says. *If you have to use a wire brush and/or a harsh chemical, The method is abrasive.*

I strongly urge you to put together your own small laboratory of coin-cleaning chemicals to experiment with on *coins from circulation.* You'll then become familiar with the effects of certain coin cleaners. If you do experiment, follow the warnings on the label, and always wash your hands well after each use. Wear gloves if possible during your experimentation. *Remember, always experiment with coins which are not valuable.*

CLEANING THAT IS ABRASIVE
ONLY SOME OF THE TIME

Acidic "Dips"

Some coin cleaners, for example, those designed to remove light tarnish or oxidation, are mildly abrasive. Acid-type solutions used for "dipping" are often abrasive. These "dips" are controversial because they are used so often. Many dealers, however, insist that they are not abrasive at all. They might be right under some circumstances. A split-second dipping might not be very harmful, but immersing a coin for more than a couple of seconds could be. *Do not dip any valuable coins until you have mastered the technique of dipping.* The A.N.A. Certification Service has taken the stance of not stating that a coin has been dipped, even if ANACS knows the coin has been, because, ANACS claims, dipping cannot be proven in a court of law.

   Many century-old coins have been dipped. It just isn't possible for 100-year-old silver coins to be as brilliant as when they were minted. Toning is a natural part of a coin's aging process. Contrary to popular belief, dipping is abrasive and can be proven in a court of law.

---

* Coins discovered at sea as part of underwater treasure are sometimes cleaned abrasively so that they can be identified. This is the only acceptable numismatic use for abrasive coin cleaning.

Fig. 12–1.   Scanning-electron-microscopic view of the undipped portion, magnified 3,500 times. Many lines which the coin was made with are visible and cause the coin to reflect light. (Photograph courtesy The Swiatek Numismatic Report)

Each coin has many little flow lines which can be most clearly seen under a scanning electron microscope. These flow lines are a result of the Minting process and are responsible for a Mint State coin's reflective properties. The depth and quality of these tiny little lines produce a coin's gleam. If these little lines are flattened or eliminated, a Mint State coin loses luster. It's like flattening the waves on an ocean; the ocean wouldn't reflect light at every angle you looked at it under.

Abrasive cleaning removes these flow lines; mildly abrasive cleaning reduces their intensity. Anthony Swiatek studied this subject in his *Swiatek Numismatic Report.* Swiatek had photographs taken of a 1964 Kennedy half-dollar—half of which had been dipped for fifteen seconds— under a half-million-dollar scanning electron microscope. The results caused a furor in the numismatic industry.

Look at the surface of an undipped area of that Kennedy half shown in Fig. 12–1 (magnified 3,500 times). Notice the hundreds upon hundreds of little lines. These are Mint-made flow lines, and they are responsible

Fig. 12–2. Scanning-electron-microscopic view of the dipped portion dipped for fifteen seconds, magnified 3,500 times. The lighter color accounts for the oxidation having been removed. The acidity of the dip caused the lines to be removed, causing the quality of the coin's luster to be lowered. (Photograph courtesy The Swiatek Numismatic Report)

for luster. Now look at a dipped area of the half-dollar (Fig. 12–2). The color appears lighter from the oxidation removed from the cleaning. Most important is the reduction of intensity and quality of those little lines, which have been smoothed out as a result of the dipping. Swiatek's title is most appropriate: "So Dipping a Coin in Tarnish Remover Doesn't Hurt the Coin?"

Some people may feel these results are inconclusive because coins are only dipped for a few seconds. However, coins retone and are dipped again and again. Dipping is cumulative; coins lose another tiny layer from each dipping. Further, some coins have no high-quality flow lines to begin with (e.g., poor minting process, weak strike). If dipped, the grade of these coins will be lowered substantially. Overdipped coins are lackluster and very unattractive. The appearance of some coins can be improved by dipping, but you have to know coin surfaces very well to know which coins can be dipped and which will lose luster.

Do not dip coins unless you are very experienced at doing so. Some coins have a surface not conducive to dipping and will be downgraded if dipped. At least 90 percent of all brilliant, untoned Mint State silver dollars have been dipped.

Hairlined Proofs

Hairlines are patches of parallel striations that interrupt a coin's reflective properties. Hairlines do not appear on Proof coins exclusively, but their presence on a Proof is detracting on a coin that is supposed to have fully reflective surfaces. Hairlines are often caused by a light cleaning, such as with a facial tissue to remove a fingerprint.

Hairlines usually end up as a primary grading criterion for Proof coins, because Proofs were made for collectors and usually didn't circulate. However, many Proofs were mishandled by collectors. And the Proof surface is so fragile that the least contact causes hairlines. Take a look at the closeup of the 1861 Liberty Seated quarter Proof shown in Fig. 12–3. Those annoying lines on the surface are hairlines. Take another look at those hairlines, this time in Fig. 12–4, and you will see that these can detract considerably from the grade. Contrary to popular belief, a Proof-65 does not have to be completely free of hairlines. A moderately hairlined Proof, though, often grades Proof-63; and a severely hairlined Proof often deserves to be given the Proof-60 designation.

Fig. 12–3. Blowup of hairlines on a Proof 1861 Liberty Seated quarter. (ANACS photograph)

Fig. 12–4.   Blowup of hairlines on another section of that Proof quarter. (ANACS photograph)

Do not confuse hairlines with *die-polishing marks,* which are also patches of parallel striations. The difference is that these resulted from the polishing of the die, not of the coins. *Die-polishing marks are raised, whereas hairlines are indented.* Take a look at the 1938 Mercury dime in Fig. 12–5. It has die-polishing marks, not hairlines. Since die-polishing marks are Mint-made, they don't detract from the grade, just the price.

Fig. 12–5.   Die-polishing marks on a Mercury dime obverse. Die-polishing marks are Mint-made and raised. (Photograph by Steven Ritter)

NONABRASIVE CLEANING

Nonabrasive coin cleaning does not adversely affect a coin's top layer of metal and, in a sense, does not "eat into" the coin to achieve its effect. Submersing a coin in water, for example, is a nonabrasive cleaning method. Nonabrasive cleaning methods are used to help preserve coins, for they remove particles and other chemicals from the surface which might later negatively affect the coin. For example, if you accidentally sneeze on a coin, you should use a *nonabrasive* method of removing the saliva. Saliva later tones the surface a dense, dark color.

Nonabrasive cleaning methods are becoming increasingly recommended before long-term storage. One chemical in particular, trichlorotrifluoroethane, is very popular and safe to use on most coins. The primary advantage of this chemical is that it evaporates without leaving any residue. Trichlorotrifluoroethane is available in kits with gloves and applicators. It is available as a product marketed as "Dissolve" from:

> E & T Kointainer Company
> P.O. Box 103
> Sidney, OH 45365

Follow the directions carefully, and do not use any rubbing action on Mint State business strike or Proof coins.

An equally good product, which some people prefer, is "Test-N-Safe," which contains trichlorotrifluoroethane and acetone. The acetone seems to help in removing stubborn residue and surface stains from coins. Test-N-Safe is great for removing the unsightly green residue from coins that builds up as a result of storage in PVC coin holders (discussed in the next chapter). If you use this product, don't use the cotton swabs it comes with on Mint State business strike or Proof coins (as the instructions warn). Test-N-Safe (Fig. 12–6) is available from:

> Equi-Safe Corporation
> 315 West 57th Street
> New York, NY 10019

How to Clean Coins Nonabrasively

Even the most harmless products can be misused. And even good products used correctly might have a negative impact on some coins. The best way to test the impact of a coin-bathing solution is by applying a small amount to the coin's edge and observing the result (see Fig. 12–7). Since the rim is made from the same material and dies as the rest of the coin,

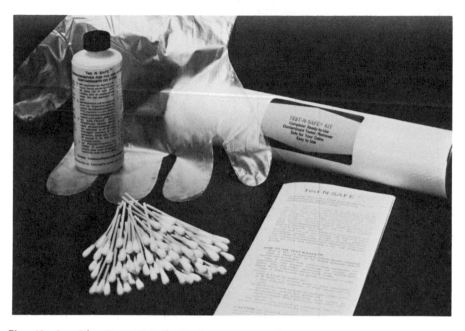

Fig. 12–6. The Test-N-Safe Kit from Equi-Safe. Not harmful to coins if the directions are followed closely. (Photograph courtesy Equi-Safe Corporation)

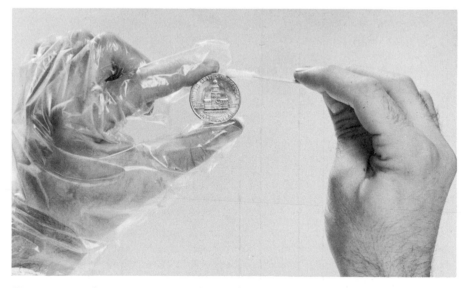

Fig. 12–7. The proper way to test a coin's reaction before cleaning it. (Photograph courtesy Equi-Safe Corporation)

you know not to use a certain bathing solution if it reacts negatively with the edge. However, this still is not a complete assurance that the coin product tested will not harm your coin.

ARTIFICIAL TONING

Often, coins which have been cleaned to appear Mint State and aren't are artificially toned to hide the cleaning. Artificial toning can be nonabrasive, but usually is abrasive. This toning is caused by a chemical reaction that resembles the slow, regular, natural process by which a coin tones or acquires patina. Anthony Swiatek, again writing in the *Swiatek Numismatic Report,* made a study of artificial toning and how it is created. Here are his findings, slightly abridged:

- Directing cigar or cigarette smoke at silver coins will produce a very light brown tone. Repeated blasts will cause color to "darken to taste."
- A coin placed in a coin envelope and in an oven at 300°F for a half-hour will result most often in a dull appearance. Colors of dull purple, yellowish-green, and bluish-purple can result.
- A weak concentration of a sulfur solution (dissolved in alcohol or water) can cause creation of a gold to golden-brown tone. A stronger solution produces purple and peacock-blue colors.
- A coin baked inside an Idaho potato covered with corn oil and wrapped in foil can result in the creation of a purple-blue to an orange color.
- A mixture of motor oil and corn oil will create a bluish-purple color when placed on a coin and baked for a period of time (275°F to 300°F for one hour or less).
- Gun bluing can be painted on a coin or an ammonia-base chemical solution used to see a sunrise color blend behind, perhaps, the Seated Liberty on that coin type.
- A sulfur shampoo can create green, yellow, and brown colors if left on the coin for a day or longer.
- A coin placed in a toaster or frying pan might have its surfaces appear dull gray to black.

Artificially toned coins are often identified by an imperfect toning job. Examine the 1899 Morgan dollar obverse shown in Fig. 12–8. The coin has been artificially toned and displays a crescent of polychromatic toning. However, look at that area of experimentation on the left side. Many of the people who tone coins are not professionals and leave tell-tale signs. Another tell-tale sign is the coin's smell. Many toning prod-

Fig. 12–8. Artificially toned Morgan dollar. (ANACS photograph)

ucts (and cleaning products, too) contain sulfur bases which leave an unpleasant smell on the coin. Many homemade toning recipes also contain sulfur, such as sulfur dissolved in petroleum jelly to induce toning on copper coins. If all else fails, smell the coin.

The primary use of artificial toning, as I've stated before, is to hide imperfections. Once you've viewed a number of coins with real toning and have also sharpened your ability to spot imperfections, you will have a hard time being fooled by a cleaned coin or an artificially toned one.

13

How to Choose the Right Coin Holder

Several years after the introduction of polyvinylchloride (PVC) to the coin storage market, some collectors began to notice greenish or bluish flecks and stains on their coins stored in PVC holders. When viewed with magnification, these flecks appeared to be thick, sticky, colored liquid which rested on the coin surface, or else appeared as patches of colored stains. Often, when the coin was removed from the holder, a green or blue "ring" remained on the plastic where the coin rim pressed against it . . . In extreme cases, coins "stuck" against the plastic so firmly that they had to be pried off, with severe damage resulting to the coin . . . Recently, due to the increase in knowledge about all plastics, it has been determined that the blue/green colored flecks and stains . . . [are] due to chemicals in the PVC bleeding out of the film onto the coin.

—George Klabin
"Understanding PVC Damage"

Storing your coins. How simple it seems. You buy a coin from a dealer, and it's protected—so you think. You reason that the dealer wouldn't sell you a coin in a holder which might ruin the coin. So you take your valuable MS-67 rare coin in its pliable plastic holder and put it away in a safe-deposit box. What will happen? The coin could lose much of its premium value if the holder is made from polyvinylchloride (PVC), a plastic film which can deposit sticky chemical plasticizers on a coin and release hydrogen chloride gas at high temperatures. The hydrogen chloride gas can react with humidity in the air and form hydrochloric acid, which can eat into the surface of your coin.

Improper coin preservation is the silent killer. Every year, improper storage methods cost the collector a fortune. But most improper storage methods can be corrected. And if detected early enough, coins affected by PVC holders can be saved. Dealers don't care how your coins are preserved. If a coin isn't in the same level of preservation as it was when you purchased it, the dealer has no obligation to buy it back or be held to a guarantee, if one was issued. (Don't think that if you store your coins properly, though, a dealer will say that they are in the same level of preservation that they were when purchased. The "not in the same level of preservation" argument is a classic for a grading guarantee not being honored.)

PVC is in more coin holders than you think. Many of the most widely used holders contain PVC, including all of the pliable-flip-types, except one brand: "Saflips," a holder made of pure polyethylene terepthalate, known as Mylar. These are the only safe coin flips available. Dealers don't have to worry about the negative effects because they move their inventory so quickly. In fact, I recommend the PVC flip-type holders if you're taking a lot of coins to a coin show for a couple of hours. These pliable pouches allow ease of handling, as well as an unobstructed view of the rim and edge. Just don't leave the coins in these holders for more than an hour or two. And don't expose the holders to heat.

Fig. 13–1 shows a grouping of coins, all ruined from improper storage. The 1951, 1951-D, and 1951-S Lincoln head cents were stored in a PVC album for several years, resulting in what preservation authority George Klabin terms "severe plasticizer damage and residue." The quarter and cent on the second row from the top display ugly tarnish. The third row from the top consists of a nickel and cent with corrosive verdigris. And the Jefferson nickel in the holder on the bottom of the photo developed a tarnish spot "about 2 years" after contaminants reacted with its surface from a pinhole in the clear plastic window of this most dangerous type of 2×2 holder (sulfur in the paper). As explained in the cleaning chapter, the plastic residue can be removed with Dissolve or Test-N-Safe—with *no* damage to the coin. The tarnish, verdigris, and toning spot are, for all practical purposes, beyond removal.

Some roll holders are also made from PVC. In Fig. 13–2, you can see a closeup of the edge of a 1960 Small Date Lincoln cent contaminated by PVC damage. The coin was stored in a PVC tube. If you need to use roll tubes, buy the squared-off milky polyethylene ones, which are inert.

The effects of PVC holders have been explored and documented in a study conducted under a grant from New England Rare Coin Galleries. Dr. Thomas W. Sharpless, Professor of Chemistry at the University of Hartford, reports his conclusions in a "Report on the Relationship Between Polyvinylchloride and Coin Corrosion." Sharpless's study was conducted a few years ago at the height of the preservation craze. This was a time when numismatic publications were paying a great deal of attention to the problems of preservation. Dr. Sharpless concluded that the PVC holders left a ring of stain when the coin was removed. Thus, just because pliable flip-type holder manufacturers advertise their products as "oil-free" or "safe" doesn't mean they are, if they contain PVC.

Fig. 13–1. *A grouping of coins ruined by improper storage methods.*
(Photograph courtesy Equi-Safe Corporation)

Fig. 13–2.   The edge of a Lincoln cent stored in a PVC tube. (Photograph courtesy Dr. Thomas W. Sharpless)

The modern attention to preservation, however, began in 1977 with the introduction of Walter Breen's "talking book record," "The Care and Preservation of Rare Coins." On it, Breen states, in part:

> The problem of preservation of coins is essentially two-fold: preventing abrasion by dusts and other contaminants or by cleaning agents; and preventing access to the coins of chemical or electrochemical processes attacking the surfaces. The vast majority of these chemical agents are smog components. Others include biological residue such as cough or sneeze or sweat droplets, excreta of rodents or insects, byproducts of molds, fungi, or bacteria. Most of these require the presence of moisture. All vary in speed of action, some working in seconds, others only over the years. Ancient bronze patina is said to take centuries.

Suddenly, the numismatic community became aware of the fact that coins had to be cared for. You can't buy a coin and put it away for a few years without expecting some deterioration unless you take some necessary precautions. Dr. Sharpless, in an exclusive test for *The Coin Collector's Survival Manual* which he entitled "Test of Coin Containers for Their Ability to Exclude Moist Air," tested the two best "airtight" holders for their "airtightness." His conclusions for the Capital and Whitman Mylar holders surprised even me! Sharpless writes:

> The change of cobaltous chloride from its blue to its pink hydrate indicates exposure to moist air. No significant differences were found among the coin containers. Each admits moist air in a matter of hours.

PRESERVATION PRECAUTIONS

- *Store your coins in a cool, dry place.* High temperatures cause some plastics to give off harmful gases. Humidity can cause negative surface reactions, even on coins which have developed a natural oxide coating. Excessive moisture causes corrosion. Copper coins are particularly vulnerable to high levels of moisture in the air, for they can suddenly break out with big black spots for apparently no reason. If you live in Florida, sell your cent collection. (Some dealers will not bring any copper coins to Florida coin shows, even for a few days.) If you do have coins in a humid environment, store silica gel with them. This will absorb the moisture.
- *Select a safe-deposit box room that will not harm your coins.* Select an air-conditioned safe-deposit box room, if you store your coins there. Breen warns that the safe-deposit box room should not contain an ozone purification system for destroying microorganisms. This system, according to Breen, emits a germ-killing agent as harmful to coins as chlorine gas, "and will corrode silver and copper coins very rapidly." Select a safe-deposit box room that is not kept humid. Many are kept humid because safe-deposit boxes are often used to store important documents which have to be kept moist.
- *Keep coins away from paper.* Paper contains sulfur, which can react with the coin and lower the level of preservation. Envelopes and some cardboard folders contain sulfur. Circulated coins are not as much at risk as Mint State business strike and Proof coins.
- *Keep coins in an airtight environment.* A primary goal should be to protect the coins from airborne pollutants. A coin cannot be in an air-free environment unless it is embedded in Lucite, highly impractical at best. Choose an inert airtight holder, such as those displayed in Figs. 13–3 and 13–4. The blue plastic boxes manufac-

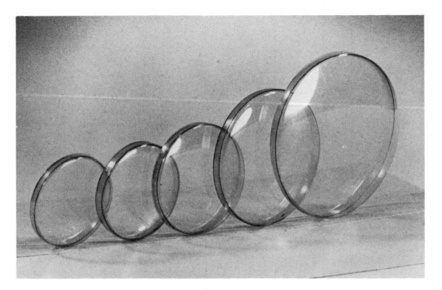

Fig. 13–3. Popular Kointain-brand triacetate holders, designed for safe long-term storage. (Photograph courtesy Equi-Safe Corporation)

tured by Whitman Coin Products which close tight are good for storing your coins, which also should be in inert holders.

• *Don't store coins in albums with sliding windows or slides.* These slides, if moved back and forth enough, could cause friction on the coin's high points.

Fig. 13–4. Equally popular Lucite sandwich-type holders, manufactured by Capital Plastics with safe long-term storage the aim. (Photograph courtesy Capital Plastics, Inc.)

- *Prevent deterioration chemically.* Mothballs are excellent preventers of tarnish. Place one or two mothballs in an empty tea bag, and place a string at the top. Put these in the safe-deposit box with your coins. A product available in plastic capsules called Metal Safe Corrosion Inhibitor is available through Equi-Safe, whose address is listed in chapter 12. This product works by changing the molecular composition of the air. Place one capsule in the blue Whitman airtight box with your coins; and place another capsule in the safe-deposit box. You'll know it's working when the clear plastic coin-holder screws turn yellow over several months.

14

Safekeeping

Ben, who had accumulated a respectable holding of coins, was proud of himself. He knew how not to get ripped off by dealers. Each coin was accurately graded, fairly priced, and in a high level of preservation. Ben had spent a good part of his life haggling with coin dealers and other sellers of coins over price. His own brother-in-law wouldn't even talk to him, for Ben had bought several coins from his brother-in-law and paid $500—for a collection worth over $5,000! And Ben was careful with each new acquisition. He made sure the coins were stored in the highest-quality Lucitelike holders available and placed in a bank safe-deposit box along with a corrosion-inhibiting product. He was paying high insurance premiums for what he thought was an all-inclusive homeowner's policy. But after all, he thought, what difference does it make if the coins are stored in a bank safe-deposit box?

One day he went to his bank and discovered that his coins, along with the contents of everyone else's safe-deposit box, had been stolen. He felt confident in knowing that he had a lot of insurance. So he contacted his insurance agent. He found out the hard way that he was only covered for $100 and that banks usually neither assume responsibility for such thefts nor do they insure the contents of safe-deposit boxes. He later learned that if he wanted to press his case in court against the bank, it would help to have photographs of every coin (which he didn't have). Poor Ben. Besides learning a very expensive lesson, something else positive came of Ben's misfortune: his brother-in-law now talks to him.

SAFE-DEPOSIT BOX STORAGE

Statistically, bank safe-deposit boxes are among the safest places to store things, although they are designed for the storage of documents, not rare coins. Mishaps do occur.

Banks rarely insure the contents of safe-deposit boxes. These boxes are provided as a service at a nominal yearly charge. Most safe-deposit box rental agreements say this in small print. Banks cannot be held responsible for negligence in guarding your valuables, and you would not be able to press a case if you were to sue a bank for negligence. However, you might be able to press a case for gross negligence—if you can prove it.

If you're going to store your coins in a bank safe-deposit box, take some precautions:

- *Make sure you know what's in the box.* Even people with ample insurance coverage sometimes don't bother to make an inventory of what's in their safe-deposit boxes. If you have to file an insurance claim or take a tax loss, the more detailed and itemized your listing, the better off you are. Photographs are of immense help, as I'll explain later.
- *Don't allow an attendant to hold your key.* Allowing a safe-deposit box attendant, even one that you've known for years, to hold onto your key when the attendant is out of your view is asking for trouble. Take a few seconds more to put the key in your pocket. That way, you increase your chances of your coins not going into a thief's pocket.
- *Keep your box at a consistent weight, and don't let anything jiggle around.* A considerably lighter-weight safe-deposit box after you leave your bank alerts the attendant to the fact that you removed some of the contents. The attendant would then be in a position to tip off a mugger that you have valuables on your person. If you make a major withdrawal from your safe-deposit box, replace what you have withdrawn with a ''filler'' of equal weight. Don't store anything in your safe-deposit box that jiggles. If the jiggle stops, the attendant will think you have removed the valuable contents.
- *Carefully read your safe-deposit box rental agreement.* This alerts you to what rights you do and don't have. If there are any unreasonable terms, change banks.
- *Store proof of purchase for coins in a separate box.* It wouldn't make any sense for you to store your receipts with your coins, for the receipts could be stolen with the coins. Make copies of all receipts and photos that you store in the separate safe-deposit box, and keep the copies in a safe place at home.
- *Carefully read your insurance policies.* Some people are covered for safe-deposit box storage of coins, but most are not. If your insurance coverage isn't adequate, buy more. Remember that just because your coins are being stored in a bank doesn't mean that they are insured. If you want your coins to be stored by your bank, check out bank custodial plans. For a fee, the bank will hold your coins for you and be responsible for each one.

HOME SECURITY

Home Safes

During many home burglaries home safes are either lifted away or wheeled away—sometimes on their own wheels! Many people make the mistake of buying fire safes, as opposed to burglar-resistant safes. Safes are available to suit both purposes, but are extremely expensive. If you buy a home safe, follow these guidelines:

- *Bolt your safe to the floor.* Securing your safe so it cannot be easily transported is one of the most important steps you can take in protecting your rare coins with a home safe. Bolting your safe to the floor helps to compensate for underweight safes, too.
- *Buy a burglar-resistant safe, not a fire-resistant one.* Make sure the lock is of high quality and that the door and structure are steel. If you absolutely insist on using a fire-resistant safe, buy a burglar resistant safe that it will fit into. Fire resistant safes have walls that are well insulated and conducive to moisture absorption. That's why fire-resistant safes are fire resistant: they have moist insulation that keeps the temperature inside the safe low. Moisture, as discussed in the last chapter, is potentially harmful to coins. Store silica gel inside a sealed inert plastic box with your coins, and store the box in the fire-resistant safe.
- *If you use a fire-resistant safe, weight it down.* Fire-resistant safes are big and bulky, not heavy. The bulkiness is due to the thick insulation. Place boxes of cents, available at face value from some banks in boxes of $25, in your safe to weight it down if you have any space left over.
- *Pay attention to the U.L. rating.* The better the rating of your safe from Underwriters Laboratories, the more favorable your insurance rates will be. Some insurance companies require safes to meet a certain minimum rating before issuing a policy for coins stored in them. Check with your insurance company before buying a safe.

Protecting Your Home or Apartment

Some commonsense precautions can be taken to protect your place of residence from a break-in:

- *Don't have coin publications delivered to your home.* These are a tip-off that you collect and might have some valuable coins at home. Rent a Post Office Box. Some people have no coins at home, but receive these numismatic publications at a P.O. Box anyway, just to make sure they have no confrontations with an intruder who gets upset that no coins are available. Don't read coin publications in public places. There's no need to give the wrong person any ideas. Similarly, if you order by mail, make sure the package gives no hints of what it contains. Tell the dealer to leave off words such as "coin" and "numismatic."

- *Don't leave a message on your telephone answering machine which states that you're not at home.* I have a friend who recorded a message which says that he is "not available to answer your call and available by appointment only." Anything is better than saying you're not at home. If you don't have a telephone answering machine and are out of the house, unplug your phone from the wall. Burglars sometimes call from a phone booth and then go to your house to find out if the phone's still ringing and you're not at home.

- *Use timers to fool people into thinking that you're at home.* Timers can be used to turn lights or radios on and off at different times of the day. A radio turned on for a few hours each day when you aren't at home is helpful. A car parked in the driveway, as well as children's toys scattered throughout the yard, is also helpful.

- *Use a good burglar alarm, and test it periodically.* Check with reputable alarm companies to see which alarm is most suited to your needs. Also ask your local police station's opinion about the effectiveness of certain types of alarms and locks for your area. An impressive alarm which notifies the police that you need help at the touch of a button doesn't appear that impressive after you find out that the notification by alarm is given a low priority by police and may not be responded to for an extended period of time. Use an electrical burglar alarm with a battery backup, and test the batteries at regular intervals.

- *Most important, use common sense.* Use the peephole on your door to screen visitors. Don't let strangers in. Ask repair people for identification. And if you go out of your house or apartment, lock all doors and windows. Some burglars make their livings by going from door to door and entering only those dwellings which have open doors. You would be amazed at all of the people with the most advanced alarms available who leave their homes and don't lock the door!

- *If all else fails, file an insurance claim.* Even people who take every possible precaution are sometimes the victims of theft. Make sure your insurance policy covers your risks. Many homeowner's policies do not cover coin collections. Check the fine print. If you want insurance designed especially for your collection, the group insurance plan offered by the insurance company contracted by the

American Numismatic Association might interest you. You must be an A.N.A. member to qualify. For more information, contact: A.N.A. Group Insurance Plans, A. H. Wohlers Company, 1500 Higgins Road, Park Ridge, IL 60068.

This firm will not issue insurance to any individual who falls under the category of "dealer." If you buy and sell coins on a regular basis, you might fall under the dealer category. If so, contact: Director of Marine Insurance, Gilbert-Martin Agency, Inc., 287 Northern Boulevard, Great Neck, NY 11021.

PHOTOGRAPHS

A photograph is like a fingerprint. Many fingerprints look similar; but if you look closely, you'll discover that each fingerprint is unique. It's the same with coin photographs. Although a coin in a photograph may at first glance resemble a coin other than the one photographed, if you closely compare photo to coin, you'll discover there's no way of switching. Use a magnifying glass and look for some tiny characteristic on the coin. That same characteristic will be on the photograph.

Photographs are an important identification aid and might even lower your insurance premiums. ANACS-certified coins are photographed. Even if the certificate itself is stolen, A.N.A. still has the negative on file at its headquarters in Colorado Springs.

Coin photography is almost impossible with a regular camera. In order for the coin to appear perfectly round in the picture, it has to be slightly tilted. A company in California makes the highest quality coin camera. The camera has a special built-in Lucite table which places the coin at precisely the correct angle to be photographed. It also allows you to photograph both obverse and reverse and have these two sides appear on the same exposure or print. I highly recommend the coin cameras made by: Aries Photo Documenting, Inc., 850 Charter Street, Redwood, CA 94063.

If you're not up to spending the $300 or more that a coin camera costs, you can still document your coin holdings. An ingenious product called Coin Detector™ (distributed and sold by Coinhunter, 1616 Walnut Street, Philadelphia, PA 19103) is a kit that provides special coin charts for you to record the imperfections manually. There is also room on each chart for background information. The kit includes two hundred registry cards, a code card, and a gauge.

Appendix A

VALUE CHART FOR UNITED STATES AND CANADIAN SILVER COINS

Silver Price Per Ounce	$9.00	$9.25	$9.50	$9.75	$10.00	$10.25	$10.50
U.S. 5¢ .350 Fine (Wartime Nickels)	.51	.52	.53	.55	.56	.58	.59
U.S. 50¢ .400 Fine (1965-1970 Clad)	1.33	1.37	1.40	1.44	1.48	1.52	1.55
U.S. $1.00 .400 Fine (Collector Coins)	2.85	2.93	3.00	3.08	3.16	3.24	3.32
U.S. 10¢ .900 Fine (Pre 1965)	.65	.67	.69	.71	.72	.74	.76
U.S. 25¢ .900 Fine (Pre 1965)	1.63	1.67	1.72	1.76	1.81	1.85	1.90
U.S. 50¢ .900 Fine (Pre 1965)	3.26	3.34	3.44	3.53	3.61	3.71	3.80
U.S. $1.00 .900 Fine (Pre 1971)	6.96	7.15	7.35	7.54	7.73	7.93	8.12
Canada 10¢ .800 Fine (1920-1967)	.54	.56	.57	.59	.60	.62	.63
Canada 25¢ .800 Fine (1920-1967)	1.35	1.39	1.43	1.46	1.50	1.54	1.58
Canada 50¢ .800 Fine (1920-1967)	2.70	2.78	2.85	2.93	3.00	3.08	3.15
Canada $1.00 .800 Fine (1935-1967)	5.40	5.55	5.70	5.85	6.00	6.15	6.30
Canada 10¢ .500 Fine (1967 & 1968)*	.34	.35	.36	.37	.38	.38	.39
Canada 25¢ .500 Fine (1967 & 1968)*	.84	.87	.89	.91	.94	.96	.98

Silver Price Per Ounce	$14.00	$14.25	$14.50	$14.75	$15.00	$15.25	$15.50
U.S. 5¢ .350 Fine (Wartime Nickels)	.79	.80	.82	.83	.84	.86	.87
U.S. 50¢ .400 Fine (1965-1970 Clad)	2.07	2.11	2.14	2.18	2.22	2.26	2.29
U.S. $1.00 .400 Fine (Collector Coins)	4.43	4.51	4.59	4.66	4.74	4.82	4.90
U.S. 10¢ .900 Fine (Pre 1965)	1.01	1.03	1.05	1.07	1.09	1.10	1.12
U.S. 25¢ .900 Fine (Pre 1965)	2.53	2.58	2.62	2.67	2.71	2.76	2.80
U.S. 50¢ .900 Fine (Pre 1965)	5.06	5.15	5.24	5.33	5.43	5.52	5.61
U.S. $1.00 .900 Fine (Pre 1971)	10.83	11.02	11.21	11.41	11.60	11.79	11.99
Canada 10¢ .800 Fine (1920-1967)	.84	.86	.87	.89	.90	.92	.93
Canada 25¢ .800 Fine (1920-1967)	2.10	2.14	2.18	2.21	2.25	2.29	2.32
Canada 50¢ .800 Fine (1920-1967)	4.20	4.28	4.35	4.43	4.50	4.58	4.65
Canada $1.00 .800 Fine (1935-1967)	8.40	8.55	8.70	8.85	9.00	9.15	9.30
Canada 10¢ .500 Fine (1967 & 1968)*	.53	.53	.54	.55	.56	.57	.58
Canada 25¢ .500 Fine (1967 & 1968)*	1.31	1.34	1.36	1.38	1.41	1.43	1.45

* The 1967 Canadian 10¢ and 25¢ were produced in both .800 and .500 Fine.

$10.75	$11.00	$11.25	$11.50	$11.75	$12.00	$12.25	$12.50	$12.75	$13.00	$13.25	$13.50	$13.75
.60	.62	.63	.65	.66	68	.69	.70	.72	.73	.75	.76	.77
1.59	1.63	1.66	1.70	1.74	1.78	1.81	1.85	1.89	1.92	1.96	2.00	2.03
3.40	3.48	3.56	3.64	3.72	3.80	3.87	3.95	4.03	4.11	4.19	4.27	4.35
.78	.80	.81	.83	.85	.87	.89	.90	.92	.94	.96	.98	.99
1.94	1.99	2.03	2.08	2.12	2.17	2.22	2.26	2.31	2.35	2.40	2.44	2.49
3.89	3.98	4.07	4.16	4.25	4.34	4.43	4.52	4.61	4.70	4.79	4.88	4.97
8.31	8.51	8.70	8.89	9.09	9.28	9.47	9.67	9.86	10.05	10.25	10.44	10.63
.65	.66	.68	.69	.71	.72	.74	.75	.77	.78	.80	.81	.83
1.61	1.65	1.69	1.73	1.76	1.80	1.84	1.88	1.91	1.95	1.99	2.03	2.06
3.23	3.30	3.38	3.45	3.53	3.60	3.68	3.75	3.83	3.90	3.98	4.05	4.13
6.45	6.60	6.75	6.90	7.05	7.20	7.35	7.50	7.65	7.80	7.95	8.10	8.25
.40	.41	.42	.43	.44	.45	.46	.47	.48	.49	.50	.51	.52
1.01	1.03	1.05	1.08	1.10	1.13	1.15	1.17	1.20	1.22	1.24	1.27	1.29

$15.75	$16.00	$16.25	$16.50	$16.75	$17.00	$17.25	$17.50	$17.75	$18.00	$18.25	$18.50	$18.75
.89	.90	.91	.93	.94	.96	.97	.98	1.00	1.01	1.02	1.04	1.05
2.33	2.37	2.40	2.44	2.48	2.51	2.55	2.59	2.62	2.66	2.70	2.74	2.77
4.98	5.06	5.14	5.22	5.30	5.38	5.45	5.53	5.61	5.69	5.77	5.85	5.93
1.14	1.16	1.18	1.19	1.21	1.23	1.25	1.27	1.28	1.30	1.32	1.34	1.36
2.85	2.89	2.94	2.98	3.03	3.07	3.12	3.16	3.21	3.26	3.30	3.35	3.39
5.70	5.79	5.88	5.97	6.06	6.15	6.24	6.33	6.42	6.51	6.60	6.69	6.78
12.18	12.37	12.57	12.76	12.96	13.15	13.34	13.54	13.73	13.92	14.12	14.31	14.50
.95	.96	.98	.99	1.01	1.02	1.04	1.05	1.07	1.08	1.10	1.11	1.13
2.36	2.40	2.44	2.48	2.51	2.55	2.59	2.63	2.66	2.70	2.74	2.78	2.81
4.73	4.80	4.88	4.95	5.03	5.10	5.18	5.25	5.33	5.40	5.48	5.55	5.63
9.45	9.60	9.75	9.90	10.05	10.20	10.35	10.50	10.65	10.80	10.95	11.10	11.25
.59	.60	.61	.62	.63	.64	.65	.66	.67	.68	.68	.69	.70
1.48	1.50	1.52	1.55	1.57	1.59	1.62	1.64	1.66	1.69	1.71	1.73	1.76

KPP8302N

Appendix B

VALUE CHART FOR COMMONLY TRADED
U.S. AND WORLD GOLD COINS

Gold Price Per Ounce	$360	$370	$380	$390	$400	$410	$420	$430	$440	$450	$460	$470
USA $1.00 .900 Fine	17.42	17.90	18.38	18.87	19.35	19.84	20.32	20.80	21.29	21.77	22.25	22.74
USA $2.50 .900 Fine	43.53	44.74	45.95	47.16	48.37	49.58	50.79	52.00	53.21	54.41	55.62	56.83
USA $3.00 .900 Fine	52.29	53.75	55.20	56.65	58.10	59.56	61.01	62.46	63.91	65.37	66.82	68.27
USA $5.00 .900 Fine	87.07	89.49	91.91	94.33	96.75	99.17	101.59	104.01	106.42	108.84	111.26	113.68
USA $10.00 .900 Fine	174.15	178.99	183.82	188.66	193.50	198.34	203.17	208.01	212.85	217.69	222.52	227.36
USA $20.00 .900 Fine	348.30	357.97	367.65	377.32	387.00	396.67	406.35	416.02·425.70		435.37	445.05	454.72
Australia $200 .916 Fine	106.10	109.05	112.00	114.94	117.89	120.84	123.78	126.73	129.68	132.63	135.57	138.52
Austria 1 Ducat .986 Fine	39.84	40.95	42.05	43.16	44.27	45.37	46.48	47.59	48.69	49.80	50.91	52.01
Austria 4 Ducat .986 Fine	159.36	163.79	168.21	172.64	177.07	181.49	185.92	190.35	194.77	199.20	203.63	208.05
Austria 10 Francs .900 Fine	33.60	34.54	35.47	36.40	37.34	38.27	39.21	40.14	41.07	42.01	42.94	43.87
Austria 20 Francs .900 Fine	67.21	69.08	70.94	72.81	74.68	76.54	78.41	80.28	82.14	84.01	85.88	87.75
Austria 10 Corona .900 Fine	35.29	36.27	37.25	38.23	39.21	40.19	41.17	42.15	43.13	44.12	45.10	46.08
Austria 20 Corona .900 Fine	70.57	72.53	74.49	76.46	78.42	80.38	82.34	84.30	86.26	88.22	90.18	92.14
Austria 100 Corona .900 Fine	352.87	362.67	372.47	382.28	392.08	401.88	411.68	421.48	431.29	441.09	450.89	460.69
Belgium 20 Francs .900 Fine	67.21	69.08	70.94	72.81	74.68	76.54	78.41	80.28	82.14	84.01	85.88	87.75
Britain ½ Sovereign .916 Fine	42.38	43.55	44.73	45.91	47.09	48.26	49.44	50.62	51.79	52.97	54.15	55.33
Britain 1 Sovereign .916 Fine	84.75	87.11	89.46	91.82	94.17	96.53	98.88	101.23	103.59	105.94	108.30	110.65
Britain 2£ .916 Fine	169.51	174.22	178.92	183.63	188.34	193.05	197.76	202.47	207.18	211.88	216.59	221.30
Britain 5£ .916 Fine	423.77	435.54	447.31	459.08	470.85	482.62	494.40	506.17	517.94	529.71	541.48	553.25
Canada $100 .583 Fine	90.00	92.50	95.00	97.49	99.99	102.49	104.99	107.49	109.99	112.49	114.99	117.49
Canada Maple Leaf .999 Fine	359.60	369.59	379.58	389.57	399.56	409.54	419.53	429.52	439.51	449.50	459.49	469.48
Chile 100 Pesos .916 Fine	215.70	221.70	227.69	233.68	239.67	245.66	251.65	257.65	263.64	269.63	275.62	281.61
Colombia 5 Pesos .916 Fine	84.75	87.11	89.46	91.82	94.17	96.53	98.88	101.23	103.59	105.94	108.30	110.65
France 10 Francs .900 Fine	33.60	34.54	35.47	36.40	37.34	38.27	39.21	40.14	41.07	42.01	42.94	43.87
France 20 Francs .900 Fine	67.21	69.08	70.94	72.81	74.68	76.54	78.41	80.28	82.14	84.01	85.88	87.75
German States 10 Mark .900 Fine	41.48	42.64	43.79	44.94	46.09	47.25	48.40	49.55	50.70	51.86	53.01	54.16
German States 20 Mark .900 Fine	82.97	85.27	87.58	89.88	92.19	94.49	96.80	99.10	101.41	103.71	106.02	108.32
Hong Kong $1000 .916 Fine	169.51	174.22	178.92	183.63	188.34	193.05	197.76	202.47	207.18	211.88	216.59	221.30
Hungary 10 Korona .900 Fine	35.29	36.27	37.25	38.23	39.21	40.19	41.17	42.15	43.13	44.12	45.10	46.08
Hungary 20 Korona .900 Fine	70.57	72.53	74.49	76.46	78.42	80.38	82.34	84.30	86.26	88.22	90.18	92.14
Hungary 100 Korona .900 Fine	352.87	362.67	372.47	382.28	392.08	401.88	411.68	421.48	431.29	441.09	450.89	460.69
Iran 1 Pahlavi .900 Fine	84.38	86.72	89.06	91.41	93.75	96.10	98.44	100.78	103.13	105.47	107.81	110.16
Jamaica $100 .900 Fine	118.13	121.41	124.69	127.97	131.25	134.53	137.81	141.10	144.38	147.66	150.94	154.22
Mexico 2 Pesos .900 Fine	17.35	17.84	18.32	18.80	19.28	19.76	20.25	20.73	21.21	21.69	22.18	22.66
Mexico 2.5 Pesos .900 Fine	21.70	22.30	22.90	23.51	24.11	24.71	25.31	25.92	26.52	27.12	27.73	28.33
Mexico 5 Pesos .900 Fine	43.40	44.60	45.81	47.01	48.22	49.42	50.63	51.83	53.04	54.25	55.45	56.66
Mexico 10 Pesos .900 Fine	86.80	89.21	91.63	94.04	96.45	98.86	101.27	103.68	106.09	108.50	110.92	113.33
Mexico 20 Pesos .900 Fine	173.61	178.43	183.25	188.07	192.90	197.72	202.54	207.36	212.19	217.01	221.83	226.65
Mexico 50 Pesos .900 Fine	434.03	446.08	458.14	470.20	482.25	494.31	506.37	518.42	530.48	542.53	554.59	566.65
Mexico Onza Oro .900 Fine	359.99	369.99	379.99	389.99	399.99	409.99	419.99	429.99	439.99	449.99	459.99	469.99
Netherlands 10 Gulden .900 Fine	70.09	72.04	73.99	75.94	77.88	79.83	81.78	83.72	85.67	87.62	89.57	91.51
Netherlands 1 Ducat .986 Fine	39.87	40.98	42.09	43.20	44.30	45.41	46.52	47.63	48.74	49.84	50.95	52.06
Panama 100 Balboa .900 Fine	85.00	87.36	89.72	92.08	94.45	96.81	99.17	101.53	103.89	106.25	108.61	110.97
Peru 1/5 Libra .916 Fine	16.98	17.45	17.92	18.39	18.86	19.33	19.81	20.28	20.75	21.22	21.69	22.16
Peru 1/2 Libra .916 Fine	42.38	43.55	44.73	45.91	47.09	48.26	49.44	50.62	51.79	52.97	54.15	55.33
Peru 1 Libra .916 Fine	84.75	87.11	89.46	91.82	94.17	96.53	98.88	101.23	103.59	105.94	108.30	110.65
Peru 100 Soles .900 Fine	487.61	501.16	514.70	528.25	541.79	555.34	568.88	582.43	595.97	609.52	623.06	636.60
Russia 5 Roubles .900 Fine	44.80	46.05	47.29	48.54	49.78	51.03	52.27	53.51	54.76	56.00	57.25	58.49
Russia Chervonets .900 Fine	89.61	92.09	94.58	97.07	99.56	102.05	104.54	107.03	109.52	112.01	114.50	116.98
South Africa 1 Rand .916 Fine	42.38	43.55	44.73	45.91	47.09	48.26	49.44	50.62	51.79	52.97	54.15	55.33
South Africa 2 Rands .916 Fine	84.75	87.11	89.46	91.82	94.17	96.53	98.88	101.23	103.59	105.94	108.30	110.65
South Africa Krugerrand .916 Fine	360.00	370.00	380.00	390.00	400.00	410.00	420.00	430.00	440.00	450.00	460.00	470.00
Switzerland 10 Francs .900 Fine	33.60	34.54	35.47	36.40	37.34	38.27	39.21	40.14	41.07	42.01	42.94	43.87
Switzerland 20 Francs .900 Fine	67.21	69.08	70.94	72.81	74.68	76.54	78.41	80.28	82.14	84.01	85.88	87.75
Turkey 100 Piastres .916 Fine	76.57	78.70	80.83	82.95	85.08	87.21	89.34	91.46	93.59	95.72	97.84	99.97
Turkey 500 Piastres .916 Fine	382.85	393.48	404.11	414.75	425.38	436.02	446.65	457.29	467.92	478.56	489.19	499.83

These values reflect the approximate gold value contained in standard coins of the indicated units, and do not take into consideration wear to which a coin might be subjected in circulation. Neither do they allow for numismatic value considerations. All values, except the per dollar values in the extreme right column, are rounded to the nearest cent.

$480	$490	$500	$510	$520	$530	$540	$550	$560	$570	$580	$590	$600	$610	$620	Change in value per dollar
23.22	23.71	24.19	24.67	25.16	25.64	26.13	26.61	27.09	27.58	28.06	28.54	29.03	29.51	30.00	.0484
58.04	59.25	60.46	61.67	62.88	64.09	65.30	66.51	67.72	68.93	70.13	71.34	72.55	73.76	74.97	.1209
69.72	71.18	72.63	74.08	75.53	76.99	78.44	79.89	81.34	82.80	84.25	85.70	87.15	88.61	90.06	.1453
116.10	118.52	120.94	123.36	125.77	128.19	130.61	133.03	135.45	137.87	140.29	142.71	145.12	147.54	149.96	.2419
232.20	237.04	241.87	246.71	251.55	256.39	261.22	266.06	270.90	275.74	280.57	285.41	290.25	295.09	299.92	.4837
464.40	474.07	483.75	493.42	503.10	512.77	522.45	532.12	541.80	551.47	561.15	570.82	580.50	590.17	599.85	.9675
141.74	144.42	147.36	150.31	153.26	156.20	159.15	162.10	165.05	167.99	170.94	173.89	176.84	179.78	182.73	.2947
53.12	54.23	55.33	56.44	57.55	58.65	59.76	60.87	61.97	63.08	64.19	65.29	66.40	67.51	68.61	.1107
212.48	216.91	221.33	225.76	230.19	234.61	239.04	243.47	247.89	252.32	256.75	261.17	265.60	270.03	274.45	.4427
44.81	45.74	46.67	47.61	48.54	49.47	50.41	51.34	52.27	53.21	54.14	55.07	56.01	56.94	57.87	.0933
89.61	91.48	93.35	95.21	97.08	98.95	100.81	102.68	104.55	106.42	108.28	110.15	112.02	113.88	115.75	.1867
47.06	48.04	49.02	50.00	50.98	51.96	52.94	53.92	54.90	55.88	56.86	57.84	58.82	59.80	60.78	.0980
94.10	96.06	98.02	99.98	101.94	103.90	105.86	107.82	109.78	111.74	113.70	115.66	117.62	119.58	121.54	.1960
470.49	480.30	490.10	499.90	509.70	519.50	529.31	539.11	548.91	558.71	568.51	578.32	588.12	597.92	607.72	.9802
89.61	91.48	93.35	95.21	97.08	98.95	100.81	102.68	104.55	106.42	108.28	110.15	112.02	113.88	115.75	.1867
56.50	57.68	58.86	60.03	61.21	62.39	63.57	64.74	65.92	67.10	68.27	69.45	70.63	71.80	72.98	.1177
113.00	115.36	117.71	120.07	122.42	124.78	127.13	129.48	131.84	134.19	136.55	138.90	141.26	143.61	145.96	.2354
226.01	230.72	235.43	240.14	244.84	249.55	254.26	258.97	263.68	268.39	273.10	277.80	282.51	287.22	291.93	.4709
565.02	576.80	588.57	600.34	612.11	623.88	635.65	647.42	659.20	670.97	682.74	694.51	706.28	718.05	729.82	1.1771
119.99	122.49	124.99	127.49	129.99	132.49	134.99	137.49	139.99	142.49	144.99	147.49	149.99	152.49	154.99	.2500
479.47	489.46	499.44	509.43	519.42	529.41	539.40	549.39	559.38	569.37	579.36	589.34	599.33	609.32	619.31	.9989
287.60	293.60	299.59	305.58	311.57	317.56	323.56	329.55	335.54	341.53	347.52	353.51	359.51	365.50	371.49	.5992
113.00	115.36	117.71	120.07	122.42	124.78	127.13	129.48	131.84	134.19	136.55	138.90	141.26	143.61	145.96	.2354
44.81	45.74	46.67	47.61	48.54	49.47	50.41	51.34	52.27	53.21	54.14	55.07	56.01	56.94	57.87	.0933
89.61	91.48	93.35	95.21	97.08	98.95	100.81	102.68	104.55	106.42	108.28	110.15	112.02	113.88	115.75	.1867
55.31	56.47	57.62	58.77	59.92	61.08	62.23	63.38	64.53	65.68	66.84	67.99	69.14	70.29	71.45	.1152
110.63	112.93	115.24	117.54	119.85	122.15	124.45	126.76	129.06	131.37	133.67	135.98	138.28	140.59	142.89	.2305
226.01	230.72	235.43	240.14	244.84	249.55	254.26	258.97	263.68	268.39	273.10	277.80	282.51	287.22	291.93	.4709
47.06	48.04	49.02	50.00	50.98	51.96	52.94	53.92	54.90	55.88	56.86	57.84	58.82	59.80	60.78	.0980
94.10	96.06	98.02	99.98	101.94	103.90	105.86	107.82	109.78	111.74	113.70	115.66	117.62	119.58	121.54	.1960
470.49	480.30	490.10	499.90	509.70	519.50	529.31	539.11	548.91	558.71	568.51	578.32	588.12	597.92	607.72	.9802
112.50	114.85	117.19	119.53	121.88	124.22	126.56	128.91	131.25	133.60	135.94	138.28	140.63	142.97	145.31	.2344
157.50	160.78	164.07	167.35	170.63	173.91	177.19	180.47	183.75	187.03	190.32	193.60	196.88	200.16	203.44	.3281
23.14	23.62	24.10	24.59	25.07	25.55	26.03	26.51	27.00	27.48	27.96	28.44	28.92	29.41	29.89	.0482
28.93	29.53	30.14	30.74	31.34	31.94	32.55	33.15	33.75	34.36	34.96	35.56	36.16	36.77	37.37	.0603
57.86	59.07	60.27	61.48	62.68	63.89	65.09	66.30	67.51	68.71	69.92	71.12	72.33	73.53	74.74	.1205
115.74	118.15	120.56	122.97	125.38	127.79	130.21	132.62	135.03	137.44	139.85	142.26	144.67	147.08	149.50	.2411
231.48	236.30	241.12	245.94	250.77	255.59	260.41	265.23	270.06	274.88	279.70	284.52	289.35	294.17	298.99	.4822
578.70	590.76	602.82	614.87	626.93	638.99	651.04	663.10	675.15	687.21	699.27	711.32	723.38	735.44	747.49	1.2056
479.99	489.99	499.99	509.99	519.99	529.99	539.99	549.99	559.98	569.98	579.98	589.98	599.98	609.98	619.98	1.0000
93.46	95.41	97.35	99.30	101.25	103.20	105.14	107.09	109.04	110.98	112.93	114.88	116.82	118.77	120.72	.1947
53.17	54.27	55.38	56.49	57.60	58.70	59.81	60.92	62.03	63.13	64.24	65.35	66.46	67.56	68.67	.1108
113.34	115.70	118.06	120.42	122.78	125.14	127.50	129.86	132.22	134.59	136.95	139.31	141.67	144.03	146.39	.2361
22.63	23.11	23.58	24.05	24.52	24.99	25.46	25.94	26.41	26.88	27.35	27.82	28.29	28.77	29.24	.0472
56.50	57.68	58.86	60.03	61.21	62.39	63.57	64.74	65.92	67.10	68.27	69.45	70.63	71.80	72.98	.1177
113.00	115.36	117.71	120.07	122.42	124.78	127.13	129.48	131.84	134.19	136.55	138.90	141.26	143.61	145.96	.2354
650.15	663.69	677.24	690.78	704.33	717.87	731.42	744.96	758.51	772.05	785.60	799.14	812.69	826.23	839.78	1.3545
59.74	60.98	62.23	63.47	64.72	65.96	67.20	68.45	69.69	70.94	72.18	73.43	74.67	75.92	77.16	.1245
119.47	121.96	124.45	126.94	129.43	131.92	134.41	136.90	139.39	141.88	144.36	146.85	149.34	151.83	154.32	.2489
56.50	57.68	58.86	60.03	61.21	62.39	63.57	64.74	65.92	67.10	68.27	69.45	70.63	71.80	72.98	.1177
113.00	115.36	117.71	120.07	122.42	124.78	127.13	129.48	131.84	134.19	136.55	138.90	141.26	143.61	145.96	.2354
480.00	490.00	500.00	510.00	520.00	530.00	540.00	550.00	560.00	570.00	580.00	590.00	600.00	610.00	620.00	1.0000
44.81	45.74	46.67	47.61	48.54	49.47	50.41	51.34	52.27	53.21	54.14	55.07	56.01	56.94	57.87	.0933
89.61	91.48	93.35	95.21	97.08	98.95	100.81	102.68	104.55	106.42	108.28	110.15	112.02	113.88	115.75	.1867
102.10	104.22	106.35	108.48	110.61	112.73	114.86	116.99	119.11	121.24	123.37	125.50	127.62	129.75	131.88	.2127
510.46	521.09	531.73	542.36	553.00	563.63	574.27	584.90	595.54	606.17	616.81	627.44	638.08	648.71	659.34	1.0635

Index